THE FLOURISHING TREE

by

MABEL RINGEREIDE

COVER DESIGN   JEAN STEWART MCGILL

HERITAGE HOUSE PUBLISHERS LTD.

Ottawa, Ontario, Canada

TO TRYGVE

whose honest individualism has always been

a joy and inspiration to me

THE FLOURISHING TREE

ACKNOWLEDGMENTS

PREFACE

INTRODUCTION

ILLUSTRATIONS

Chapter I   HAPPY CHANCE

Chapter II   BECKWITH 1833

Chapter III   THE BUILDING OF A MANSE

Chapter IV   TAIN, ROSS-SHIRE, SCOTLAND

Chapter V   CROMARTY, ROSS-SHIRE, SCOTLAND

Chapter VI   A MINISTER FOR BECKWITH

Chapter VII   JOHN SMITH OF BECKWITH

Chapter VIII   THE CHURCH

Chapter IX   THE CONGREGATION

The Heirs of The Rev.John Smith

Chapter X   THE MINISTER'S WIFE

Chapter XI   THE MINISTER'S BAIRNS

Chapter XII   OF KIN AND SUCCESSORS

Genealogical Chart

Notes on Bibliography

Appendices

ACKNOWLEDGEMENTS

The assistance of the following Institutions is gratefully acknowledged by the author.

The General Assembly Office of the Church of Scotland
The National Library, Edinburgh, Scotland
Hugh Miller Museum, Cromarty, Scotland
The Royal Commission of the Ancient and Historical
Monuments of Scotland
Kings College Archives, Aberdeen
The Glasgow University, Scotland
Public Archives of Canada, Ottawa
Archives of Ontario, Toronto
Douglas Library, Archives Queens University, Kingston, Ont.
United Church Archives, Toronto
St. Andrews Presbyterian Church, Ottawa
Knox United Church, Owen Sound, Ontario

Specific people are mentioned in the book for their help and interest. However, I would like to pay tribute to the following for their correspondence and encouragement.

Miss Jess Dunbar, Tain, Scotland
Miss Jay Duff, Cromarty, Scotland (now resides Fortrose)
Rev.James Ewing, former Minister, Cromarty Parish Church
Sir Kenneth Murray, "Geanies" Ross-shire, Scotland
Miss Eveline Barron, M.A."The Inverness Courier"Scotland
Bruce F.MacDonald of Invergargill, New Zealand
Rev.Sinclair, Westminster Church, Smiths Falls, Ont.
Rev.Glenn Lucas, Archivist, United Church Archives
Dr.Elizabeth McDougall, Montreal, Que.
Miss Evelyn Taylor, Britannia, Ottawa, Ont.
Miss Jean McGill, artist, Toronto, Ont.
My husband and son who sustained me with patience and
humour.
The Wardell, Wyld and Neame families - descendants of the Rev. John Smith who are in a class by themselves in this moment of recognition. Without them the story would be hollow indeed.

My sincere thanks to all   *Mabel Ringereide*

1

PREFACE

Mabel Ringereide's interest in people and their families
combined with her love of pastoral beauty, be it weath-
ered old buildings or lovely sweeps of countryside, led
her directly to the Rev.John Smith, nineteenth century
Church of Scotland clergyman in Beckwith Township,Lanark
County, Upper Canada. Her home in Beckwith, a solidly
built house marred by successive renovations and additions, when brought back to it's original form proved
to be a beautiful, warm, stone house and a delight to
the Ringereides. She discovered that it had been built
as a manse for a young Scottish clergyman, the Rev. Mr.
John Smith and determined to find out more about him.
Her search led her into exhaustive research in both
Canada and Scotland.

She ascertained that Smith was the son of the Rev. Mr.
Robert Smith, Church of Scotland clergyman at Cromarty,
a sea coast town north of Inverness in the Black Isle
of Scotland. Her account of conditions in Cromarty when
John Smith lived there with his family provide interesting and useful background material for her Canadian
story---and it is a Canadian story.

Smith brought two sisters with him to the Manse at Beckwith and both he and his sisters married in Canada and
were thus brought firmly into the main stream of nineteenth century colonial life.

Although Mrs. Ringereide's admiration and sympathy for
the Smith family is apparent, at no time does she sacri-
fice accuracy for grandiose statements. She has relied
heavily on authentic Presbyterian records in writing of
the church on the 7th Line of Beckwith. Indeed, her work
abounds in direct quotations taken from reputable sources
in Scotland as well as Canada.

Interest in her work should extend well beyond the bounds
of Lanark County.

                              E.A.K.McDougall, phD.

THE FLOURISHING TREE

Introduction:

To pick up the threads of genealogy or family history from an older member of the family who has had the forethought to keep a diary or record of people and events, covering perhaps a comparatively few years or centuries in time is an exciting and worthwhile venture.

To try to pick up the threads of an unknown quantity with no ties of relationship on a romantic whim is quite a different matter. However, one can easily become as obsessed with the latter as the former.

It is often a hard, rugged trail with many dead ends and disappointments but once engrossed in the hunt, one cannot shrug off involvement lightly or forget what one has learned.

It is also impossible to throw away the desire to bring facts to light and to put flesh on the bones of the skeletons of long-gone people who contributed in their own way to the sum of Canadian heritage.

To find an old derelict house and feel it had a story to tell was an adventure. To find the minister for whom the house was built was named John Smith, was a challenge in itself. To go over archive records, church records, registry records; to take trips to Scotland and other places tracking him down was, you will realize, to become very involved in his life.

To have to admit defeat many times but always to re-joice when one small lead proved valuable and fruitful and go joyfully on to the next step of discovery, brought a glow of achievement.

Now, almost ten years later, to say it must be recorded, because whatever else there is will come from readers truly interested in the Reverend John Smith and his kin.

This has been no light decision. One can only hope that for local historians it will serve as a reference and perhaps bring to light for them many hitherto unknown facts of the early Beckwith ministry.

John Smith's years at Beckwith, his highland family
and early Rockliffe connections were known to him.
His descendants at Ottawa, Hamilton, Dundas, Toronto
and in Great Britain would have pleased him. That his
beloved Jane lived to be 83 years of age and his youngest son, I04 years, might have amazed him but, that
his little Manse should be restored to life again in
the I960's after long periods of disuse, would have
caused that gentle, shy man to smile happily, I am sure.

This is the story of a manse, a minister, his congregation and his family.

Mabel Ringereide,
Como, Quebec

June I977.

THE FLOURISHING TREE

ILLUSTRATIONS

Numbers

1-5   Before and After Views of Manse, 1965-1970

  6   Exterior of Manse, 1970

  7   St. Duthac Memorial Chapel, Tain
         Courtesy of Jess Dunbar, Tain, Scotland

  8   High Street, Tain, Ross-shire, Scotland
         Courtesy of Jess Dunbar, Tain, Scotland

  9   Reformation Memorial Window, Mem. Chapel ruin, Tain
         Courtesy of Jess Dunbar, Tain, Scotland

 10   Pastoral Scene 1821, Cromarty
         Permission National Library, Edinburgh,Scotland

 11   Cromarty Homes

 12   Plaque to Rev.Robert Smith in Cromarty Parish Church
                    (known as East Church)
         Permission of Royal Commission on the Ancient and
         Historical Monuments of Scotland

 13   Interior Cromarty Parish Church, Cromarty, Scotland
         Royal Comm. on Ancient and Hist. Monuments

 14   Ruins of Church of the 7th Line, Beckwith, 1937
         Sketch, kindness of Jean S. McGill, from article by
         J.T.Kirkland given to author by Beth Kirkland

 15   Tombstone of Rev. John Smith

 16   Jane Morson, wife of Rev.John Smith and daughter
         Jane, Britannia, June, 1899
         This, and all photos of Smith family unless other-
         wise stated - courtesy Miss Dorothy Wardell

 17   Isabella Rose Smith, wife of A.R.Wardell, Dundas Ont.

Nos.

18 Lindsay A. Wardell, grandson of Rev.John Smith
    and family.

19 Photo of proposed plans for Restoration of Fort
    Marie near Midland, by Lindsay Wardell
    Courtesy of his son, Jack Wardell, Toronto

20 Father Henry and Father Thomas Wardell, July 1945

21 Dorothy Wardell, standing beside her painting
    "The Crucifixion" 1944,
    Courtesy of Jack Wardell

22 Jack Wardell, portrait by his sister,Dorothy Wardell

23 Margaret Crawford Smith Wyld, daughter of Rev. John
    Smith.

24 Ottly Wyld Neame and son Shirley, England, prior to
    World War II
    Courtesy Mrs. Ottly Neame

25 William Wyld, N. B., gr.-grandson, Rev. John Smith
    Courtesy Marie Babineau Wyld

26 Robert Smith, eldest son of Rev. John Smith, 1914

27 John Rose Smith, photo taken when nearly 100 yers old.

28 The 4th Laird of Nigg, wife and daughter - great-
    grandparents and grandmother of Rev. John Smith
    from The Story of the MacDonald Family, New Zeal-
    and, 1866-1966. Courtesy Bruce F. MacDonald

6

CHAPTER I

HAPPY CHANCE

It had been a very hot summer and we were thankful to
have a cottage on Lake Mississippi in the vicinity of
Carleton Place, near Ottawa, Ontario - to be away from
the city heat.

At the end of the summer an errand took us for a visit
on a short country road near the Lake and that is when
it happened. We called it "serendipity".

To the left, as we entered the dusty concession road,
we caught a glimpse through the trees of a small storey
and a half Georgian style cottage set in it's own meadow with log outbuildings.

The friends we visited told us the house belonged to an
elderly bachelor who probably would not sell; that he
owned several hundred acres of land, raised beef cattle and the house was of no importance to him as such
being much in disrepair with no amenities for modern
living. They advised us to contact him to satisfy ourselves.

On our return trip we drove in through the gateway and,
derelict though she was, the Georgian lady , in her own
small way, had been a true beauty.

Now, sagging floors caused by a crack in the stonework,
holes in the plaster, wallpaper hanging in ribbons, rat
holes in the floor boards all gave expression to the
neglect, abuse and vandalism she had suffered. Only one
24 pane window had survived intact.

Amaingly, we were not at all discouraged by these things.
We felt only the peace, quietness and gentle grace per-
meating under all the debris, dirt and disregard for her
basic beauty that was evident. We had a feeling of coming home.

Our reasons varied, of course. Our son saw the trees,
the meadow, the log buildings and space. The engineer-
husband was immediately caught up in plans for restor-

ation and I, feeling the enchantment and romance of its
pioneer days sensed I could become willingly entangled
in its history. We all three decided that it must be
ours.

Aflame with the desire to obtain it, we visited the
owner at the local hospital where he was laid up with
a leg injury. No, he wouldn't sell - not at the moment
- but, if he did, we should have the first chance to
buy. We were to contact him later.

January snows and winter winds gave way to thaw and with
the scent of a false spring, we once again journeyed
forth to see if we could at least get a signed "option
to buy" from our reluctant "party of the first part".

Believe it or not, we took a portable typewriter and
typing paper and descended on him at his home farm with
such enthusiasm he agreed to sell the house and outbuildings but only about six acres of land. We were to
measure out the terrain we would like and have it sur-
veyed.

Despite the return of the cold weather, the next Sunday
saw all three of us out tramping kneedeep in the snow,
measuring from tree line to tree line and from gate to
a distance behind the barns. By spring the surveyor had
done his part.

In June, we were legally responsible for our charming
Georgian girl. That she was referred to by descendants
of descendants of pioneers as the "Old Manse" did not
detract from her glamour. Indeed, we almost named her
in Gaelic,"Furan Suidhe" (pronounced Fooran-soo-yu)
meaning "peaceful green place" which quite expressed
the aura of her years. And, had not both English and
Gaelic been spoken within her walls !.

To the artist and sculptor bone structure, form and
clean lines inspire creation. If these are enhanced
by a sad, mischievious or wise expression, by great
beauty or character, then he has a masterpiece.

The engineer assessed our "derelict" and decided all
camouflage and bits and pieces that had been added over
the years must go.

We set to work to scrape off the make-up - coats and
coats of paint - down to the natural wood and smooth

8

the wrinkles; removing all plaster and wallpaper; bringing her back to the bare bones, or stones, of her original form.

The walls were a foot-and -a-half thick and built of field stone. The exterior had latterly been covered with a heavy substance called harling - similar to stucco.

We uncovered an extra fireplace, making four in all. We discovered the inside shutters were of oak, golden and beautiful when cleaned down.

The beams were strong, sure and axe-hewn. The roof beams were secured with wooden dowels. Such nails as had been used originally were square and rate as museum pieces to-day.

It was all hard work and joyful adventure. It was several years before we moved in for year-round living.

Self appointed historian of the venture, it took me many years before I could pin down the date of it's beginnings - 1834.

In 1838 the Rev.John Smith brought his bride to the Manse, an English girl of gentle upbringing. I had suspected she was of special background when, on July 1st, 1967, I laborously and tenderly was able to take from the rough stone fireplace wall of the living room, a section of the first wallpaper. Made up of cameo scenes of a lover and his lass by a woodland stream. The girl sitting barelegged, dabbling her feet in the water, dressed in a lovely deep blue silk gown and the gallant lounging lazily on the grass watching her, dressed in French style blue knee breeches and lace trimmed jacket - his white periwig tied with a black ribbon. Both watched over by a serious looking duenna, standing to one side.

It was, I must admit, basically this small piece of wallpaper that set me off seriously on the trail of the Rev.John Smith, leading to fascinating facts of family, places and pioneer history.

A many-faceted gem of adventure that brought the Beckith Manse of the Seventh Line back into the local history scene once again.

#-1   BEFORE-----
THE MANSE KITCHEN SHOWING COOKING
                              FIREPLACE

-2   BEFORE RESTORATION
SHOWING THE OLD KITCHEN IN RUINS

10

#-3   BEFORE ------
A CORNER OF THE LIVING ROOM

Small, quiet place of beauty rare,
Fields and meadows, country air
Fills the lungs, renews the mind;
Far from the city, one can find
Time to think and meditate;
Time to wonder and create.
A vibrant home, full of song,
Golden sunshine all day long.

Fond memories, tales to tell
In every beam doth dwell,
Linking past and present days-
Pioneer and modern ways.
May God bless the little manse
And coming years re-enhance
It's beauty, built long ago.
May it's hearths forever glow
Giving visions in their gleams,
To help unfold other dreams.

                    M. Ringereide

#-6

THE MANSE---------1970

11

#-4   AFTER RESTORATION
        THE OLD KITCHEN AS FAMILY ROOM

#-5   AFTER------
        SHOWING LIVING ROOM AREA AND OLD
        BYTOWN STAINED GLASS WINDOWS

CHAPTER II

BECKWITH 1833

The early settlers had arrived in Beckwith in 1818 and the concessions from three to nine became busy with land clearing and cabin building; the settling in to a new way of life in a wilderness of forest and swamps and summer scourge of black flies and mosquitoes.

It must have been a surprising ordeal and rugged challenge to the men and their families learning a new way of life far from the Perthshire hills of Scotland.

The Rev.William Bell was the minister for a widely scattered district and it was through his efforts that George Buchanan was sent by the Edinburgh Secessionist Presbytery in Scotland, to be minister to what was to become known as the Congregation of the 7th Line, Beckwith.

The Rev.George Buchanan, who had served a short while as a military chaplain was entitled to a grant of land under the military regulations and for this he applied in 1824. The Crown Grant, however, was not officially issued until October 1831 (see Appendix). He staked out his claim to Lots 14 and 9, Concession 6, Beckwith Township, County of Lanark, Upper Canada. Within a year of his arrival he had built a large log house to accommodate his family of ten children, on Lot 14.

A makeshift barn was used for his ministerial efforts and one day, after holding services in same for about ten years, it burned down. The idea nurtured for a long time by some members of the congregation to build a proper church, now became a decision.

The problem was whether to build it of logs on Buchanan property, as he wished, or of stone on McArthur's land over the road on Concession number 7. The congregation decided on a stone church and although the church never owned the property on which it was built, it thrived for over forty years on that spot.

One of the early settlers, a man named Alexander Fisher, who arrived in 1818, secured his grant (see Appendix)in 1824 of Lot 12 SE, Concession 7, Beckwith.

After building a log house and barn, digging a well and clearing ten acres he sold this property to the Trustees of the Presbyterian congregation of the 7th Line in connection with the Church of Scotland, namely - Alexander Dewar and John McTavish - in 1826, for thirty pounds.

This was not an unusual procedure to conclude the deed in trust for a congregation. Dr.E.McDougall in her thesis "Presbyterian Church in Montreal" page 49, writes:

> Parish churches in Scotland were held in trust by the heritor or landlord of the parish. In North American Presbyterian Churches, the heritor obviously had to be replaced in some manner. Trustees were usually appointed by the congregation to hold the church property in their names, before Churches were allowed by law to become incorporated.

We will probably never know why the church built in 1832 was built on McArthur's property (lot 14, Conc. 7) and not on the church property on Lot 12 of the same concession.

We do know there had been dissension and dissatisfaction among the Beckwith settlers on the matter of church and worship and a group insisted on writing to the Glasgow Colonial Society for a new mininster, despite objections to this by the Rev.William Bell.

The Rev.George Buchanan who had come at the age of sixty was now in "retirement" years and in ill health. He was, in the opinion of some, we understand, actually more doctor than minister.

The stone church was begun in 1832 and by autumn 1833 was basically completed and a newly ordained minister had arrived in October.

He preached his first sermon at The Scotch Church on the 7th Line, in connexion with the Church of Scotland, November 3, 1833.

Thus began the Beckwith Ministry of the Rev.John Smith.

13

THE OLD MANSE

"Around some fireside he
hears - the language of
the soul"

Unknown

14

CHAPTER III

THE BUILDING OF A MANSE

During the years we lived at the old Manse on the 7th
Line, the following Bible quotation came often to mind.

> I will liken him to a wise man,
> which built his house upon a rock:
> And the rain descended and the floods
> came, and winds blew, and beat upon
> that house, and it fell not: for it
> was founded upon a rock.   Matt.7-24,25.

In the present day when information is properly recorded
so that one can say - in such a year, in such a way, for
such a price, this or that building was constructed, it
is hard to assemble a picture of the building of a little
Manse in more or less wilderness settlement without aid
of letters, diary or written word pertaining to same to
give colour and credence to it's creation.

The Rev.J.Croil, when making a survey of the Presbyterian
Churches in Canada in 1867, wrote in his notebook that
the Beckwith Manse was built of stone in 1834.

It is said that in the early days a stonemaon went from
district to district and worked for a specific period of
the year building stone houses. This could be how the
Manse came into being.

I choose to believe the congregation, each in his own
way, contributed to the work to build a special residence
for the new minister. Such details as the Georgian panel-
led inside shutters, three big stone fireplaces and a big
double fireplace in the kitchen as well as lovely smooth
beams, were for the times very special.

It was a small house. No additions were made to it in the
years between 1834-1970.

In 1970 a small stone entrance room to the backdoor was
built by my husband who gained a great respect for the
men who had built the original house. Collecting field
stone and building a room approximately 10 ft. X 6 ft.
was heavy work and took much ingenuity to harmonize it

gently with the rest of the house and not detract from
the basically simple lines.

It should be mentioned here that some stones from the
Church ruins on Lot I4 went into it by the kind permission of Jack and Barbara Harris who owned the McArthur
property on which the church had been built.

The terrain of Lot I2 and further west on Concession 7,
Beckwith, consists, for the most part, of rock and shale
-soil not too deep and lots of natural springs that create ponds in the meadows in the Spring.

To choose a special spot for the Manse must have been
quite a problem and whoever made the decision was very
wise. When, in I967, we installed a septic tank the
neighbouring sceptics were sure it was going to be a
very expensive dynamiting job. However, the "engineer"
drew up his plan and , as th old farmer over the way
said, he was "certainly born under a lucky star" for
the septic tank location turned out to be at the very
edge of a drop of a six foot wall of rock.

The house itself then was built on rock - solid rock,
the original underflooring beams resting on a rock shelf.
The site was indeed well chosen.

The center hall plan of it's architectural design, though
small, was gracious and sensible. It's proportions were
in absolute symmetry.

Two large rooms, two small rooms and upstairs two long
attic rooms under the eaves with a storage room at the
end of the stair well. A room over the kitchen and, under
the latter, a six foot deep cellar.

Let it be said the solidity of it's beams, wood trim and
stonework in walls and fireplaces, gave strength and beauty to it's twentieth century revival.

Therefore, one can see whoever built it, or however it
was begun, it was a worthy effort and must have caused
no little pride to the congregation of the Seventh Line,
Beckwith.

The Church of Scotland contributed a sum toward the building. The minister himself, or his sisters perhaps, expressed special desires in it's design. It is very much
akin to small houses in his hometown in Ross-shire and

Georgian cottages were very popular in Scotland in the
nineteenth century.

Some artistic member of the congregation must have thou-
ghtfully made the buttermilk stained semi-circular piece
of wood carved to simulate a sunburst design fanlight
over the front doorway.

That it was begun soon after the Rev.John Smith's arrival
is certain. He did not mince words in writing to the Glasgow Colonial Society April 2I, I834, regarding the lack
of a proper home for the minister.

> With regard to the state of my temporal
> circumstances here, I experienced much
> inconvenience from finding that there
> was no house built for me as your Soc-
> iety had assured me. One of my hearers
> very kindly gave me possession of a
> log house built for his own use until
> another could be fitted up. Had prev-
> ious notice of my appointment been sent
> to the people, some sort of dwelling
> should have been prepared for me. This
> however was not done and most unfortun-
> ately a letter which I wrote to our
> Trustees on arriving at Quebec was
> detained at Perth, so that until a day
> or two previous to my appearance in
> Beckwith no notice was given to my
> appointment. There is but one hundred
> acres, two hundred was the quantity
> promised me. But these wants have been
> more than compensated by the kindness
> of the people.   GCS V 28

These remarks tend to convince one that the first log
building of big squared-off logs in the Glebe (in ruins
I964) was a double purpose structure. Half part used as
a cattle shed, half part as a dwelling place. It is possible Alexander Fisher lived in this domicile.

It took settlers some time to wholly complete the Manse
but at least, when John Smith married it was a "neat
little house" according to the Rev.Bell's jottings in
his diary after assisting at a Beckwith service in I839.

Real or imaginary - the mind must allow itself poetical
license to visualize the daily life of those who dwelt

17

in it. The tea cupboard built between the two fireplaces
in the west wall, the small study with it's built-in
bookshelves* and eastern window - with a door to the back
hall and one from the parlour where Jane decorated the
fireplace wall with her very elegant, hand printed 18th
century wallpaper, perhaps from a roll brought to her as
a gift from the Continent by her brother. The evidence
of these things was real enough.

One can visualize the students gathered around the kitchen fireplace when being tutored in the catechism. The
hearthstone there was one solid piece 8ft. by 4ft. In
1970 we built a stone "kettle shelf" in front of this
fireplace from stones of the "auld kirk" ruins. Again
through the kindness of the late Jack Harris and his
wife, Barbara.

Thus some stones from the Rev.John Smith's church were
incorporated into his Manse in 1971 - commemorating in
a small way the relationship of both.

The old kitchen restored then from almost impossible
ruins (see illustrations) became well named "the family
room" and when it was in order, July 1st, 1971 - we hung
a plaque over the fireplace there with a quote from the
Rev.Van Dyke of 1909.

> Every task however simple
> Sets the soul who does it, free -
>
> Every deed of love and kindness
> Done to man is done to me.
>
> Never more need you seek me-
> I am with you every where,
>
> Raise the beam and there you'll find me
> Lift a stone, and I am there.

This we felt expressed for us the aura of the Old Manse!

---

* The top half of the bookshelves is now closed in by a
leaded stained glass door, formerly a window from the old
Bytown Inn, Ottawa. Another pair of stained glass windows
made room dividers between kitchen and dining room area
when the interior was renewed and remodelled to modern
living. My husband purchased all three windows at the
time of the demolition of the Bytown Inn, Ottawa.

#-7   ST.DUTHAC MEMORIAL CHAPEL
        TAIN, SCOTLAND

#-8   HIGH STREET,TAIN,
        ROSS-SHIRE, SCOTLAND

HERITAGE

That the great light be
clearer for our light,
And the great soul stro ng-
er for our soul;
To have done this is to
have lived, though fame
Remembers us with no
familiar name.

Archibald Lampman

\#-9   REFORMATION MEMORIAL WINDOW
        MEMORIAL CHAPEL RUIN, TAIN

21

CHAPTER IV

TAIN

Tain is a very old and historical town in Ross-shire, Scotland. Perhaps it would be of interest to know something of the church where the Rev.Robert Smith, father of John, was assistant for a time.

The Rev.Robert Smith was born in 1764 to Robert Smith, Saddler of Inverness and his wife Catherine Grant.

After graduating M.A.from King's College, Aberdeen, March 30th, 1784, he became a tutor to the family of Donald MacLeod of Geanies.

"Geanies" is an estate about eight miles from Tain and the MacLeods at one time were High Sheriffs of Ross-shire. Later, the MacLeod estates were sold to the Murrays and a sister-in-law of Robert Smith, Christine Rose, married William Murray of Pitzculzean. Christine and Isabella, Robert's wife, were granddaughters of the 4th Laird of Nigg, Ross-shire.

Robert Smith was licensed by the Presbytery at Tain, December 12th, 1787, presented by George III, June 9th, 1788 and became Assistant at the St.Duthac Parish Church, an earlier Collegiate Church. It is now a historical shell and known for the huge Reformation window which glows like a jewel in the sunlight, set in the wall of this now memorial edifice.

As one enters Tain, one can see the whole High Street stretching before one to the hotel at the far end. Lined with shops and very old grey stone buildings, one can well visualize how it appeared in the early centuries of it's beginning.

If you stand by the stone wall on one side of the street on entering the town and look down to the mud-marshes when the tide is out, then further seaward, you can see a grassy headland on which a lonely ruin stands with crumbling walls overgrown with vines, encircled by an old, old cemetery protecting it's solitude.

This was the Chapel of St.Duthac - not used as a parish
church but a memorial cell - a place of prayer. An acc-
ommodation for a resident hermit to guard the shrine
of St.Duthac. It was destroyed by fire in 1427, sixty
years after the Church of St. Duthac had been built up
in the town.

A sanctuary - in fact, there was an area around "Tayne"
between four crosses called the "Sacred Girth of St.
Duthac", which was regarded as a place of safety from
enemies of whatever kind, personal or political, for
anyone who had once gained their sanctuary.

The disregard for this law brought horror and shame to
the religious orders of the times when the wife of
Robert the Bruce and her daughter, Marjorie, while on a
pilgrimage to Tain, were captured by the Earl of Ross
(a partisan of Edward I) and sent to London as prisoners.

To-day, upon a hillside in the town of Tain where the
small museum stands and a well-kept cemetery is cherished
behind the iron fence, stands the small memorial church
of St.Duthac. This then, is where the Rev.Robert Smith
started as an Assistant Minister.

Now it is absolutely empty. There is a stone floor and
stone walls decorated with plaques to long gone ministers
(one of whom was the Rev.Lewis Rose who recommended John
Smith for the ministry in Canada), provosts and other
worthies.

No pews or benches within - only the high Murray pulpit
recovered and brought back into place. The stained glass
windows letting in colourful gems of sunlight, causes one
to tread softly.

As one turns to leave, the huge Reformation window by the
doorway holds the eye and one stops to ponder on the religious history of this well-kept sanctuary.

The illustration photograph in black and white does not
do justice to the rich colours and drama of the scene -
Munro of Foulis (an ancient Ross-shire family), the Bish-
op of Ross, the Regent Murray and John Knox reading the
Confession of Faith to the Scottish Parliament in mid-
August 1560. Reading across the bottom of the panes it is
recorded:

23

This Church was first used for the reformed worship when the Scottish Parliament
of 1560 adopted the Confession of Faith
drawn up by John Knox and his associates
Robert More Munro, 17th Baron of Foulis
and Nicholas Ross Provost of Tain and
Abbott of Fearn being the members present from Rosshire. The building continued to be used as a Parish Church until
1815 and was afterwards left unprotected
and ruinous for upwards of 40 years, when
it's restoration by public subscription
was undertaken and conducted until 1877
by John McLeod, Provost of Tain. In con-
tinuation of his efforts and to his memory this window has been placed by his
son, George McLeod 1882.

It is easy to understand why this big memorial window is
of major importance in the little church when one realizes that in 1488 James IV came to the throne of Scotland and continued, so it is recorded, the royal tradition of contributing generously to the Church of St. Duthac. As he grew older he paid frequent penitential visits
to the shrine of St. Duthac at Tain. Perhaps, it is said,
to atone for his part in the rebellion which had led to
the death of his father.

The late Alan G.R.Robertson, whom I met while visiting
Tain, wrote in his book "The Lowland Highlanders":

James IV paid his last visit to Tain in
1513. A month later he fell on the field
of Flodden.....

His son James V is presumed to have made
at least one pilgrimage to Tain and is
traditionally believed to have walked
barefooted through the streets of Tain, as
his father is said to have done.....

The route or bridle path taken by the royal
visitors at the approaches of Tain is known
as the King's Causeway and vestiges of the
original which still exist are pointed out
to this day.

A window in the St Duthac Memorial Church shows the Provost of Tain receiving the charter from Malcolm Canmore.

Yes, the town had a long religious history and in the Council Chamber is preserved the charter of James VI confirming the privilege of the Burgh in I588. The parchment Bull of Pope Innocent VIII recognizing the Collegiate Church in I492 (presented by Andrew Carnegie) and the notarial copy of the inquest of I439 relating the immunity of Tain, was founded by Malcolm Canmore.

However, during the reign of James V - Patrick Hamilton The Titular Abbot of Fearn (near Tain) was burned at St. Andrews as a heretic. He was the first preacher of reformation in Scotland and though he probably did not really reside at Fearn, it is said his martyrdom aroused feelings in that district that caused the "winds of change" to be felt most strongly in the north.

In I549 Sir Nicholas Ross, who was the Provost of the Collegiate Church of St. Duthac, was appointed Abbot of Fearn but later embraced the Protestant faith and in mid-August I560 he sat among the representatives of the three estates of the realm in the "Reformation Parliament" at Edinburgh and voted with the majority for accepting the reformed Confession of Faith.

Such a step in the sixteenth century was almost like the "giant step on the moon" in the twentieth.

After I560 the Church of St.Duthac came into use for the reformed worship. A fine oaken pulpit was presented to the church by the Regent Murray, a friend of John Knox, in recognition of the "zeal of the people of Tain in the cause of Reformation".

Other churches came into the life of the town and much water had flowed under the bridge between the I500's and 1974 when I visited Tain but, I think standing in the center of that empty church one felt most sympathetic to all those who, by conviction, had contributed on that long variegated trail down the centuries to our own day of freedom of thought and an ecumenical understanding of man's personal belief and his right to it.

The old church left uncared for and unused for generations became prey to vandalism and decay. In I857 some people whose relatives were buried in the adjacent

churchyard sought and obtained permission from the
heritors to carry out repairs. By subscription work began
and by 1870 the roof and walls had been completely re-
paired and the stonework of the windows renewed. The
church was cleared of pews and seats and the ST.Duthac
Church deserted in 1815 for a new parish church, came
into it's own again - acquiring dignity and grace and
bringing peace and pleasure to the town and tourists
within the coolness of its preserved walls.

It seemed to me, in spirit, Tain was not much changed
from the days at the end of the 18th century when Robert
Smith walked to services at St. Duthac or courted his
wife to be, Isabella Gair Rose of Nigg.

The past is ever part of the present as each man's
heritage contributes to the future.

CROMARTY IN 1821
From a Drawing by William Daniell
"I used, too, to climb, day after day, a grassy protuberance of the old coast-line immediately behind my mother's house, that commands a wide reach of the Moray Firth"

n.10.

Page 26

#-11 CROMARTY HOMES
      NOTE SIMILAR DOORS TO
                  THE MANSE

27

DEDICATED
BY THE **PARISHIONERS**
OF **CROMARTY**,
TO THE **MEMORY** OF
THE **REVEREND**
ROBERT SMITH,
THEIR HIGHLY ESTEEMED
AND MUCH BELOVED
MINISTER,
WHO DEPARTED THIS LIFE
ON THE 20TH MARCH 1824.
IN THE LXI YEAR OF HIS AGE,
AND XXXV. OF HIS OFFICE.
HIS LIFE
WAS A BRIGHT EXAMPLE TO HIS FAMILY
AND TO HIS FLOCK,
HIS DEATH
A POWERFUL AND STRIKING EVIDENCE
OF THAT JOYFUL CONSOLATION WHICH
FAITH DERIVES THROUGH
JESUS CHRIST.

#-12   PLAQUE TO REV.ROBERT SMITH
CROMARTY PARISH CHURCH

#-13   INTERIOR CROMARTY PARISH CHURCH
        SCOTLAND

CHAPTER V

CROMARTY

Heritage is becoming more and more important in this era. Genealogists and historians rely often on the social facts of other days to portray people and places with understanding and sensitivity.

John Smith, son of the Rev.Robert Smith, was born January I9, I80I, at Cromarty on the Black Isle, Ross-shire, Scotland.

"The Black Isle" is rather a magic phrase to me. Perhaps because on my first visit I encountered so much kindness, made some special discoveries and just fell in love with - Cromarty by the sea.

It was unknown to me until I began research on the Rev. John Smith. Then I spent much time over maps trying to find Cromarty and other places close to it associated with the background of the Smith family - Geanies, Nigg and Tain.

In I972, after a quick, brief visit to Tain, I had taken a bus thinking to have an equally quick, brief look at Cromarty before going on to Inverness. The last person on the bus, on arrival in town I asked the driver when he made the trip to Dingwall. He did not. There was no bus out of Cromarty until noon the next day.

I suppose my consternation must have shown on my face and asking where he thought I might find a room for the night, he pondered then said: "Just sit. I'll drive you around to the hotel and see if they have one available."

After circling some short, narrow streets we drove up in front of a long, low-slung building on the waterfront. A room was available. Later, after a short walk in town, a cozy chat with friendly folk over coffee in the lounge and a saunter along the esplanade, I had a good night's sleep.

The next morning was bright and sunny and I had several hours of exploration before taking the bus to Kessick to catch the ferry for Inverness.

That morning still stands out as a highlight in my research endeavours. Walking up the hill in the sunshine and the clear air, the view of the sea and the town nestled into the hillside are all imprinted on my mind and while the Miller monument reaching needlehigh into the sky and the absence of cattle make it a different scene from I82I, the essence was very much the same - of peace and contentment and a lovely tranquility.

I discovered plaques in the old cemetery by the ruins of the Gaelic chapel on the hilltop, to the Rev. Robert Smith, his wife Isabella, two of their children who died in infancy and one to his mother, Catherine Grant, who died in I800. Another one to a John Duff MacDonald , Naval Officer, intrigued me. It was of special interest because a man of that name was a doctor at Perth, Upper Canada, at the time of John Smith's death at Beckwith in I85I and was chief executor of Smith's will.

Later, I found out he was a nephew and the son of a man married to John Smith's sister Catherine. But I did not know it at the time - only that the man who had died at Cromarty had the same name as the man in Perth, Canada. All this, of course, proving the worth of tombstone markings and recordings.

On top of the small hill overlooking the sea one had the feeling, as said, of the pastoral scene portrayed in the I82I drawing. The ruins of the little church fascinated me as did the monument to Hugh Miller, born I802, the year after the Rev.John Smith.

Hugh Miller, as a boy, was interested in the rocks and seashore out-croppings. He became a Geologist, a stonemason, a writer and a sculptor. His small cottage home with the crowstep gables, so typical of the town, is now a museum under the National Trust of Scotland.

I wandered down the hillside path which led to it and spent most of my time in the museum reading through some of his books in the hope of finding mention of youthful friends and possibly John Smith who had, at one time, lived but a few doors away from the Miller home, but no luck!

Time flew by and too soon I had to catch that bus. Driving away, I was not even aware I had passed the house where

John Smith's sister Margaret, who married Dr. George Mc-Donald , had lived. These facts came to light later through correspondence and proved more fruitful when I revisited Cromarty in 1974.

In August, 1974, my arrival at Cromarty just missed, by two days, the spectacular launching of the Highland One, the tremendous oil rig that was so newsworthy, as it was floated down between what are called "the Sutors" - the two rocky promnotories of the Cromarty Firth where it joins the sea.

Thousands of visitors and local people had watched this notable event. The Queen had been there to see this fantastic engineering feat take the community into the late twentieth century limelight. There is no turning back the explorations, the work and the equipment necessary to them. A fact which has saddened many old timers up on the Black Isle.

At Nigg, the Highland Fabricators Company who are behind the venture, have restored "Pitculzean" a one-time Murray house, owned by the relatives of John Smith earlier in the century. It is now a V.I.P. Reception House for the Company's special occasions and visitors. Nigg is just across the water from Cromarty and a few miles from Tain.

Thus began the web with fragile threads of history and family, from early days to the present.

The high point of my four days was really visiting the Cromarty Parish Church and meeting the minister, the Rev. Mr. Ewing with whom I had had correspondence and who gave me some historical notes.

The Rev.Robert Smith, the father of John, was ordained as minister of the Cromarty Parish Church in 1789 and he ministered to that congregation for thirty-four years. The plaque to his memory in the Church expresses the congregation's esteem of him.

In 1791 he married Isabella Gair Rose of Nigg and it is reported their first home in Cromarty was in the gatehouse of the Ross estate, next to the church. It is a fine two-storey sandstone building - impressive still to-day.

They later moved to "Denoon Villa" at the other end of the Main Street , near the entrance to the town and here Isabella lived at the time of, and after, the death of her husband in 1824. This is a lovely house, still inhabited.

To find the boy, John Smith, in Cromarty proved futile. The school, unfortunately, had no records of that time and one can only imagine that he might have attended the Academy there as a very small boy and even sat with hisfellow students in the Students' Loft for service on Sunday, in his father's church.

At 13 years of age, as his father had done before him, he went to King's College, Aberdeen, to study.

The history of the town is another matter and maybe knowing some of it may give life and meaning to the person of the Rev.John Smith, the man.

In January, 1973, "M.E." wrote in "Scotland's Magazine" in an article entitled - "A Walk in the Black Isle" -

> The Black Isle is still unspoiled. It is
> not an island as the name implies, but a
> splendid fertile peninsula of dark woods
> and agricultural land across which a nec-
> essary major road will soon be driven.

At the beginning of the 19th century Cromarty was alive with seafarers - for the in dustry of the town was the sea. It was a center of fishing and a section called "Fishertown" (conservation area to-day) had many boats at anchor and the air was always heavy with the tang of fish.

Manufactures of that time were hempen cloth, linen, lace, ale, nails and spades. All these were shipped around the coast of Scotland and to the Continent in tall masted sloops. This was the prosperous state of the town when John Smith was born in 1801.

The town on the Cromarty Firth was protected from east winds and open seas by the Sutors - the two headlands where the Firth met the open sea. This had made it a haven for shipping and it's geographical situation well adapted it to be a center of coastal trading. The population, like many places on the east coast of Scotland, was of Lowland and Scandinavian origin.

According to the Rev. Ewing, it's history was colorful but it had really only come into historical prominence under the Stewarts. At that time the Urquharts were lairds.

The story is told that the most famous of the Urquhart
family was the whimsical Sir Thomas Urquhart, trans-
lator of Rabelais, (French humourist who died I553) and
author of several rare and eccentric works. Sir Thomas,
continuing in the family tradition of royalist, fought
at Worcester. He died in exile on the Continent, so it
is said, of joy at hearing the news of the Restoration.
Tribute is paid to him by the Saltire Society with a
memorial plaque in the Cromarty Parish Church.

The Cromarty Parish Church is one of the few buildings
of the old town that remains. The seventeenth century
town built to the north of the present site had been
washed, house by house, into the sea.

The church built to the south of the old town, escaped
erosion. It is a T-plan kirk dating from I700. It has
harled walls and a simple belfry (added I799) with
large round-headed windows flanking the pulpit. The I8th
century Cromarty House Loft at the east end is decorated
with pillars and panelling and there is a simpler, or
poors' loft and a students' loft.

The Rev.Robert Smith was called as minister to this
church in I789.

Earlier, the Union of I707 had brought depression to Cromarty and failure of fishing made the first half of the
century a black time for the town.

However, a merchant and native of the town by the name
of Forsyth was mainly responsible for the return of prosperity by helping the fishing trade institute a bounty on
herrings which encouraged the fitting out of boats and
later he provided the fishers with tackles and nets.

He also expanded his father's importing and exporting
interests and in I746 was appointed agent of the British
Linen Company in the north of Scotland.

Flax was shipped from Holland and prepared at Cromarty
then shipped to ports of the north. Employment thus provided for linen spinners made up for the loss of herring
fisheries. These and other local resources were put into
use by George Ross who bought the Cromarty Estate in I722
and, it is said, did more for the town than anyone else
was able to do.

He began the manufacture of cotton bagging from imported

hemp and this became a flourishing industry. He built
a brewery to encourage ale-drinking rather than whiskey
drinking. Lacemakers were brought from England. Such was
the consequent trade that Ross persuaded the Government
to contribute seven thousand pounds for the building of
the pier to which he also gave liberally and which was
constructed in 1785.

Thus it was when Robert Smith brought his bride to Cromarty the town was on the upswing. The employment created
coupled with the breaking up of the clan system in the
highlands earlier, had caused immigration of Gaelic
people into Cromarty and Mr.Ross had built for them the
Gaelic chapel on the hill above the town in 1783.

A visitor to Cromarty once recorded it as one of the
neatest, cleanest and prettiest towns of it's size in
Scotland at the time.

By 1829 boats left from Cromarty for London every Tuesday.

When John Smith was young, tremendous business was done
by sea at Cromarty. Hugh Miller published January 6.1830,
in the "Inverness Courier" an account of the launching
from Hugh Allan's shipyard in the town, a large and
handsome schooner which was christened "The Sutors of
Cromarty".

The harbour under George Ross and his successors became
the artery through which much of Scotland's lifeblood
ebbed in emigrant ships. These ships left Cromarty for
Canada and Australia, taking with them emigrants from
Ross and Sutherland, not all of whom - at least in the
earlier days - were impoverished. It has been recorded
"many possessed property, many were young and eager for
adventure".

A changing social structure and competition from the
steamlooms of the industrial south robbed the local
weavers of employment. Cromarty shared depression with
the highlands. The railway stations were to bypass the
town, leaving it in isolation and at the same time under-
cutting the economy of the coastal trade. It was doomed
to become a quaint, neglected backwater in the mid 1800's.

During the thirty-four years of the Rev.Robert Smith's
ministry at the Parish Church, the Smith household - in

35

tneir childhood and youth, must have made quite a lively family circle when they were all home together.

The two first born children, Isabella and Robert, died in infancy. Of the others, John was the fourth oldest. His sister Margaret Crawford Smith, born in 1802, later married a Dr.George MacDonald and had numerous children. After her husband's death she went to live in New Zealand. Catherine married Lieut.John Duff MacDonald and lived in Cromarty. Helen and the youngest daughter, Isabella, went with John to Canada. Robert, the youngest brother, became a doctor and was at Fort Chambly, Lower Canada for a time, died at Stuttgart, Germany, in 1880. Barbara married a man named Joyner and also moved to New Zealand. Hugh is still the unknown on the Family Tree. Their mother died at Cromarty in 1844.

In 1833 John Smith decided he wanted to go to Canada and through tne recommendation of the Rev.Lewis Rose of Nigg and otner friends to the Glasgow Colonial Society, he was considered for Lancaster, Glengarry or Beckwith, Lanark - both in Upper Canada and both wanted ministers fluent in the Gaelic.

He chose Beckwith. Perhaps he may have felt some kinship with the settlers from Laggan, Perthshire, where he had spent some time before being ordained, but on this one can only surmise.

As one can only surmise how he journeyed forth. Did he travel by ship from Cromarty to Greenock to board the brig "Canada" - (Captain James Allan). And was the latter related to Hugh Allan who had a shipyard at Cromarty? We do know the ship sailed from Greenock, August 31st and arrived at Quebec City approximately six weeks later.

What of the quiet backwater town he left?

History records that during World War I (1914-1918) the army encamped nearby the ships of the navy once more used the Firth and the streets echoed with the voices of young seamen again.

Then - back to peaceful-off-the-beaten-track isolation until World War II (1939-1945) when its seaport was used once more. To-day, in the latter 1970's, there is a stirring and busyness and a growth of prosperity from oil activities causing both joy and sadness!

John McLennan has written that Cromarty set on a narrow
strip between high ground and the shore, presents some
physical difficulties to development. But the pressure
of oil related industry at Nigg, just a mile across the
water, has pre-empted any claim the town may have had
to be left in peace.

However, Cromarty's conservation area which already in-
cludes the picturesque old Fishertown is being extended
to cover the whole of the older part of this delightful
town on the Black Isle.

NOTE--
The Cromarty Parish Church known as the
EAST CHURCH - will be celebrating the
establishment of the East Church next
year. It was either the fourth or fifth
church to be constructed in Scotland after
the Reformation (1560), and there are records from 1580 forward concerning the East
Church at the Church Offices, Edinburgh,
so 1980 will be a very significant date.*

*This information and token from the Rev.R.Galloway, now
Minister of the Cromarty Parish Church or EAST Church as
it is called.

The illustration shown is of a Communion token No.47, from
1833...These tokens were distributed by elders to members
before communion and the member returned it to Church on
Communion Sunday. Thus the record was kept of those who
attended the communion as each is numbered.

Courtesy of Rev. R. Galloway.

CHAPTER VI

A MINISTER FOR BECKWITH

It would be foolish to state the Rev.John Smith arrived at Beckwith under ideal conditions. From authentic records we know that this specific congregation had had problems for m any years. This became obvious in I83I when they wished to call a minister of the Church of Scotland for their n ew church which they intended to build of stone. The background of their petition was given by a Beckwith Presbyterian (unnamed) who wrote to a Mr. Wilson of Glasgow from Beckwith, September 28th, I83I, as follows:

> In the beginning of the winter of I8I9 the Residenters wrote a petiton to the Governor of Quebec to see if the Township could be supplied with a clergyman of the Kirk of Scotland, and also some aid from Government for his support. To this petition they received no reply. They then applied to the Rev'd Wm.Bell of Perth to see if he would send a petition to the old country for a minister. I believe between 70 and 80 members subscribed two bushels of wheat for his support.
>
> Bell wrote the Petition in which he desired that they would send out one of the profession of Hall and Peddie, Edinburgh.
>
> We wished for one of the Kirk of Scotland and we did not know at that time BUT that these men in Edinburgh were of our own opinion nor did we know at that time BUT the Kirk of Scotland might be established in Canada as in Scotland without any trouble; but now we know otherwise.

This latter paragraph seems to contain the kernel of the matter in the proverbial nutshell.

The letter continues:

> A minister came but several breaches in
> the congregation have taken place. At
> last Sacrament there were about 120
> communicants. The present minister is
> disesteemed and he cannot preach in
> Gaelic.
>
> A petition was sent to the Society
> signed by between 70 and 80 individ-
> uals, preparations are making for
> building a place of worship and the
> erection is to commence in the Spring
> of 1832.

The foregoing was recorded in The Glasgow Colonial Society Minute Book I - January 19, 1832.

These records are a great source of information as to
what took place in Presbyterian congregations in early
Canada.

On November 22, 1832, the Rev.Wilson of Perth (who had
been sent out earlier by the Church of Scotland) on authority of the Presbytery wrote to the Secretary of The
Glasgow Colonial Society concerning the Beckwith petition.

This letter reads in part:

> We, the Presbytery, have judged it
> expedient, earnestly to request that
> some information may be sent without
> delay by the Society in regard to the
> steps which have been taken as to what
> prospect there is of a minister being
> sent out. I may mention that a good
> stone church has been erected at
> Beckwith. The people are in general
> industrious and comfortable in worldly
> circumstances, and warmly attached to
> the Church of their fathers. And I
> know of few country places where a
> faithful minister may be more agree-
> ably situated. *
>   GCS III 141

We find a Rev.Peter McLaren, a Church of Scotland minister at Lecropt, near Stirling, Scotland, also had an
interest in Beckwith. He had some relatives from Perthshire among the settlers there and he communicated with
the Glasgow Colonial Society in regard to the matter.

Some of the letters are being quoted quite extensively
as they are documents of the time and in considering
some extracts there might be descendants living in
Beckwith and elsewhere in Canada to-day who may be dis-
tantly related to this man and others mentioned who will
find much of interest in same.

The Rev.McLaren's letter is first hand information of
the conditions of the time as reported to him by kinfolk.
He writes to the Rev.Robert Burns at Paisley from the
Manse at Lecropt on <u>December 12, 1831</u>, as follows:

> My dear Sir:
>   From the last report of the
> Society in Glasgow for promoting the
> religious interest of Scottish settlers
> in North America of which you are a
> Secretary, as well as from other sou-
> rces, I learn that an application was
> made to that Society from Beckwith,
> Upper Canada, for a pastor and also
> for aid but for reasons assigned "no
> arrangement has been made in regard
> to it."
>
> I feel some interest in this case,
> many of the applicants having gone
> from my native parish, Comrie, and
> some of them being distant relations.
> I take the liberty of troubling you
> to request that you will at your
> earliest convenience favour me with
> the particulars of the Memorial
> presented to your Society and also
> the recommendation of Mr.Morris of
> Perth which accompanied it.
>
> There is a Gaelic preacher who ex-
> presses a desire to go to America,
> about whom I have been making inquiry
> and if arrangements could be made in

the event of obtaining tne favourable
answers, as to his sentiments, talents,
piety, attainments, etc., he might be
sent to Beckwith, it would afford me
peculiar pleasure. To obtain this object
I nave sometimes thought of applying to
the clergymen of those parishes from
which most of the applicants emigrated
for Collections and perhaps a little
might be got from some friends in this
neighborhood.

I am informed the building of a church
at Beckwith will be commenced in Spring.
And were a Pastor appointed, perhaps
before setting out he might be disposed
to attempt something in the way of preaching and making collections in certain
quarters. The interest which I take in
object in question will I am sure be
sustained as my apology for this trouble. Give me your opinion of the case.

                    (Signed) PETER   MCLAREN
        *GCS iII 76

Further references are made to Beckwith in another letter
from Rev.Peter McLaren to the Rev.Robert Burns. A letter
dated <u>January 2I, 1833</u>, contains some noteworthy ones.

I feel almost ashamed to address you again.
You must have been not a little surprised
at not hearing from me in answer to your
favour of the 20th January I832.

Indeed I had almost despaired of finding
a suitable person for Beckwith and as you
stated in your letter that the only difficulty of the Society was the want of a
proper person, I was unwilling to trouble
you unnecessarily on the subject. However,
I continued to correspond with various
individuals though with little success.

Lately I saw a letter from Beckwith stating "that the Church was built, the windows

and doors ready, if not on, and all the
wood for the seating, etc., ready and
Church would immediately be finished
if a minister were appointed...

I begin to feel anxious for the poor
highlanders of Beckwith. At present I
believe they form one of (?) congregations in Upper Canada, but should
they not get a minister soon it is not
unlikely that some in the outskirts of
the township may join other congre gations though at greater inconvenience
and thus weaken that at Beckwith. From
your letter I perceive the interest you
take in the subject.....

Evidently the Beckwith settlers were Scots for the most
part who worked hard, needed the stability of church
and religion and were dedicated to education and expected a minister to be beneficial to them on both counts.
Now, it is implied, if not in our own section of the
Township, we will go farther afield and join other
groups to give some stability and discipline. The remark made in the Rev.Peter McLaren's letter was more
important than it may seem at first glance as proved
later when a minister came and got involved in remarks
and reports made by the Church of Scotland missionary
at Coburg, on this same matter. McLaren continues-

I trust your Society will still be disposed to give the fifty pounds, which
you mentioned in your last, should Mr.
McEwen or any other properly qualified
young man be found.

The answers to Mr.McEwen's queries is
by a young man attending Glasgow College
from America, who is a distant relation
of my own and whose father I believe
was the Contractor for the Church of
Beckwith. *
                                GCS V 8
Now let us consider the young man, John McEwen, who had
written to the Rev.McLaren of his interest in the ministry in Canada. He seems to have had some ambitions
toward authorship. It would also seem from the Rev.

42

McLaren's remarks to Robert Burns in the letter January 2I, I833 - just quoted, that McEwen was a son of a Beckwith settler who had gone over to Scotland as a student of divinity.

Let us examine some extracts from his letter, a long epistle written in flowery, religious terms, which portrays the young man as something less than enthusiastic.

He writes to the Rev. McLaren from Auchterderainan on April 25, I833.

> I am fully aware that you have just
> grounds to be surprised at my delay
> in replying to your kind letter con-
> taining so minute and satisfactory a
> solution of the question regarding
> Beckwith which I proposed for your
> consideration. I may state at once
> that I am completely pleased with
> your answers, and when I consider
> the condition of that people, de-
> prived in great m easure of that
> which alone can support them under
> the trials of life, and gild even
> the brightest scenes of earthly
> prosperity, my heart glows ardently
> with the desire of being the unworthy
> instrument of diffusing the knowledge
> of Christ among them, and by the Grace
> of God, of guiding their steps thro'
> the wilderness of time to a home of
> brightness and blessing in the clime
> of everlasting joy......

He goes on to say he has reflected seriously, etc... and gives the reasons for declining (should he be accepted) at that time - the Beckwith ministry! He says if it were the next Spring (I834) he'd be very interested.

The letter continues in part:

> But altho' my resolution of emigrat-
> ing to Canada is as fully fixed as ever,

> I find it will be impossible to leave
> Scotland this season without incurring
> disadvantages which could not be easily
> repaired afterwards. One of these I may
> mention knowing that you will sympathize
> with the feeling I experience.
>
> My library is but small altho' I have
> for the last 12 months devoted all my
> spare money in making additions to it,
> and as I am at present in the course of
> collecting a number of works favoured
> to authors, and without which the sol-
> itude of the Back Settlements would to
> me at least be dreary indeed were I to
> go this season, I would be completely
> deprived of this prized and invigorat-
> ing source of enjoyment and which I
> would not procure there without diff-
> iculty and at an enormous expense. GCS IV 100

Another paragraph gives yet another reason and this one
really touches the crux of the matter at Beckwith. It
may help to understand the line in the unknown writer's
letter to Mr.Wilson of Glasgow on the background of the
petition from Beckwith. He stated, referring to the
Rev.George Buchanan - "and he cannot preach in Gaelic".

Down through the years inferences have always been made
that the Rev.George Buchanan had the Gaelic, thus the
remark quoted above tends to make one wonder and the
answer may lie here. Perhaps it not being his mother
tongue as he got older and ailing, it was more and more
difficult to concentrate and PREACH in Gaelic.

Here is what young John McEwen writes in his letter to
the Rev.McLaren, which may substantiate such a view.

> There is another circumstance you men-
> tion which has somewhat staggered me
> I do not read my sermons as I find
> little difficulty in committing to
> memory. BUT I AM AFRAID OF THE GAELIC,
> for altho that language is native to
> me, and altho I was in the habit of
> SPEAKING IT WHILE I LIVED WITH MY FATHER.

I have never employed myself in writing it, and from the course of my education being wholly in English, I find
that I have considerable difficulty in
expressing myself in that language, and
I fear it would be out of my power for
some time at least to undertake the duty
of preaching in it without notes. At
least I would feel reluctance with my
present knowledge of it to pledge myself
to do so. I am in the habit of reading
the Gaelic Scriptures privately but I
have made but few attempts at compostion.
I am now however to commence its study
more systematically and vigorously and
I cherish the hope of mastering it in
the course of sometime at least to such
an extent as will enable me to convey
my sentiments intelligently. GCS IV I00

Therefore, we can see the Rev.Archibald Young's comments
on John Smith's trial sermon for The Glasgow Colonial
Society was of great importance, and I quote:

May 27, 1833
That Mr. Smith preached yesterday an
orthodox Gaelic sermon for me with such
propriety and facility of expression
that I could not have discovered that
Gaelic was an acquired language had he
not told me so. GCS IV I33

Once again the Rev.Peter McLaren of Lecropt writes to the
Glasgow Colonial Society and this time we sense it is
with relief.

June 28th, 1833
From a recent newspaper I saw stated
that a Rev.Smith from Cromarty was
appointed to Beckwith, Upper Canada,
America. I rejoice to see this appointment, as I feared from Mr.McE's
last letter that he was not so hearty
in the cause as we could have wished.
This I think I ventured to hint in my
last to you. I rejoiced the more; assur-
ed, from the caliber and determination

> of the Colonial Society to see none
> but men of talent, unblemished char-
> acter and evangelical principle, the
> pastor appointed for Beckwith was a
> man who possessed these qualifications.
> And besides knowing that you held,
> that Gaelic was a sine qua non in
> that station, I felt that Mr.Smith
> must know Gaelic and be able to preach
> in it. I felt therefore satisfied that
> Beckwith is to enjoy the labours of a
> talented, pious and faithful pastor.
> I hope Mr.Stewart of Cromarty knows
> and has recommended him.
>   GCS IV I49

The Rev.Alexander Stewart had succeeded John Smith's
father as minister of the Cromarty Parish in I824 and
the Smith family were members of that congregation.

The Beckwith station incidentally had been written up
in The Glasgow Colonial Society report No.7, I833,
as follows:

> The case of Beckwith has occupied
> much of the attention of the Direct-
> ors during the year and they are not
> without hopes, that a well-qualified
> clergyman, able to preach in English
> and in Gaelic, will soon be sent to
> that very promising settlement. A
> Church has been built, a lot of hun-
> dred acres has been secured, and
> government aid is expected in addit-
> ion to the engagement by the people
> and the Society. Thus this station
> does not owe it's want of a minister
> to any deficiency in the way of liber
> al encouragement.

On May 29th, I833, John Smith wrote from the Manse at
Dunoon, his acceptance to Archibald Young, Glasgow, of
the Beckwith charge:

> Allow me to express to you my gratit-
> ude for your kind attention and for
> your proffer of assistance in prepar-
> ation for my intended transatlantic

voyage and the kindness of every
member of your worthy committee towards me was most generous and kind,
and sincerely anxious, believe me, do
I feel, that through the Grace of God
I may be enabled to justify the good
opinion regarding me which they have
been pleased to express. Of the two
stations offered me by the Society I
have determined to accept of Beckwith
and hope that with as little delay as
possible, you will have the kindness
to forward to me at Cromarty any document in the shape of Bond or Letter
of Recommendation which may be required by our Presbytery previous to grant-
ing an ordination. Something of the
kind they will of course require. Could
you give me any information about securing the means used either in this
country or in Canada, for the promised
Government allowance at Beckwith? Have
the kindness also to say whether in add-
ition to defraying the expense of my
passage the Society will have any objection to advance me before leaving this
country any part or the whole of their
allowance of forty pounds. Along with
this, I beg to return the papers regarding the Lancaster Station given to me by
the Society.

>   Yours with great regard,
>   JOHN SMITH   GCS IV I34

Mr. Young then wrote the North American Society quoting
the foregoing letter and added a postscript which read:

Has the bad spirit which at one time
existed at Beckwith subsided? If not,
would it not be well to give Mr.Smith
some kind line regarding it? As from
his modesty and I would almost say
bashful manner, he might not be able
to bear up against such a spirit and
thereby materially injure his usefuless.GCS I36

It might be enlightening to consider at this time the station decided upon - BECKWITH, Upper Canada - mentioned by the Rev.Archibald Young as having a "bad spirit".

There were inferences of a split in the congregation over the new stone church and Bell had already written in his diary of dissatisfaction of the congregation with the Rev.George Buchanan. It has been implied this dissatisfaction began shortly after his arrival because he was not Church of Scotland, as the settlers in 1819 had wanted. His Gaelic fell short also of their expectations and since some of them no doubt did not speak English at that time, this would be important to them.

What of Buchanan's background? Did it have any bearing on all this uncertainty and disagreement with regard to St. Andrews in connexion with the Church of Scotland, the new stone church of which the building began in Spring 1832.

Small's History of United Presbyterian Congregation, has this to say:

> George Buchanan, described in the minutes of the Relief Synod for 1797, as "student of divinity" who thoroughly understands the Gaelic language. Licensed by Perth Presbytery and employed two seasons in the Highland Mission of Argyleshire. With the view of being ordained at Strathkinnes he was certified to Dysart Presbytery in April 1800. In July 1808 he demitted his charge, but, the congregation having promised to be more regular in paying up his stipend, he agreed to remain. On the 18th May he resigned a second time.
>
> After parties had been heard, the Presbytery blamed the people for having proved undutiful to their minister, but it carried to accept the resignation and grant an ample certificate of ministerial and moral character.
>
> Mr.Buchanan now acted as a preacher for a number of years, but in 1816 a sphere of labour opened for him at Kirkcaldy. When Thomas Nairn left the Associate Presbytery

and joined Mr. McMillan, a few of his
people built a place of worship for him
in Linktown. For forty-four years this
straggling remanent had for their minister, Mr.James Kirkcaldy. In I8I6 they
were vacant and Mr.Buchanan was without
a church, and in some way the parties
were brought together. The Cameronian
Presbytery found that Kirkcaldy congregation had been admitting "a number of
vagrant preachers to their pulpit" and
had also subscribed a call to one of
these preachers without their concurr-
ence. This was the Rev.George Buchanan,
who without ecclesiastical recognition,
became minister of this little society
of Cameronians. For renouncing their
authority the Relief Presbytery of Dysart
cut him off from their connection and when
he applied for readmission in I8I9 they
found it inexpedient to receive him.

Somewhere along the line he was chaplain in the military -
perhaps in the years between I808-I8I6 or I8I6-I8I9 but
this has not been verified.

Small's History continues:

In the Spring of I822 when an application came from Beckwith in Upper
Canada to some members of Edinburgh
Seccesionist Presbytery for a missionary who could preach both in Gaelic
and English, they made the choice of
Mr.Buchanan. His testimonials were
considered highly satisfactory, and
he possessed medical skill, this
with the gift of the two languages
fitted him as a triple blessing to
his countrymen in the far West.

Much has been written about George Buchanan's ministry
of a decade I822-I832. His daughter, Jessie Buchanan
Campbell, in her book, "The Pioneer Pastor", wrote
glowingly, sometimes bitterly,(but not always factually)

recalling from memory extending over approximately seventy years, from when she was a child of eleven on arrival to an elderly lady in her late 80's.

The Rev.William Bell, Buchanan's friend, or at least the man instrumental in securing him as a minister for Beckwith, wrote up many incidents in his diary:

> In 1828 he records that Mrs.B.(Bell) and he started July 18th to Beckwith. "No horse for road full of trees since great storm of June 27th. At places water so deep that we had to take off shoes and stockings and wade. Reached Beckwith at 9 P.M. Preached Saturday 19th. Sabbath - not very big congregation not so much because of roads as I found, but dissatisfaction at Buchanan.

> Feb.20, 1830. -State of Buchanan's congregation discouraging. To arouse them it was proposed to build a church and form a Missionary Society.

> March 2, 1830. - I went to Beckwith, preached and discussed building afterwards. But most were unwilling and unfriendly to Buchanan.

And again in October 1831 he writes:

> A collection has been ordered this fall, in all churches to aid the synod fund but Mr.Buchanan and his congregation being upon bad terms, he was afraid they would rebel, and therefore he proposed he exchange with me the day of collection....

Again, the Rev.Bell in his diary May, 1832, wrote about the Fair, May 1st and continues:

> Two days after this we received intelligence that Mr.Buchanan's barn was burnt, with all it contained. He had been burning chips, and all the rubbish around it on a windy day, and before the fires were out he left them and went to work in the

garden. In a little after, when he looked
around, the barn was in a blaze. His neighbours saw the fire and came to his assistance, but to no purpose. In half an hour
the barn was consumed together with the
hay, grain, cutter, harness, saddle, seed
potatoes, pulpit and seats for it was used
as their place of worship, and everything
else it contained. The dwelling house was
saved with great difficulty for at this
time the shingles were very dry.

The dissension of several years standing came to a head
with this event and the building of a new church became
expedient. The congregation had already made up their
minds in 1831, it was to be of stone and "in connexion
with the Church of Scotland", as they had wished originally.

No doubt it seemed a long time, although it was only two
years until the arrival of a new minister and the finish-
of the new church building.

Why the church was built on McArthur's property and not
the glebe belonging to the congregation and held in trust
by the trustees - Alexander Dewar and John McTavish - is
a mystery that might in time come to light if there were
any old McArthur papers available of that time.

The variety of groups of religious break-offs from the
Church of Scotland were many and varied and it is not
my intention to go into them here. However, I have included in an appendix at the back of the book (through the
kind permission of Mr.Donald Steel, author of several
books on historical research, genealogy and education,
brief and concise summaries he has written on Secessionists, Free Kirk, Relief Synod, Burghers and Anti-Burghers
and Cameronians. From his book, National Index of Parish
Registers Vol.XII -"Sources for Scottish Genealogy and
Family History"by D.J.Steel - pages 190-193).This will
help those interested to understand what was meant by the
different names, the times and how they related to the
Church of Scotland.

We know the Rev.Buchanan and Rev.Bell were Secessionists
from Edinburgh - Burghers - and the Church of Scotland
Assembly recorded in their minutes of Synod August 2nd

1832 the following:

> The report of t he Committee appointed
> to collect information respecting Pres-
> byterians in Canada NOT in connexion with
> the Church of Scotland as to the exped-
> iency of admitting them into the commun-
> ion with this church, being called for,
> was given by Mr.Rintoul, and approved
> the tenor - as follows:

> The community met with the Rev. Wm. Smart,
> Brockville, Convenor of the Committee for
> the United Synod of Canada for treating
> in the matter of the Union, and received
> from him the following information - that
> the ministers of the United Synod were I5
> in number.

Among the names were included the Rev.William Bell of
Perth, Rev. Boyd of Prescott, Rev. Gemmel of Lanark,
Rev. Smart of Brockville AND the Rev.George Buchanan
of Beckwith.

This would seem to disprove Jessie Buchanan Campbell's
statement that her father was a staunch Secessionist and
refused to give up his convictions. However, the culmin-
ation of this re-admittance to the Church of Scotland
took time and when it became fact, the Rev.George Buchanan had died.

It is also interesting to note an item of December 26th,
I823, in Bell's Diary which reads - "We met, at my suggestion, at the house of Mr. Buchanan in Beckwith and
after hearing a sermon from Dr. Gemmill, the ministers
and elders present were formed into a Presbytery called
the Presbytery of Perth. They declared their adherence
to the principles of the Church of Scotland and appointed
to meet four times a year."

Beckwith, "the trouble spot" for whatever reasons, finally got a new minister and the announcement was made
in "The Scottish Guardian" a paper established in I832
by the evangelical party of the Church of Scotland, June
I4th, I833 issue, page no. 4:

> The Glasgow North American Colonial Soc-
> iety have lately been pleased to make the

following appointment: The Rev.John Smith,
Cromarty, to the English and Gaelic congregation, Beckwith, Upper Canada".

The new minister of course had to be properly ordained
in his charge and the Presbytery of Chanonry minutes the
event:

> At Chanonry, the ninth day of July, one
> thousand eight hundred and thirty-three
> years, which day the Presbytery of Chan-
> onry was constituted by prayer. Inter alia:
> Mr. John Smith, preacher of the gospel who
> had been taken on trials for ordination at
> ast meeting of Presbytery with a view to his
> settlement in the congregation in connexion
> with the Church of Scotland at Beckwith, Up-
> per Canada, appeared at this meeting and ha-
> ving presented a certificate of having qual-
> ified to Government, he delivered the sev-
> eral pieces of trial formerly prescribed to
> him all of which the Presbytery approved of
> and sustained. And the Presbytery having
> again maturely deliberated on the whole
> circumstance of this case now before them,
> unanimously resolved to proceed forthwith
> to ordain Mr.Smith. Where upon the Moderator
> did, in presence and by appointment of Pres-
> bytery, put to Mr.Smith the questions in the
> prescribed formula and having received sat
> isfying answers, Mr.Smith was by solemn
> prayer and the imposition of the hands of
> the Presbytery, set apart and ordained to
> the office of the Holy Ministry at Beckwith,
> Upper Canada, or wherever thereafter the
> Great Head of the Church may see meet to
> cast his lot. And all the Breth n of the
> Presbytery having given Mr.Smith the right
> hand of fellowship, the Moderator in a
> suitable address exhorted him to maintain
> a doctrine and conversation becoming a min-
> ister of Christ and encouraged him as to
> the interesting department of Our Lord's
> Vineyard in which he was called to labour.

The original Bond granted by the Trustees
of the Congregation at Beckwith, and the
original Minute of Mr.Smith's appointment
by the Director of the Glasgow North American Colonial Society, were at his request
returned to him coram; and the Clerk was
instructed to furnish him with an extract
of this Minute when required. (Certified
true extract - G.V.R.Grant - Clerk to the
Presbytery of Chanonry, Dingwall and Loch-
carron, MARCH, 1977).

The choice made, the solemn ordination service behind him,
we find the Rev.John Smith arriving at Quebec City, together with his two sisters, Misses H. and I.Smith on
October 8th, 1833.

The Rev.Clugsten of St.John's Church, Quebec City, (now
Chalmers Wesley United Church) seems to have entertained
new arrivals and shown them around the city as an introduction to their new country.

In a letter to Rev.Burns, Paisley, November 12th, 1833,
he writes:

I will not say anything of the missionaries
who came out in the early part of the season. You will most likely have heard from
themselves individually. John Leach and
John Ford arrived on or about the 9th of
October and after spending a day in Quebec
proceeded onward to the U.P. Messrs McNaughton and Smith arrived about the same
time. Rev.McNaughton preached for me on
the 15th of October, the Thursday previous to the dispensation of Lord's Supper in my congregation. Then Rev.Smith
and he set off for Montreal the following
day. *
*This information courtesy of Rev. Cook
of Chalmers Wesley United Church, Quebec
City.

He also mentioned Smith and McNaughton in a letter to a
friend in Montreal, to the effect their stations at Beckwith and Glengarry would find them very worthy ministers.
The Rev.McNaughton was minister ordained to Lancaster,

Glengarry and arrived on the same boat as John Smith,
October 8th, 1833 - the "Canada" from Greenock.

BECKWITH

"Every blade o' grass
has it's ain drap o'
dew."
Unknown

#-14   RUINS OF CHURCH 7TH LINE, 1937
        BECKWITH   Jean S. McGill

CHAPTER VII

JOHN SMITH OF BECKWITH

The Rev.John Smith - Minister of Beckwith!

Have you ever suffered the frustration at a party of trying to put a name to a face? Then you will know it is even more difficult to put a face to a name. I mean someone about whom you have read or whom you've researched and you try in your imagination to conjure up what he or she was like in the physical sense.

With the Rev.John Smith, this was for a long time an unrewarding challenge. Jessie Buchanan Campbell wrote: "a quiet, unassuming man". A Glasgow Colonial Society official wrote: "this modest (bashful) man". And, the Rev. Rose of Nigg in commending him wrote:" shy almost to a fault, causing diffidence of speech."

At Presbytery meetings and Synod gatherings the records merely list among those present - John Smith, Beckwith". Woe is me, I thought - how can I make this person real to readers, especially those interested in the history of the Beckwith congregation?

Years of fruitless searching in Church records of Bath-hurst Presbytery; then finding a tombstone had been erected to his memory by the congregation in connexion with the Church of Scotland.(thanks to Howard Brown, historian). His obituary in the paper when discovered told of his qualities and abilities in English and Gaelic and that he left a widow and six children.

His marriage record finally found at St.Andrews Pres-byterian Church, Ottawa, and the announcement of the wedding published in the"Quebec Mercury " two weeks later; as well as interesting relatives, continued to pique my curiosity. A copy of his will written gently, sensibly and listing friends and relatives of some import in the early Bytown area was an important add-ition to research papers. But still the "man" eluded me as to character and personality.

I collected photographs of family - his mother in her
youth, sisters, daughters, son, nephews, great-grand-
children. Looking at them I tried to visualize a composite
picture but alas I could not put "flesh on the bones"!

A letter written when he was twenty-one years old showed
him as an ordinary young man who felt he had displeased
his mother on his last holiday home by going shooting at
Nigg; who teased a newly married sister not to become too
matronly and lose her spirit of fun; who was disappointed
over pots of jam sent to him at Aberdeen that had been
broken en route and which meant the jam could not be
eaten; who writes of having a cold and being spoiled by
some ladies of the church.

But ten years later - what of the man?

I almost gave up in despair after being informed that some
references made to him in correspondence which had been
promised by some relatives in New Zealand, had been lost
in a fire.

Then, a Glasgow Colonial Society letter brought me a
personality portrait of the Rev.John Smith, in his own
words, through a long letter-report sent by him from
Beckwith, April, 1834, to the Rev.Archibald Young telling
it as it was - in the Beckwith settlement. The words portray a practicable, factual man, kindly, responsible and
one who could be very definite in expressing himself in
writing.

Therefore, I am going to let the Rev. John Smith speak
to you himself for your own consideration of the type of
man this quiet, unassuming, modest, bashful person really
was!

The extracts from his letter-report are not written here
in the exact order they appear in his letter but they are
quoted exactly as he wrote them to the Glasgow Colonial
Society six months after his arrival in Beckwith.

First, let me quote once again from the Rev.Bell's diary
- date - October 1833.

> Near the end of the month, the Rev. Mr.
> Smith, minister of the Kirk for Beckwith
> arrived. This afforded another proof of the

insincerity of the Kirk ministers in this
quarter. They were sending in ministers
to divide our congregations at the very
time they were professing friendship and
offering to receive us and our congregations into their connection. Mr.Miller, too,
one of their missionaries had among other
falsehoods, stated in the printed extracts
from his journal, that in Beckwith the
gospel was NOT preached, although he well
knew that the Rev.Mr.Buchanan had been
settled 13 years. Mr.Phillips,* Mr. Buchanan's son-in-law, on this gave him a
severe but deserved castigation in the
"Coburg Reformer".

*(Anthony Phillips married Isabella Buchanan, daughter of
the Rev.George Buchanan at St.Andrews Presbyterian Church,
Bytown, in 1832. The minister officiating at the service
- Rev. John Cruichshank.)

Would that we could   ain copies of the "Coburg Reformer"
covering these articles but so far neither archives nor
libraries have been able to turn one up of the time mentioned.

Bell and Buchanan, Secessionists, were on the list to
return to the Church of Scotland and after Buchanan's
death, Wm.Bell did come under the Kirk umbrella.* (*See
Appendices). But in October 1833, he is writing bitterly
in his diary that while the Church of Scotland was courting them back it was sending new ministers, (i.e.John
Smith).

But let us look at the other side of the coin, and realize
a"minister disesteemed" in the eyes of his congregation -
elderly and ailing - and for sometime unable to fulfil his
duties of preaching, was hardly a force for unity and stability in a pioneer community. A congregation would soon
break up under such circumstances with families going to
a variety of religious m eetings, wherever available.
This was what Mr Miller had stressed. He evidently tried
to bring home to the Glasgow Colonial Society and the
Presbyterian communities in Upper Canada the need to have
active Church of Scotland affiliations and ministers at
the established stations (he had mentioned Beckwith in
particular), or the people would go elsewhere to worship.

John Smith refers in his letter to groups with "heresy tendencies" and "bigoted sectarianism", and also mentions that the Covenanter faction would have gained much ground with the congregation if he had not arrived when he did.

For sometime before this the Church of Scotland Assembly had been doing "battle" for recognition in Canada and records show they were trying to stress that while the Church of England was the State Church in England, it was not necessarily so in the colonies and the Church of Scotland had equal rights to Government allowances for ministers and to clergy reserves.

It was a long, hard argument but eventually Government allowances were granted and we find the Rev.John Smith applied to Lieut. Gov. Rowan for his the day after his first sermon - November 4th, 1833.

We also find in the records a petition to the Lieut. Governor from Alex Dewar and J. Carmichael in June 1833, stating Buchanan had preached for so many months and they felt he was entitled to a Government payment.

It was more or less the termination of the Rev. Buchanan's preaching days, apart from his own family worship, five months before the arrival of Smith, which shows Miller was right in saying the Beckwith settlement was without a preacher.

These are facts, not now of much importance, but at the time there was a hard core to them. One feels had Buchanan been twenty or thirty years younger and had had this irreparable disagreement with the congregation, he'd have sold his property and moved to another settlement to minister to a new group. All kinds of opportunities for such service were possible in the expanding and extending of settlements further westward in the province of Upper Canada and beyond. But again, it must be remembered, his age and health were against another colorful step in the mosaic of his life.

One is saddened by the thought that his family were his prime promoters but, not always in his best interests. Perhaps as Bell so graphically wrote and implied in his diary on many occasions, had they been more industrious and concentrated on keeping and making the property a worhty farm, he could have retired with dignity

He might well have become - as his family did after his death, a member of the Church of the 7th Line, working with the Rev.John Smith in brotherly harmony - not become a symbol of disunity in the tales which have been misinterperted down the years.

The Church of Scotland, it must be admitted, was late out in sending missionaries and ordained ministers to Canada. It was chiefly through the Glasgow Colonial Society the real need for more effort in this direction was made known to them and thus invigorated them to action.

There were certainly Secessionist ministers sent out by the Edinburgh Synod earlier but the basic difference in promotion of the work was that the Secessionist ministers, as Dr.Elizabeth McDougall suggests, were older men either without a church, retired or ready for retirement and they were not provided with assistants.

Whereas the policy of the Church of Scotland was usually when ministers in charge became elderly they were provided with a young assistant to help with the ministerial duties. The Church of Scotland, however, chose for Canada and the colonies, younger men who, it was felt, would withstand the rigours of pioneer living. Even so, some of them, for example, the Rev.Wm.Hutcheson, Minister of the 7th Line, Beckwith, 1956-186i, returned home to Scotland, broken in health.

Thus it would seem reasonable to assume an old, ailing man could not carry on adequately the burdens of a wilderness ministry.

Another point, we might emphasize again, is that the letter written to Mr.Wilson, Glasgow, states:"The present minister is disesteemed and cannot preach in Gaelic".

Ten years in the life of a man from sixty to seventy, suffering from gout and asthma, can bring about many changes in ability and thinking and, as young John McEwen wrote to the Rev.Peter McLaren, he could speak Gaelic in his father's house, but would not want to preach a sermon, or write it.

Gaelic was not Buchanan's first tongue - earlier it was written he "understood" Gaelic. It is often the case as

one gets older it is more difficult to think quickly
and fluently in an acquired language. Perhaps this was
the reason the Gaelic settlers felt he had failed them
and the need for Gaelic became more and more the reason
for seeking a new minister.

We can sympathize with the congregation also, or should
be able to do so in this day and age, when language has
become so important. How many of them must have missed
the scenes of their childhood and the language of their
birth - often not being at all comfortable in English.
Old people who relied on the minister to bring comfort
and inspiration in a way they could understand, might
indeed get a bit querulous on the letter of the law of
their religious service.

The younger ones, as has always been the way, would
accept changing times and adjust to them and evolve with
them to create new ideas in the new world.

This, of course, is all speculation. There are those, it
is written, mostly family, who remained "faithful" to
George Buchanan. In doing so in the way they did, they
seem to have caused ill feelings in the early days of
the Rev.John Smith's ministry. It was a pity. Always
when a candle burns out there is need for new light.

The foregoing has, of course, just been written to make
the reader think a little about the situation at Beckwith.
Certainly, John Smith had not taken on an easy station,
as his superiors in Scotland well knew, and the first
few months must have been very upsetting at times to his
basic nature.

However, we find in his own quiet way he was equal to the
task.

His letter-report of April 1834 is well worth considering
for it's many facets of information.

Here are some excerpts:

> To Archibald Young:
> The only reason for my long delay in
> addressing you or any other member of
> your valuable society was my wish to
> be able to speak from experience, as
> regarding my prospects of usefulness
> and comfort in the situation to which

I have been appointed. It will no doubt
be gratifying to you to know it, and I
trust that it is with a sincerely thankful heart I inform you that all the success which I could have anticipated has
attended my labours here and that my
prospects of usefulness are most encouraging.

Difficulties of one or other unknown in
Scotland are attendant on the work of the
ministry in most situations amongst us.
On my arrival here, the divisions and
party feeling existing among the people
of my congregation were alarming; these in
a great measure originated from the presence of the Scotch Burgher clergyman who
was settled here before I came. And at
this time also it was expected that he
along with the list of his brethren in
the Province were about to be received
into a connexion with our Synod. For various good reasons the portion of the people
here who applied to your Society became
discontented with Mr.Buchanan (for this
you will perhaps know is the name of the
gentleman in question) - a number more
were less displeased with him; a good
many, including several respectable families related to himself continued to
adhere to him, and wished that he should
have got possession of the Church; much
division had its origin in this.
                                    GCS V 28
John Smith mentions the matter connected with Mr. Miller.
The latter had been sent to Upper Canada as a licentiat-
ed missionary through the Glasgow Colonial Society and
eventually was ordained to the Coburg Church. Tragically,
his career ended in death by drowning shortly after John
Smith's arrival.

Smith, referring to him says: "Mr.Miller's death to all
appearances the greatest loss we could have sustained in
the present circumstances of our Church here; he was peculiarly fitted to be useful; he left my house two days
only before his melancholy death".

64

In his letter to Young, he refers to the matter that Bell
had written up in his diary re the Coburg Reformer.

A very short time before the lamented death
of Mr.Miller, a series of most abusive letters
were published in one of the Provincial news-
papers (The Coburg Reformer) and some addressed to Mr.Miller by the son-in-law of Buchanan.
The letters as I have observed were low and in
bad taste written with a view of hurting the
feelings and sullying the fair and blameless
character of Mr.Miller, with the view also of
falsifying many of the statements made in his
journal and reported to your Society.

The first of these letters a reply was made by
Mr.Miller thr' the medium of the paper in which
they were published. What had been reported to
your Society regarding the Township of Beckwith
was the chief subject of controversy in both
matters, and immediately upon their appearance
and before having the happiness of personal as-
quaintance with him, I wrote to Mr.Miller saying that if agreeable to him, I myself and the
people of my congregation would in some public
manner express our sense of the entire propriety of his conduct, and likewise our feeling of
deep obligation to him. The only reply made by
Mr.Miller was the publication of an extract of
my letter, which of course, was the cause of
the outpouring of torrents of abuse upon me.
Upon the whole I thought it best to allow it to
pass unnoticed.

This detail will I fear be uninteresting to
you, I mention it merely as it was likely to
have awakened occasioned division among my people. This difficulty is now however completely
overcome. The writer of the letters (Anthony
Phillips) referred to has been obliged to leave
our Township, and his father-in-law has now,I
understand entirely given up preaching;except
for his own immediate relations the people
ceased to attend him and have joined our congregation.

65

During the interval between the time of the
application made to your Society and the time
of my appearance to take the pastoral charge
here the feeling of party spirit and animos-
ity reached its height.This with the desire
among some of the better disposed among the
people to live in the use of the means and
observance of the ordinance of the Gospel,
induced a few to connect themselves as regular hearers of a Cameronian clergyman named
McLaughlin. He came to this neighbourhood
about a year ago at the suggestion I believe
of people of his own persuasion living in
Ramsay and some of the townships near it.

I heard this gentleman once preach a plain
gospel sermon and from what I can learn the
tendency of his preaching generally must be
good. His appearance however at the time he
came was an additional cause of disunion among the Presbyterians of Beckwith.

Notwithstanding of all these causes operating
rather in opposition I am rejoiced to have it
in my power to inform the Society that as one
called to minister in Holy things among them
I have met with every mark of esteem and respect from my congregation; in every way also
in which they can add to my personal comfort
they have shown the utmost kindness - the
most cheerful willingness to oblige. GCS V 28

The Rev.Smith then reports some statistics that are rather interesting at this point in time as they imply the
settlers certainly made it their business to travel to
Church in all seasons and the numbers of hearers were on
an average quite high - by modern standards.

His Township visiting is mentioned and the teaching of
the Sabbath School. One gets a fairly graphic idea of his
ministry and plans.

Upwards of 300 regularly attend my public ad-
ministrations. On some favourable days during
the sleighing season, the number attending
could not have been less than 500. During
summer months when our roads are passable, I

66

hope the average number of hearers will be
400 or rather more. This in one of the back
townships is considered a very respectable
audience.

Frequently I go to preach in some of the
remote corners of the Township; on these
occasions the places of preaching are not
large, hitherto have been crowded to excess.

I regularly keep a Sabbath School. The number attending is considerable and much benefit
may be communicated in this way, not only to
the scholars who generally are from 8 to 15
years of age, but also to many of every age
who attend and listen to the instructions
and explanations of the Scripture given to
the scholars. Last Lord's Day for instance,
from 50 to 70 were present besides our shc-
olars.

During the winter months I visited the greater number of families connected with my charge.
I did so partly with the view of communicat-
ing instructions, but chiefly for the purpose
of obtaining some personal knowledge of their
characters and mode of living; in every instance during the course of my visits I met
with cordial welcome.

Sometime between Spring and Harvest seasons
I purpose doing what I can in the way of cat-
echisming. At our meeting of Presbytery called
for the purpose of ordaining Mr.Romanes to the
charge of Smith's Falls (about 12 miles distant
from us) Committees of Presbytery were appointed to ordain Elders in connexion with the congregation here, at Ramsay, and at Smith's Falls.

I think it best at present to have three only
ordained. Two of these are disciples of the
late worthy Mr. Russel of Muthill; the third
is a prudent, pious man. There are several
others in the Township in whose ordination
to the Eldership I should not have much hes-
itation but the matter seems to me so important and involving so much of the spiritual

prosperity of the congregation, that it is
best to postpone it. The opinion and wish
of the Heads of Families have of course
been held in view in this matter.

The Heads of Families were the important core of the
Church. These could form a nucleus of say 70 to 80
members - with hearers numbering 300 or more. The
communion roll would vary in between as children
grew old enough to "join the church on their profession of faith".

Smith continues his report:

The ordination of the Ramsay Elders takes
place about the end of th is month, that
of the Elders here, during the second
week of May.

I have had the happiness of assisting my
co-Presbtyters McAllister and Cruickshank
in dispensation of the Sacrament of the
Lord's Supper.

The Rev.Mr.Wilson of Perth also assisted
at Bytown where you will of course know
that Mr.Cruickshank is settled and where
his ministry is justly and highly valued.

GCS V 28

On spiritual things he ends;

That the Ordinances of Christ are thus
decently administered; that scenes, but
a short time a wilderness and desolate,
frequented only by the savage beasts of
the forests should thus be sanctified by
the voice of praise and prayer must
gratify the heart of every member of
our benevolent Society.

Now we come to the more immediate practical matters of
everyday living in the physical sense. It has been previously quoted regarding his disappointment over housing
on arrival.

On the Church building he remarks:

Our Church is NOT yet finished; if it is
roofed in, floored and pulpit is erected

in it by the end of harvest, I hope we
may have it decently finished.

These remarks lead one to realize that some of the reports
on the church building made to Rev.Peter McLaren were
a bit premature, although no doubt it was meant the mere
framework (albeit in stone) of the church had been constructed and the interior finishing had to be done. As
the report was written in April, it is fairly safe to
assume the church was all in order by the autumn of 1834
and the building of the Manse had begun.

He finally comes to his own personal business and again,
one is struck by a factual,straight forward approach - no
flowery phrases. He calls a spade a spade or, a pound a
pound!

We have, of course, realized he was not in a strong financial position when he left Scotland. The Glasgow Colonial Society had paid him 3 guineas for travelling expenses when he gave his trial sermon. He had requested
some advance on his salary for the year of forty pounds
to travel to Canada. He was advanced twenty and under the
Government allowance he was allowed fifty pounds per year.

However, it would seem he found expenses to Beckwith to
have exceeded his expectations as he writes:

> Is it too much to ask you to use your
> kind influence with the Society to make
> me some allowance for travelling from
> Montreal to Beckwith; owing to the seas-
> on of the year when I came the expense
> of this journey was very heavy upon me.
> Altho it cost me a great deal more I
> shall consider say a sum between five
> and ten pounds sufficient renumeration.

One can't help but wonder the route he took. Was it by
boat from Montreal to Lachine to Ottawa and thence overland to Franktown by the Richmond Road? Or, by batteau
on the St. Lawrence to Brockville and overland to Smith's
Falls to Perth? In any case, he writes:

> In case the Society may think it right
> to make me some allowance say five pounds
> itself, may I further beg of you to ask
> Mr.Montgomerie to pay the money falling

due to me this year by the Society, in
the following sums:

To - the Rev.Peter McLaren of Lecropt,
fifteen pounds.

To - the order of Robert Smith of Bais-
hay near Paisley, five pounds

To - the order of Mr.John Joyner, Merchant, Tain, Ross-shire, five pounds.

The first mentioned sum is intended
for the use of a son of one of my
Parishoners who is now in Scotland
engaged in the study of divinity.

The last mentioned sums go in part-
payment of old debts.

Robert Smith was, of course,his younger brother and
Joyner was possibly related to his sister Barbara's
husband. John Smith continues:

When I left Scotland Mr. Willis talked
to me of the intention of your Society
to establish Tract and Book depositories
in our neighbourhood. We are much in want
of such. We particularly require books
for our Sabbath School.

He ends this long report with this sentence:

I had late accounts from Mr.McIntosh of
Charlottetown. He says, "My congregation
is large and prospering and I trust that
few have by Grace been brought to a knowledge of the Faith.

One wonders was this a personal friend? The son possibly
of the Rev. McIntosh of Tain?

John Smith's signature is large and generous and destroys
the image of an insipid, lukewarm character - apologetic
and stammering. He comes through - to me at least - as
a man able to assess a situation honestly and well, not
playing down the difficulties but not puffing himself up
nor being dismayed by the challenges. His tolerance,
opinions, optimism and love of people has no face yet
the spiritual essence of the man gives body to his personality.

70

His happiness over helping with the Sacraments; his dis-
may over the death of Mr.Miller; his disappointment
over housing; his concerin to secure books and his joy
over his scholars and congregation make one - almost a
century and a half later, feel that any church would
find such a man very worthy to-day.

NOTE

In doing research on the Church of the Seventh Line I often came across some confusion as to remarks and events.

It seemed as though the verbal historical tales intertwined one church with another and some people were thinking of the Church at Black's Corners - THE FREE KIRK - built in 1844, when discussion was made of the stone church on the 7th Line, in connexion with the Church of Scotland, built in 1832.

The disruption did make a split in the congregation and to a layman not aware of the specific family backgrounds of the individual members of the congregation, the idea suggests itself that many newcomers in the 1840's would have been seriously affected by the changing viewpoints in Scotland. The Irish Presbyterian element would not be too tied to the Church of Scotland ideas and the Presbyterians from the United States were a more independent group.

The churches at Carleton Place and Franktown were, of course, under the Presbyterian Church in Canada within a few years of building. The Manse of the 7th Line sold through trustees of whom Robert Bell, the son of the Rev. William Bell, was the chief negotiator with the Ottawa Presbytery for permission to sell the Glebe, Lot SE 12, Concession seven, Beckwith. This was accomplished in 1878. (*Appendices)

The Church not owned by the congregation was simply closed, the pews and trimmings removed, leaving the building a shell to the elements.

The forty-two years, more or less, of it's activities however, should not be negated. Nor should the lives and efforts of the men responsible for the ongoing work, be forgotten.

CHAPTER VIII

THE CHURCH

The Church built on Lot 14, Concession 7, Township of
Beckwith, County of Lanark, District of Bathurst, has
been known by many names,

Marriage records written by John Smith are headed The
Scotch Church of Beckwith. Other names were - The Scotch
Congregation of Beckwith; St.Andrews of the 7th Line
in connexion with Church of Scotland.

Under whatever name the congregation of the 7th Line
after ten years of bickering and dissension, seemed to
settle down in 1834 to enjoy the new ministry and their
new stone church.

As mentioned earlier, there will always be several unanswered questions with not a hope of being answered.
One is - why was the church built on the McArthur's
property? There were several McArthur brothers and they
owned land on Lots 13, 14 and 15, Concession 7. Beckwith
Township. They were a prolific family according to the
church register. The first small domicile on Lot 13,
Concession 7 is no longer there but the house first built
on Lot 14 evolved into a lovely stone building and is
still inhabited to-day. The last McArthur to live there
died in the 1960's.

The McArthur's had a still. One can therefore imagine
they had many visitors. It tickles the imagination to
visualize the groups going up to visit - for a wee dram
or a jugful, on Saturday night perhaps - being the same
group to trudge up and over the Jock stream to the kirk
on the Sabbath. (This distillery licenced in the 1840's)

They were, for their time, prosperous farmers and John
McArthur became a good friend of the Rev.John Smith. He
was an Elder of the Church on the 7th Line following the
disruption in 1844. His name appears on the Rev. John
Smith's will as one of the executors, together with that
of Colin McLaren, another member of the Beckwith congregation.

73

It is said Alexander Stewart who died
in 1892 at the age of 100 did the fine
woodwork in the Scots Church of 7th
Line, Beckwith in 1834.

The Beckwith Church pulpit was so high
as to be on a level with the gallery
opposite and its canopy made of finely
carved native wood reached to the top
of the wall behind it. The precentor's
stand was placed directly in front,
and below the pulpit. It was reached
by ascending three steps. There was a
doorway in each end wall of the church.
These doors were connected by a wide
aisle, and faced the pulpit from the
east and west respectively. The gallery
was reached by two flights of steps,
one at each end of the church. An
impassable partition cut across its center.

A long table at which communicants sat
while they partook of the Sacrament
stood in front of the pulpit enroaching
somewhat on the aisle space...

Peter Hunter Drummond, the boy mentioned, uncle to Claire
Drummond of Edmonton, whose forebears lived in the house
across from McArthur's from 1865 to 1905, was born in
1880. Five years after the church was closed. Two years
after the Manse was sold and, by 1905 the Church was a
total ruin.

A McEwen was the contractor who built the Church. The
photo taken from an article by J.T.Kirkland in the
"Almonte Gazette" 1937, shows it as it was in its last
days - the beautiful woodwork and pulpit gone - stripped
of seating and the finishing that made it alive and mean-
ingful to the congregation. If stones could only talk -
what a story could be told!

As it is, when the property was sold out of the McArthur's
family, the new owners having small children bulldozed

As you will recall, when the barn on Buchanan's property where services were held from 1822-1831 burned down, the Rev. George Buchanan wanted a log church built on his property but the seeds of dissension had been sown and there were those who had already planned for a stone church for some time, so the tug of war ended with the building of the church on Lot 14, Concession 7.

The Presbytery of Bathurst met at York in August 1833, according to page No. 43 of the Minutes of the Presbytery. Ministers present were - J.Ketchum, J.Cruichshank and Matt.Miller and an extract of an item of business reads as follows.

> No. 5.BECKWITH - subscription 200 pounds. Estimated expenses 400 pounds. No. of congregation 300. No minister, but bond and application before the British North American Colonial Society, Glasgow. All but pews finished. Debt, 100 pounds.

In the Spring of 1834, John Smith wrote:

> ....if it is roofed in, floored, and pulpit erected in it by end of harvest, I hope we may have it decently finished.

And decently finished it became!

One wonders how much influence John Smith had in connection with the seating and interior design.

It is intriguing speculation. Look at the photo (see illustration) and consider the interior of the Cromarty Parish Church; then note this description of the Beckwith Church written up in G.E.Kidd's "The Story of the Derry", page 21, published in 1946.

> Peter Drummond was familiar with the Church on the Seventh line. As a boy he played in it, while the furnishings were still in place.
>
> The most unique feature of the building was the pulpit, which was placed high in the center of the north side.

the ruins to a pile of stones. And now they are merely a hillock under winter snows and a green mound during the summer.

The next owners, the late Jack Harris and his wife, Barbara, offered in Centennial year, to allow a fence to be built enclosing it as a memorial site but this offer was not acted upon.

In 1971 I suggested some sort of cairn be built to mark this site of the first Presbyterian Church in Beckwith Township and to this the Harris' were agreeable. Again, for some reason, nothing was done. Now, I hear there is a possibility of something of this nature being instigated. Let us hope so.

Though in the final sense we must admit a church is more than a building. It is in essence the people - the congregation - and, what of them?

CHAPTER IX

THE CONGREGATION

A church is simply a building until it comes alive through the congregation. It would be a fair supposition, I think, to say the members of the Scotch Church of the Seventh Line, in connexion with the Church of Scotland, Beckwith, put much of themselves into the construction and life of their church.

What kind of people were they?

Of highland ancestry most of them, more at home in the Gaelic language than in English; down to earth, hardworking, ambitious for their children in educational matters and with a strong religious fibre to their characters.

To-day, (apart from descendants lining in the district with family histories written or passed down by word of mouth from generation to generation) the congregation of the 7th Line, in the years between 1834 and 1851, are merely names recorded in the minutes of the Session, so long ago, by the Rev. John Smith.

Many moved westward to Toronto, to the far West, down to the States and East to Ottawa and Quebec. Some descendants are still active and energetic in community affairs in various places in Lanark County, alive to the heritage that is theirs because of these rugged early settlers.

They were all ardent learners of the Catechism in the Sabbath School - that much we know. It was a serious, responsible business being prepared for "joining the Church", and one can see names of families expanding and growing over the years, being added to the communion roll in a never-ending stream, as generation succeeded generation.

One doubts if the joke told in later years in Scotland would have caused any amusement in Beckwith in the mid-1800's.

A dominie (school teacher) preparing his
class for the Minister's visit to the
school, told them -

"He'll ask you questions on the catechism,
so be prepared.
He'll start with the first boy and so on
down the line, the questions will continue.
Who made you? And the first boy will answer, "God".
Of what are you made? and the second boy
will answer "Dust". And so he prompted them.

Just before the arrival of the minister, the
first boy in the row asked to leave the room
and was still gone when the minister came in
and immediately proceeded with the question-
ing.
Thus, to the second boy, he said, "Who made
you?"
The answer came loud and clear, "Dust"!
"Oh no, my boy", said the minister, "God
made you".
To which the cheery lad replied, "Oh no -
please, sir, the boy God made is out of the
room"!

In reading through the Minutes of Session, one is a bit
awed by the many instances of misbehaviours of members
of the congregation recorded which came to the attention
of the Session - Elders and Minister. These miscreants
were required to confess the sin, be admonished by the
minister and if judged properly penitent by the Session,
allowed to partake of Communion but only after appearing
in Church before the entire congregation and publicly
acknowledging the deed.

It seems a far cry from to-day's permissive society but
I suppose it was basically the strength and protection
of the community. The Rev.Smith comes through as a kindly
understanding man and his task could not have been an
easy one as Moderator. It certainly had to be mercy temp-
ered with justice in many ways - as one can see from
this item in the records, dated I839.

Nov. 10th, 1839.
....which day the Session met and was
constituted by prayer, present - Rev.
J.Smith; John McDonald; John Carmichael;
John Campbell; Alex. Dewar and Peter
Campbell, Elders.

The case of----------------was brought
under consideration of the Session.
Previous to marriage with her present
husband------------------she had on two
different occasions fallen into the sin
of fornication in both instances when
absent from this township and engaged
at a distance as a servant. Her case
being of an aggravated nature, the
session were unanimously of opinion that
without public rebuke and public confession of her sin, she should not be
admitted to the privilege of the church;
yet, considering that such public appearance might possibly induce an attack
of hysterical or epileptic fit to which
she is represented as being usually subject, the Session deem it expedient that
intimation for the reason just specified,
she is to be admitted to the church privileges on her confession of crime to the
Session.

There came a time when the Church of Scotland decided
the rules of public appearance and confessing as punish-
ment for moral misbehaviour was not the most humane or
Christain formof religion and it was eliminated from the
Church of Scotland.

The Rev.Smith suggested in 1839 it be omitted in his
church but the Elders to a man decided it was good discipline and should be continued. Dour, stubborn, inflex-
ible men, no doubt, but who felt in the pioneer settlement - especially, there had to be some code of honour
and behaviour for the good of all. One would not presume
to judge their decision but it does bring home the fact
that a Minister was but one voice on the Session.

The item January 2Ist, I839, read:

> Altho' the laws obliging those guilty
> of scandalous offences to profess pub-
> licly penitence of the same, has in
> many parishes become obsolete in
> Scotland, and has not, so far as is
> known to Session, been fully acted
> upon in any Scotch congregation in
> the province, still the Session being
> unanimously of the opinion that obser-
> vance of this law would be beneficial,
> it was resolved it be enforced.

However, a more mellow appoach to life was often expressed and a story from Smith's Falls told in this century
of a "humanity to man" tale of early times makes one
smile.

A man and a woman living together outside of marriage
for some years, became parents of a baby whom they wanted to have baptized.

They approached the minister of the time who said this
could not be done as they were not married. What to do?
The pastor stroked his beard. "No", he really could not
marry them without severe repercussions but, he suggested
they might take a journey down into the States and marry
somewhere across the border, come back and he'd baptize
the baby in the local church and the records would all
be in order.

Thus, the private lives of the congregation were inextric-
ably bound with the Church and while most church records
show it was a matter of confession, forgiveness and acceptance back into the privileges of the church communion,
there were some cases where a harder line did prevail.
For example, the school teacher who, it was decided, ex-
hibited too much immorality and was not penitent enough
to be considered a worthy communicant. He was expelled
from church privileges for several years until he made
an effort to reform. Later it is noted he is back in
good grace after having had "time to mend his ways"!

In glancing through these records one can well understand
some of Robert Burns' poetry and appreciate that in the
midst of the hardheaded, stern disciplinarians there
was some kindly leaven to help the backwoods community

accept the way of life of their times and build strong, tolerant and philosophical families to contribute to the growth of the new land.

We can understand that the Congregation was the Church. But also, the Church through its laws, in its way, made the congregation what they were.

As the hardy highlanders fought for their right to have a Church of Scotland connection in their early pioneer domain, later in 1844 some of them became "Free Kirk" advocates! Later still, in 1875, they formed one Presbyterian Church in Canada(with the exception of the St. Andrew's Church, Perth, a Montreal Church and some in Glengarry who remained in "connexion with the Church of Scotland", and the last one to give up that designation was the church in Montreal - now the Church of St. Andrew and St.Paul, in 1918; which again in 1925 went through the throes of upheaval on the Union question - out of which the United Church of Canada was created. All these decisions entailed expression of individual beliefs at different times, in different ways. In considering the records of the early congregation one cannot help but feel they contributed worthily to the future by encouraging a way of life that made for strong character and achievements, for courage and kindness, for education and daring and diversity. They moved as said, west, north, south and east, often to bring glory to the families they had left behind in the Beckwith area.

The Minutes of Session of the Church, as we have shown, gave a picture of people, their weaknesses and strengths. The events were neither lightly written up nor lightly excused. The Minister had to be a veritable Solomon of a judge and his Elders were the jury who had the final say in the matter, it seems. To"stand up and be counted" was not an idle remark in church laws.

But, like diaries, not all items recorded should be quoted for general perusal. Therefore, in listing the Minutes of Session of the Church of the Seventh Line, apart from a few special excerpts, only the communicants lists and eldership information will be given in the appendices, showing certain dates and additions from time to time during the ministry of John Smith.

of BATHURST, Upper Canada, at Smiths Falls
on the 3rd. day of March 1834 years, which
day the Presbytery met and constituted present Rev.Messers.John Cruickshank of Bytown,
Thomas C. Wilson of Perth, William McAlister
of Lanark, John Smith of Beckwith, John Fairbairn of Ramsay and George Romanes of
Smiths Falls.
Inter Alia -

The Presbytery appointed the following
committees to meet with the heads of families
and to take the necessary steps towards the
organization of Kirk sessions, for the
congregations undermentioned.

For the congregation in the Township of
Ramsay, Messrs.McAlister, Smith, and Fairbairn to be Convenor.

For the congregation at Smiths Falls -
Messrs. McAlister, Smith, and Romanes to
be Convenor.

For the congregation in the Township of
Beckwith, Messrs. Wilson, Fairbairn, and
Smith to be Convenor.

The Committees to report their proceedings
at next meeting of Presbytery. The Presbytery then appointed that their next meeting
take place at Bytown on the first Tuesday
of August next.

Extracted from the Records of the Presbytery
of Bathurst on this sixth day of March,
eighteen hundred and thirty-four years by-

                    (signed) John Cruichshank
                             Presbytery Clerk.

Beckwith, 26th May 1834
The committee appointed by the Presbytery
of Bathurst to take the steps necessary towards the election and ordination of Elders
for the Scotch Presbyterian Church in this
place, met this day with the Heads of Families for said purpose. Present Messrs. Wilson,

By 1834, some of the early older settlers had died and
others had moved on to greener pastures but with the
induction of the three Elders, John MacDonald, John and
Peter Campbell, the communicants list began for the
ministry of the Rev.Smith. It snows 161 on the Communion
Roll of February 1835.

A man's ministry would be the little every day decisions,
the comfort and advice given in a variety of ways, the
visiting and praying with families, the supervision of
children growing; tolerance, love and understanding
blended with wisdom. These must have had a great part in
the daily rapport between the minister and his people.

The Beckwith congregation of whom the Rev.Wm.Bell wrote
disparingly as not being a "giving" group in it's early
years did, under the Rev.John Smith, contribute to the
French Canadian Mission (as it was called), the work of
the Protestant Church in Quebec, and also contributed to
the fund for the College at Kingston (an act which verified their keen interest in education), and many sons
and daughters of Beckwith Township up to the present
time have been graduates of Queen's University.

You will recall that John Smith designated some funds be
paid for a young relative of the Rev.Peter McLaren studying in Scotland. Was he the son of a McLaren of his congregation? One wonders if it was a son of Alexander Mc-
Laren from whom John Smith bought land? Land that McLar-
en had purchased from Buchanan in 1834.

It is interesting to consider these matters but without
family papers or letters one can only speculate. It might
even have been a McEwen lad - the McEwens were also related to the Rev.Peter McLaren, Lecropt, nr. Stirling,
Scotland.

The Rev.John Smith's Minute Book of Session opens with
this special record:

<u>MINUTES OF THE KIRK SESSION OF THE PRES-</u>
<u>BYTERIAN CHURCH IN THE TOWNSHIP OF BECKWITH'</u>
<u>IN CONNEXION WITH THE ESTABLISHED CHURCH OF</u>
<u>SCOTLAND</u>

Extract from the minutes of the PRESBYTERY

Fairbairn and Smith - Smith Convenor.
After the sermon by the Rev. Wilson from
Rom.8 and 1st.
......the meeting constituted by prayer.
After dire consideration held between the
members of the committee and heads of families, present, with regard to those considered best qualified for the office of
the Eldership and persons herinafter named
were proposed and chosen - Peter Campbell,
John Campbell and John McDonald.

The Rev.Smith was directed to serve edict
and proceed in the ordinary way, to the
Ordination (see Appendices under "Eldership" -Ordination) of the persons named,
in case they accepted of the office of
Elder and no objection to their life and
conversation be advanced.
                    (signed) John Fairbairn
                              Clerk of Meeting

Beckwith, 25 January 1835.
The Session met and was constituted by
prayer Sederunt Rev.John Smith, Moderator,
Peter Campbell, John Campbell and John
McDonald, Elders. It was resolved that
the Sacrament of the Lord's Supper should
be dispensed in this Church on the third
Sabbath of the next month (February) being
the 15th day of the month.
Closed with prayer.
                         John Smith, Moderator

Beckwith, 7th,February, 1835.
The Session met and was constituted by
prayer, Sederunt Rev.John Smith, Moderator,
Peter Campbell, John Campbell and John Mc-
Donald, Elders.

The following list of those desirous of admission to the Ordinance of the Lord's
Supper was produced and the Session being
satisfied with the claims of those undermentioned, it was agreed that they should
be admitted.

The list consists of 161 names(lists of communicants
names are contained in Appendices for those interested
in early families of Beckwith).
Among them John Carmicail and Alexander Dewar, who had
remained loyal to George Buchanan as long as it was
possible. Alexander Dewar, a trustee for the church
property, the Glebe of Lot SE 12, was committed to
"the connexion with the Church of Scotland" and so,
the old order changed.

On the Communion Roll of February 7th, was the name
Isabella Gair Smith. This was the minister's youngest
sister who had come to Canada with him in 1833. Another
sister, Helen, also came but her name does not appear
on the Communion Roll until the 12th February, 1836.

Isabella was 22 years old when they arrived in Canada
and no doubt added a certain vivacity and charm to
the primitive dwelling when she was not visiting friends
and acquaintances. Among their friends was the Rev. Romanes, the first minister to Smiths Falls for the Church
of Scotland. He was a serious, academic man, known for
fine oratory and a certain solidity of appearance. His
was a fine old family from the Tweed Borders and he
became, in due time, one of the first professors at
Queen's College, Kingston. Having succumbed to the charm
of the bright and lively Isabella, on Aug. 12th, 1835, by
proclamation, they were married at Beckwith by brother
John. Isabella went to live in the Manse at Smith Falls
and no doubt Helen was there very often, especially after
the birth of a Romanes baby the next year. (James)

A short letter in the Glasgow Colonial Society records
Vol. V.No.175, shows John Smith was in Montreal, 24 Sept.
1835, from where he addressed a letter to Mr. Montgomerie
as follows:

> I have this day the liberty of drawing
> upon you, as Treasurer of the Glasgow
> Colonial Society for 35 pounds (say
> thirty-five pounds ster.) thro Messrs.
> Kidd Cormack Co., of this City. By a
> letter which I had the pleasure to
> receive from Mr. Young one of the
> Society's Secretaries the amount due
> to me by the Society is 45 pounds.

85

I shall soon take the liberty of
empowering Robert Smith Esq. of
BrJaishaw and Mr. John Joyner of
Tain, Ross-shire, to draw upon you
for the balance of I0 pounds still
remaining in my favour after payment
to Kidd Cormack Co.

I intend taking an early opportunity
of writing at length to my friend
Mr.Young. I may in the meantime
state that things go on as favourably
with me and my congregation at Beckwith
as I could wish, I have the honor to be
Your obed. Servt.
John Smith.

GCS V 175

This would imply John Smith was clearing his debts back
on the Scottish homefront and progressing nicely with
his new home in Beckwith but the thought crosses one's
mind - did George Buchanan and he ever pass the time of
day? There is no recording of such an encounter and yet
each, in his own way, was a tolerant man, evangelical,
with inner strength of endurance.

George Buchanan was two years older than John Smith's
father. His family was large like Smith's own. It seems
a shame that history cannot, or does not, record that
they became friends or, at least, nodding acquaintances.

The year I835 was a sad one for George Buchanan. Ill -
with still a wife and five of his offspring unmarried
and evidently living at home, life must have been very
depressing at times.

His friend William Bell, called often a man austere, was
certainly not gifted with writing with a gentle pen. His
exasperation of the Buchanan family comes through again
and again, as he makes notes in his diary during that
year, I835. He evidently had ignored the Rev.Smith until
he knew that Buchanan's death was inevitable. But his
diary is a good authentic record of George Buchanan's
last days.

March, I835 - p.24. The Rev.Geo.Buchanan has
been ill for sometime and has sent me to come
and see him. On the 24th Mrs.Bell and I set

out for Beckwith together. The sleighing
was good for there had been a fall of
snow two days before. We had William's
horse which was a fine traveller but
somewhat restive at times, when he had
little employment. The road we travelled
was one with which he unfortunately for
us, was well acquainted, and would not
pass a house at which he had ever called
- without stopping. When I would not let
him, then he became restive and ran
back, so that I was forced in every case
to get out among the snow and lead him
past. This had to be repeated so often
my feet became as cold as ice and so
remained to the end of the journey, which
made me very uncomfortable, and even
unwell.

At Mr. B's as usual, we found all in dirt
and confusion, and scarcely any fire to
warm us. Though Mr.B. was not so ill as
he had been a few days before, yet it was
evident he was going the way of the earth.
He was suffering from both dropsy and asthma, and anasart was already spreading
over his feet and legs. After a stay of
two hours, conversing and praying with him,
we proceeded to Carleton Place, six miles
farther where we arrived at sunset, very
cold. We found our sons well, and they
soon made us comfortable, beside a good fire.

March 1835, p.27.-Next day the snow was
nearly all gone and the roads near the
town covered with deep mud. Yet Mrs. Buchanan and George came in from Beckwith,
riding a cutter. The day after was warm
and hazy and the roads almost impassable.
Yet Mrs. B. with all her retinue of colts,
dogs and bundles with her, had to find her
way home. She had brought a keg with her,
as she said, to take home wine for Mr.B.
but concluded to take Gin as it suited his
trouble better. It was 12 before she went
away and the snow was all gone. She must

have found difficulty in getting home.

In June 1835, p.49 entry - we find mention of the Rev. Smith:

> Mr.B. (Buchanan) being dangerously ill
> and having expressed a desire to see me,
> I went out to Beckwith on the 23rd, on
> purpose to visit him. I found him easier
> than I expected, he having been tapped
> on the preceding day. After talking with
> him some time I called upon the Rev.Smith.
> It was the first time I had seen him. I
> found him in a ragged suit of blue, the
> coat having one of the sleeves partly
> torn away from the body. He seemed to
> have great talent for silence. I made
> my stay short.
>
> On my return to Mr. B.'s I found the
> boy contrary to my wish had turned my
> horse loose in the pasture so that
> when I was going away, we had a chase
> of near an hour before we could get
> hold of him again. I went and stayed
> with my sons in Carleton Place.

One thing is evident when reading Rev.Bell's notations in his diary - he did not suffer inconvenience gladly. He liked comfort and approved of industry and success. Yet one feels he had a sincere feeling of affection for the Rev. Buchanan. In time, after he became a minister in connexion with the Church of Scotland, he often assisted Mr.Smith at the Church of the 7th line but one never feels he ever more than just accepted Mr.Smith - though he did admire Smith's wife and relatives and was duly impressed by their background.

One also feels a certain amount of sorrow, reading two entries in September, 1835 from Bell's diary:

> p.69.-While we were at tea, David Buch-
> anan arrived from Beckwith and informed
> us that his father had died on Saturday,
> (Sept. 12th) at 10 o'clock. This was an
> event we had long expected, yet the news
> came like a thunder bolt. What was to
> become of his widow and numerous family?
> For though they were all able to do for

themselves, such was their thoughtless dis-
position and want of industry, that nothing
can be expected.

p.70.- I went to get a grave prepared for
the remains of my old friend, Mr.B. After
sending round letters inviting the inhab-
itants of the town to attend his funeral.
At two the funeral arrived and I made a
short address at the grave. A great number of Beckwith people formerly his congregation came part of the way but only
those on horseback came all the way to
the burying ground. There he was laid in
the place where I had expected to lie
myself. On the following Sabbath, I
preached a funeral sermon.

Thus departed the Rev.George Buchanan, an individual
and maverick in his day. Whether he fell into "disest-
eem" with the settlers on account of personality or
beliefs we will never know. Perhaps in 1822 he just
made the wrong move in his very chequered career to
support his numerous family.

His land secured through a crown grant and the log house
he had built had been sold to Alexander McLaren and then
to the Rev.John Smith; although his family continued to
live there until Mrs.Buchanan and her daughter Ahn went
to join the son George at Van Kleek Hill in 1839.

Meantime, Rev.Bell seemed out of duty bound to check on
the family periodically - always seeing them less than
capable. January 1836, p.132, Bell writes:

On my way home I called on Mrs. B. (Buchanan)
and her daughters. For half an hour the ladies
as usual were invisible for they are never fit
to be seen till they are dressed. Mrs. B. I
found entertained her usual quantum of visionary schemes. She talked about getting a pension
from Government to support her in decline of
life. About sending her son David to Scotland
to college, about getting a bursary for him
there. Then she talked of going to Scotland
with him herself and getting some of her
friends who she said were well off to pay
for his education. Thus she went on building

castles in the air till I left her,
wondering at her folly.

February, 1836, p.140. - Next week
our county election kept the town in
a stir, nearly all the time. To be
out of it at least for some time I
borrowed my son's horse and cutter
and on Monday afternoon, Mrs. Bell
and I set out for Carleton Place. It
was after sunset when we got to Mrs.
B.'s (Buchanan's) place where we
intended to stop half an hour, till
the moon got up. Here we found all in
darkness, dirt and confusion. Yet the
young ladies were out taking an airing
of which if we may judge from the state
of their apartments they must have had
some need. The room we were in being
quite dark, Mrs.B. called repeatedly
to the servant girl to bring in a candle, but as the candle never yet appeared,
we suspected there was none in the house.
I wanted a little water for my horse, but
neither pail nor water could be got. But
as a substitute the girl took some snow
in a tin dish held it over the fire and
then to his nose but he would not taste
it. In order to escape from this squalid
scene of misery we groped our way out of
the house, and by the light of the moon
soon reached Robert's at Carleton Place,
where we found things more to our mind.

Again, it is evident the Rev.Bell had no patience with
women's dreams. It makes one wonder about the wives of
such men and the stories of their lives.

On that theme, it is intriguing to realize that Mrs.
Buchanan was only 47 years old when she came to Canada
in 1822 with her ten children...sixty when her husband
died and, while possibly full of "visionary schemes" as
Bell wrote it - they must have been the incentive that
kept her going, from Strathkinnes to Beckwith - and on
to Vankleek Hill until her 74th year. Her young son,
David, did study theology but died before he was ordained
in Jamaica.

She herselfbecame a member of Mr.Smith's congregation in July 1837. following her children, Julia, Jessie, George and Margaret (Mrs. John Dewar) who were entered on the Communion Roll February, 1837.

John Smith's abode also came in for some scathing remarks by Bell in 1838 in July, when he tells of arriving at Beckwith to assist the Rev. Smith at the Communion.

> I reached the Manse, at 9 PM, through
> myriads of mosquitoes so that the jour-
> neywas not a pleasant one, and was little
> more comfortable at the end of it, for Mr.
> Smith's was a cheerless abode, those qual-
> ities which form the charm of social life
> being sadly deficient. The heat of the
> weather was at the asme time almost intol-
> erable.

The following year, after Mr.Smith had married, the comments in the diary were much more amiable. He evidently approved of Mrs.Smith and her brother, Dr.Frederick Morson, a surgeon at Bytown.

One can see that Bell's diaries as well as the Minutes of Session give some very interesting information of the times and the people but in case one gets the impression that Minutes of the Session were a will o' the wishp affair, nothing was haphazard about them and they were checked every once in a while by the Clerk of the Pres-bytery to make sure they were kept in accordance with the rules of the Church. For example:

> At Lanark on the sixteenth day of Jan-
> uary, eighteen hundred and thirty-six
> years, the Presbytery, in the report
> of the committee appointed to examine
> the records of the Kirk Session of
> Beckwith, being read, ordered their
> clerk to attest said records as corr-
> ectly kept, and they are hereby attached
> accordingly.
>   John Cruickshank,
>   Presbytery Clerk.

Entries such as follows continue on as regular as clockwork.

> Beckwith, 29th, Jan. 1836.
> The Session met and being constituted,
> present Rev.John Smith, Moderator,
> Peter Campbell, John Campbell, and
> John McDonald, Elders. It was resolved
> tnat the Sacrament of tne Lord's Supper
> snould be administered in this Church
> the third Sabbath day of next month.
>
> John Smith, Moderator.

> Beckwith, 12th, February 1836
> The Session met and being constituted
> present Rev.John Smith, Moderator, John
> Campbell, Peter Campbell and John
> McDonald, Elders. It was agreed that
> tne following names should be added to
> the list of communicants.

From February 7tn, 1835 when 161 communicants were listed in tne Session Minutes, to February 24th 1844 another 116 have been listed. Communicants therefore numbered approximately 300. That did not cover those people classified as hearers and Sabbath School scholars.

Of course, there were deaths, births and marriages and families moving from one township to another but generally speaking one can see the congregation grew under the Rev.John Smith's ministry during his first ten years at Beckwith.

He had had his ups and downs and been rapped over the fingers on one occasion for taking off on a trip to Scotland without proper permission from the Presbytery. From the Minutes of Presbytery of Bathurst, U.C. page109, the rebuke read:

> A letter from Mr.Smith, Minister of Beck-
> with dated 29th June 1836, and addressed
> to the Moderator of Presbytery read, in
> which he states that being called upon
> by business of importance to go on a
> visit to Scotland it was his desire that
> during his absence the Presbytery would
> appoint a supply of preaching in his church.

92

> Having left his charge without their
> knowledge or approbation the Presbytery
> in the meantime resolved to record their
> surprise and disapproval of Mr. Smith's
> conduct.The Presbytery agreed that pro-
> ceeding the 27th instant Mr.Romanes
> should preach at Beckwith.
>
> John Cruickshank
> Presbytery Clerk

On the whole, however, his life on the 7th Line, Beckwith
was successful.

Then disruption !

It would seem reasonable to suppose that not all the
congregation of the 7th Line in 1834 were Church of
Scotland enthusiasts; some had already left earlier and
were affiliated with other groups but the stone church
was the only church there and one gathers John Smith
was well liked. Their way of life had always meant att-
endance at church regularly. Religion and education were
the pillars that upheld their dreams and efforts - the
reality of living, through sad times and glad.

In 1843 in Scotland the winds of change were blowing
harder than ever and the "Free Kirk" was the banner cry.
Scotland was aflame with the advocates of the Free Kirk
doctrine and like the Secessionists versus Church of
Scotland of an earlier time, the controversies came
across the Atlantic with people, in letters by ministers,
so that congregations throughout Upper and Lower Canada
and the Maritimes felt it;with bitterness and spite and
intolerance - it had to work itself out.

We note three items in the Kirk Session Minutes of the
early disruption times:

> May 23, 1843...the Session met and was cons-
> tituted by prayer. Present: Rev. John Smith,
> Moderator, J. Campbell, John McDonald, Peter
> Campbell, Alex.Dewar and Alex Stewart, Elders.
> It was moved by Mr.Peter Campbell and agreed
> unanimously that Mr. Alexander Dewar should
> be the representative in the Presbytery of
> Bytown and the Synod of Canada. This was con-
> cluded with -

It was resolved that 15 pounds should be
given to --------widow, living at Carleton
Place and in very needy circumstances, closed in prayer.   John Smith, Moderator.

July 1, 1843. Admitted to Communion.
Catherine Duncan, Christian Fisher, John
McCuan, Duncan McCuan.

February 24, 1844 - names added:
Alexander Graham, Jane Thomson,Wm.Cochrane
Within six months - friends and even families became
enemies with religious differences of opinion.

Newccongregations were formed, churches built at new
locations. Disagreements were many. The years between
1844-1875 saw much dissension and disunion and it is
rather interesting to note some of the "Free" spirits
and some of the "Establishment" names going through
the records of Synod. The Rev.William Boyd an Irish
Presbyterian of Prescott, previously Secessionist
minister who had petitioned to return into the Estab-
ished Church of Scotland in 1832 in the records of the
Assembly, was for the FREE KIRK. The Rev.William Bell,
also earlier a Secessionist, who returned to the Est.
Church of Scotland group continued in connexion with
the Church of Scotland, to name two.

The Rev. John Smith was of the group who stayed under the
jurisdiction of the Established Church. The Beckwith
order and discipline were for a time nearly expended.
The Elders without exception ceasing to officiate, recorded in the Minutes of Session by John Smith at Beckwith,
January 22, 1846.

The effect of the unhappy disruption which
on the 9th July 1844 took place in the Presbyterian Church of Canada in connexion with
the Church of Scotland, extended more or
lwss to all the churches under the spiritual
charge of the Synod. The Beckwith order and
discipline were for a time nearly suspended,
the Elders without exception ceasing to officiate. A necessity of course arose to re-
organize the Session.
The following is an account of the steps

taken towards the legal and orderly accomplishment of this object.

John Smith, Minister.

Then follows the account of a meeting <u>1845</u>

Of the Scotch Presbyterian Church in Beckwith in connexion with the Church of Scotland.

At the Church of Beckwith the 24th day of January 1846. The Committee appointed by Presbytery of Bathurst to confer with the Heads of families regarding the election of Elders, met and according to appointment.

After a sermon by the Rev.George Romanes, the committee was constituted by prayer; present Rev.Alexander Mann; Rev.John Smith, Rev.George Romanes, Rev.Alex Mann, Convenor.

<u>The Minutes of the congregational meeting on the IIth day of November 1845</u> in reference to that subject were read by which it appeared that the following persons had been nominated being fit and proper persons to fill the office of Eldership viz. JAMES FERGUSON; JOHN MCARTHUR and DONALD MCLAREN. The members of the congregation having then declared their adherence to the election of the persons named above, it was resolved that the committee should sanction the same and that instructions be given by the minister to proceed to ordination according to the rules of the Church. For this purpose it was appointed that their edict be served on Sabbath next the 25th instant, the ordination to take place with all convenient speed thereafter.   Signed, Alex.Mann.

Convenor of Committee.
Beckwith, 25th January 1846.
Announcement of proposed Elderships *
Signed, John Smith.

* (See Appendices under "Eldership")

On June 27th 1846, a list of additional names were added to communicants roll. And it must be noted some baptisms and marriages had taken place during the years when to all intents and pruposes the church activities were seemingly suspended.

It meant a rebuilding of the congregation of course, and the Communicant list went through many changes. Many had gone, but many remained and later some returned and new names were added.

John Smith's minist ry at the Presbyterian Church of the 7th Line in connexion with the Church of Scotland continued for another five years.

He died April 18th, 1851. A descendant says he got a chill, developed pneumonia and in three days was gone. The Rev. Bell wrote in his diary - simply:

> The Rev. John Smith died to-day.

Bell ministered to the Kirk of the 7th Line until the Rev. Duncan Morrison was ordained to that charge in Uctober, 1851 and noted in the Minutes of the Session:

> On June 15th, 1851 - Sacrament of the
> Lord's Supper was administered - 94
> Members partook.
> Wm. Bell, Moderator, pro ten.

The Lanark Herald reported on April 25th, 1851, the death of John Smith at the Manse, saying in part:

> The mild and christian demeanor which he
> maintained at all times and under all cir-
> cumstances endeared him to all who had the
> pleasure of his acquaintance. The congre-
> gation have sustained a loss which will be
> severely felt, not only on account of the
> affection which existed between the pastor
> and the people but because Mr. Smith had
> been in the habit of officiating both in
> English and Gaelic, an accomplishmnet
> perculiarly grateful to our highland
> friends....

Certainly John Smith's sincerity and evangelism, his quiet gentleness must have had some influence, filter-

ing like sunlight through a shaded forest. The wording
on his tombstone, erected by the congregation reads:

ERECTED
by
THE PRESPBTERIAN CONGREGATION
OF
BECKWITH
IN CONNEXION WITH
THE CHURCH OF SCOTLAND
IN MEMORY OF
THEIR REVERED PASTOR THE LATE

REV JOHN SMITH

NATIVE OF CROMARTY, SCOTLAND

WHO COMMENCED DUTIES

AMONG THEM OCT. 1833 AND DIED
18 APRIL 1851
AGE 50 YEARS

Their "Revered" pastor. A man "held in deep affection-
ate or religious respect, venerated". The Oxford meaning puts it clearly - reverence for the Reverent. In
his shy, highland way John Smith may have smiled, tongue in cheek, to have had his "usefulness" in Beckwith
so honoured.

The Scotch Presbyterian Church of the 7th Line renewed
itself under the Rev.Duncan Morrison, who was succeeded
by the Rev. Wm.McHutcheson from Scotland in 1861, who
in turn was followed by the Rev.Walter Ross, a graduate
of Queen's College, Kingston and the last minister to
live at the Manse and to preach in the Church until it
closed. The Church Minutes of Session give a clear
picture of the last event of admitting Patrick McLaughlin and George Tait to eldership in the Spring of 1875.*
*(See Appendices).

97

The Rev. John Smith had for almost 18 years given un-
stintingly to his charge at Beckwith, the first minister
of the Scotch Presbyterian Church of the 7th Line in
connexion with the Established Church of Scotland, had
unified the congregation on two occasions. In 1834, and
again in 1846 - inspiring them to carry on the work
of the church in harmony and christian fellowship with
one another.

Twenty-four years after his death the Presbyterian Church
in Canada became a fact embracing Established and Free in
one body.

#-15

TOMBSTONE OF REV. JOHN SMITH

THE HEIRS OF THE REV.JOHN SMITH

O'er the meadows on a calm day
Sweeter than mavis to me
My lover's voice a ho, a hey -
Beautiful maid my love is she.

From the Gaelic.

CHAPTER X

THE MINISTER'S WIFE

The obituary in the "Lanark Herald" of April 25, 1851,
ended with, to me - twelve very important words:

> The deceased leaves a wife and six
> children to lament their loss.

No identification, no names, just the thought of the
grieving widow and six children suddenly fatherless.
It was, however, a lead. He had married - but when,
where and whom?

Luckily, I finally got hold of the Minutes of the St.
Andrews Church, 7th line, Beckwith on microfilm at the
Ontario Archives in Toronto and his will, of which I
obtained a copy. Therein are the names - "My dear
wife Jane Smith or Morson..." and the names of the six
children - "Robert, Isabella, Matilda, Margaret, Jane
and John Rose Smith".

Mrs. Smith is listed on the Communicants Roll of the
Church of February 17, 1839. Narrowing down the years
and spending much time at the Archives eliminating the
John Smiths who married Janes in the hope of finding
a record of the marriage, added up to many research
hours..Then one day, by the simple method of playing a
hunch, I struck gold. Walking along Wellington Street
in Ottawa, I passed the St.Andrews Presbyterian Church;
stopped and retraced my steps, reasoning it was the
oldest church in the district and John Smith might just
have been married there. The kindly secretary helped
me secure the early book of marriages and in five minutes - there it was!

> No. 141 - John Smith of Beckwith of the Bath-
> urst District in the Province of Upper Canada,
> clergyman, and Jane Morson of Rockliffe, in
> the Ottawa District of said Province, spinster,
> by license from His Excellency Sir George Art-
> hur, Knight, married by me this thirtieth day

of August, Eighteen hundred and thirty-
eight years.   Signed -
                 John Cruickshank
                 Minister.

The witnesses were - Thos.Morson and Arch.Petrie.

Now, I had established he was lawfully married but who
was Jane Morson?

Again luck was on my side! Looking through the Biog-
raphies of the Medical Profession 1893, on an entirely
different matter, I came across the write-up on Dr.
Frederick Morson and his brother Dr. Alfred Morson,
sons of Thomas Morson, lawyer from Rochester, Kent.
England. A letter from the Arnprior Macnab to his kin
Sir Allan, on the occasion of a visit of Dr.Alfred Morson to Hamilton, stated he was related to the clan Mcnab
through his sister being married to a son of the Colonel
of the 91st Regiment. Seemingly irrelevant information
but it was a great help on the trail of Jane.

Jane was, as you will have realized, daughter of Thomas
Morson, gentleman, retired, former lawyer of Rochester,
England. She was born in 1816 and would have been appro-
imately eighteen years of age when her father emigrated
to Canada at the same time as his daughter Charlotte
and her husband Duncan Rynier Macnab. The latter began
building a home called "Rockliffe" on the site where
"Rockliffe Manor", the residence of the Apostolic Dele-
gate to Canada, now stands. He died in 1837 before it
was finished. His widow, left with three children under
nine years of age, took on the task of seeing the job
completed. It was at this residence (the first substantial stone house just outside Bytown proper, on Lot A
Gore, from which the village of Rockliffe later derived
it's name). Jane Morson married the Rev.John Smith.

If we were to speculate how they met, the ideas could
be many and varied but two seem more obvious than others.
It might have been that the Rev.John Cruickshank, while
courting Catherine Fellowes, introduced the Rev. John
Smith to her kin Jane Morson. John and Catherine were
also married at "Rockliffe" in August, 1838, and John
Smith was the officiating minister at that wedding. It
is recorded in the Beckwith Church minutes.

On the other hand, he could have met her brother, Dr.
Alfred Morson, on the latter's emigration journey to
Canada in 1836. The year John Smith took off for a
trip to Scotland without official leave of the Presbytery and Alfred could well have introduced him to his
family on arrival at Bytown.

We only know they did meet, fell in love and were married.
The bridegroom was 37 years old and his bride 22 years
of age- but again, no diaries, letters or shipping lists
to make fact of fantasy so we must be content with the
knowledge that they had a wide circle of friends and the
marriage was published in the "Ottawa Gazette" and the
"Quebec Mercury" which, no doubt, means it had some
social significance.

Did they honeymoon at Quebec City or go straight out to
Beckwith Manse?

It must have been a bit of a shock for Jane to settle
into the fairly primitive conditions at the Manse but she
would have had help and encouragement from John's sister
Helen who, no doubt, was the housekeeper "extraordinaire"
of the ministerial residence. Helen was now 34 years old
and did not marry until after her brother's death.

Isabella, his youngest sister, had married in 1835 the
Rev.George Romanes of Smiths Falls, a village only twelve miles distant.   She was more Jane's age,being 27
years old in 1838,and she was the mother of 2 boys.

Jane gave birth to a son on August 16, 1839 and he was
baptized Robert, after his paternal grandfather, by his
Uncle George at the Smiths Falls Church, Sept. 19, 1839.

Thus, we can see there were happy family occasions.
Jane's brother Frederick visited her in 1839 at Beckwith
and attended church services at the Kirk on the 7th Line.
He'd recently emigrated to Canada and it is not an im-
probable assumption he brought his baby sister a wedding
gift of the hand-printed wallpaper. It was not unusual
for a bride to get a roll or panel of wallpaper in those
early days - and such a gift with it's European sophis-
tication must have delighted the Chatelaine of the Manse!

Was it a laborious labour of love to cement it on to the
rough stone wall over the parlour fireplace, we wonder?
It remained hidden under layers and layers of additional
papers of a variety of designs from different decades

103

The balance of monied property to be divided in equal shares among our daughters,
Isabella, Matilda, Margaret, Jane and our
youngest son John R.Smith.

As witness my hand and seal this 2Ist day
of October 1849.Beckwith, C.W.

              Signed - JOHN SMITH
Witnessed - Peter Comrie
            Thomas Hawkins

He concludes with a list of executors - as follows:

I appoint as Executors of my last will and
testament - Charles D.Morson; Dr.Frederick
Morson; George Byron Lyon, Esq., Professor
George Romanes; Dr.Robert Smith 23 rd Fus-
iliers; Dr.Jno.D.MacDonald of Perth;Rev.
John McMorine; Rev.William Bain; Mr.John
McArthur and Mr.Colin McLaren of Beckwith.

On the I3th September I85I, John Duff MacDonald, of the
town of Perth, Surgeon, and an executor of the will of
the Rev.John Smith, swore before the probate court that
the deceased died possessed of goods, chattels and personal estate as follows:

Bank stock	I000 pounds
Bank deposit	65 pounds
Money in hand	------
Horses & furniture	25 pounds
Horned cattle	25 pounds I0s
Swine	I pound I0s
Plate & household goods	30 pounds
corn growing	--- none
Hay & corn	I5 pounds
Debts	673 pounds I2s 6p
Total	I835 pounds I2s 6p

              Signed - J.D.MacDonald
                       John McArthur

At least Jane was not left destitute and certainly she
must have brought a good dowery to the marriage or the
Smiths had been very frugal people. On the original

until uncovered in July, 1967.

That she was indulged by her husband was obvious in this regard. It was not the type of paper one associates with the stern, straight-laced Presbyterian characters as often portrayed by early settlers.

It is said Jane Morson Smith was an inept housekeeper but no doubt Helen (known Aunt Ellen to the children) helped her over many a stile and managed the early years of the household for her.

Five more children were born. Jane, the youngest daughter born on September 2nd, was baptized at Beckwith on September IIth, I847, by a visiting minister from Scotland, a Rev. Stevenson, a member of the Assembly Deputation of the Church of Scotland.

This was the period of the rebuilding of the life and congregation of the Seventh Line church after the split of the Free Kirk element who built the church at Black's Corners.

In October, I849, the Rev.JohnSmith made out his will and again we are inclined to think that the family and friends must have been gathered fora visit at the Manse. The list of executors records interesting local names as well as relatives.

WILL OF THE REV.JOHN SMITH

Feeling the uncertainty of life and propriety of settling my temporal affairs, I, John Smith now in the enjoyment of health and of sound mind, declare this to be my will and testament. After payments of my lawful debts, for the love and great esteem in which I hold my dear wife, Jane Smith or Morson, my will is duly declared to be, that during her lifetime she possess and enjoy the whole of my property, real or personal now possessed or hereafter to be acquired land, houses, cattle, furniture, monies invested in Bank Stock due by mortgage note of hand or otherwise...at her death, our son Robert Smith to inherit the landed property together with houses thereon, furniture, cattle and I00 pounds in money.

stipend of approximately I00 pounds yearly (or $400.00) his economical status at death was worthy of admiration.

However, at 35 years of age, his wife of thirteen years was left, as they say "to mourn her loss". After John's death it is evident she moved to Perth. She is listed in the personal census of the village of Perth of I85I-I852 and her children are also recorded - five as scholars ages I3 to 5 years. The youngest, John, is simply written up as "child - 3 years".

Sometime before I86I she moved to Ottawa. In that year she released the property on Concession 6 Beckwith Township to her son Robert who was studying law in Toronto. The memorial drawn up in Toronto was registered at Perth on 2Ist day of August I86I and states it is between Jane Smith of the City of Ottawa and Robert Smith, formerly of the same place now of the City of Toronto.* (See Appendices)

She became a civil servant and raised her children as members of the Anglican faith, attending Christ Church in Ottawa. All her family lived long lives moving between Ottawa, Dundas, Hamilton and Toronto. Two daughters Isabella and Margaret married. Two died spinsters, Matilda and Jane, but one gets the impression they were well-loved aunts of nieces and nephews and grandnieces and nephews. John Rose, the youngest son, was his mother's protector and guardian in her latter years.

She died at the age of 83 at his summer home at Britannia on an August day in I899. Her obituary read:

> Friday, Aug. 4, I899
> Internment - the funeral of the late
> Mrs. Jane Smith took place this morn-
> ing from the residence of her son, Mr.
> J.Rose Smith of Britannia Bay, to Christ
> Church Cathedral where Very Rev.Dean
> Lauder conducted the funeral services.
> Internment was made in Beechwood Cemetery.

#-16   JANE MORSON, WIFE AND JANE,
        DAUGHTER, OF REV.JOHN SMITH
        BRITANNIA, JUNE 1899

OOR AIN FIRESIDE

Now the bairnies all are sleeping
Dreaming over pranks and play
Wearied out the restless rescals
With*spiering all the livelong day.

Blessed be the peace o' gloamin'
Deep the mother's joy and pride
When she settles down to share the pleasure
And comfort of her ain fireside.

Cuddled in so warm and cosy
Like wee birdies in the nest
Ilka yin that sang but's bringing
The happiness within my breast.

May the days and years before them
All that's good in life provide
And their share of all the joy they bring us
When resting at oor ain fireside.

A Scottish Ballad

*spiering--asking questions

CHAPTER XI

THE MINISTER'S BAIRNS

The Scottish ballad "Oor Ain Fireside" sung by Kenneth
McKellar brought back memories of a line from an old
Scottish dialect poem my mother used to recite – "Ah,
bairnies cuddle doon at nicht".

When we bought the Manse, the two long upstairs rooms –
the length of the house – were filled with a moasic of
many things, hornets's nests, pigeon droppings, broken
lathing and plaster, broken glass, old discarded garments
and children's books and broken playthings – scattered
hither and yon mute evidence of life, times past and
decay.

While to-day the Manse may seem a small dwelling to
have housed nine people – father, mother and six children, "Aunt Ellen" and, no doubt, hired help who possibly
slept over the kitchen, those long rooms upstairs must
have provided ample nursery and playroom space for the
energetic Smith children. Especially on rainy days! There
must have been admonitions now and then to be quiet and
let father get on with writing the Sunday sermon.

The lines of the ballad conjure up bedtime and candle-
light and young ones wrapped in warm blankets with
sleepy heads snuggled on their pillows, safe within the
stone walls of the little Manse in the mid-1800's.

John Smith in a letter written from Aberdeen, January 12,
1822, to his sister Margaret, recently married to a Dr.
George McDonald of Cromarty, wrote:

> All the Christmas parties and festivities
> will be over with you now and tho' such occ-
> asions are most calculated to give pleasure
> to young people, I hope your becoming a Mat-
> ron had anything but a tendency to counteract
> the joy you used to feel at such times – as
> to me if nothing else comes to prevent, or
> rather make it seem unbecoming, that I should
> take great interest in joys of such seasons

than changing my present state of sin-
gle blessedness, I hope that for years
innumerable I may without censure have
the full enjoyment of them...

He goes on to write: "...it is nothing but vanity your
speaking of your brother and his bairns, etc..."

This was no doubt written at the time he was studying and
tutoring as was the custom often to get through the theology courses. He was seven days short of his 22nd birthday.
His sister Margaret was 21 years old.

It is certain from such an appreciation of speacial occasions, there were many happy hours of joy under the roof
of the Manse, at which the Rev. John and his wife Jane,
shared in laughter and pleasure with their children.

When their father died in April, 1851, Robert, his eldest
child was almost 12 years old, Jane had no easy task ahead
of her, but she survived and so did her children, who all
lived over three score and ten, except the youngest daughter Jane who died in her 68th year.

They were part of the Bytown/Ottawa scene with presumably
frequent trips to Hamilton, to visit their cousin Dr. John
Duff McDonald who had settled there in 1852 with his wife
Sarah Malloch. To Dundas, to Morson relations and to Tor-
onto where Dr. Alfred Morson lived, and where later Robert
Smith studied law.

Where then is their history, or as much as can be determined. Owing to the sparsity of papers and letters, it has
not been easy to accumulate these few facts. The Beechwood
Cemetery records and wills of various family members have
been a great help in piecing together their lives after
Beckwith.

> ISABELLA ROSE SMITH
> born Beckwith, October 4, 1840
> married ca. 1871
> died Dundas, November 13, 1913

Isabella, the eldest daughter of the Rev.John Smith was
baptised by her uncle Rev.George Romanes at St. Andresw
Presbyterian Church, Smiths Falls.

Apart from the fact she was listed as a "scholar" in the
Perth census of 1851-1852, when she was almost 12 years
old, and she was a witness at the wedding of her cousin

Florence, daughter of Charlotte Morson Macnab, to
Charles Barret Grasset at Ottawa, on March 13, 1862,
there is no information available of the years between.
In Toronto Directory of 1864-65, an Isabella R. Smith
is listed as dressmaker, but it is not certain this
refers to the daughter of the Rev. John Smith.

She married in 1871, Alexander R. Wardell, (Mayor of
Dundas 1867-1871 and again 1879-1888), a widower, father
of several sons and a daughter. She became a Roman Catholic. A.R.Wardell was an active member of the St. Augustine Roman Catholic Church, Dundas, and his family were
well known in the society of the town. He died on March
3rd, 1913. Isabella bore Alexander four children --

> MAUDE OTTLEY CUMBERLAND,
> born Oct. 1872, died Nov. 1872
>
> REGINALD STEWART ROSE WARDELL
> born 1874, died 1910
>
> ApROBERTS GREIR WARDELL
> born 1877, date of death not established
>
> LINDSAY ALEXANDER AITCHISON WARDELL
> born 1879, died Jan.13, 1962

All her children were baptized at St. Augustine Church,
Dundas.

Her youngest son Lindsay A. Wardell became an architect
and lived for a time in Hamilton. He married in 1908
Mabel Theresa Barrie of Rochester, N. Y. and they had
a family of six children, two of whom, Mary and Kathleen,
died in infancy. *

The family moved to Toronto and two of his sons became
Jesuit priests. His daughter, Dorothy Wilma Wardell,
is a sculptor and lives in Toronto, as does her youngest
brother, John.

*See Genealogical Chart

Lindsay A.Wardell, the grandson of the Rev.John Smith
was well known in the field of architecture and many
churches, church halls and other buildings stand monument to his talent. He designed the restoration of
Fort Marie near Midland in 1947. (See photo illus.)

His children in turn have succeeded in their fields of
endeavour.

FATHER HENRY A' WARDELL, S.J., born
September 10, 1911, Hamilton, Ontario.
Entered the Society of Jesus, Aug. 14,
1932. Ordained July 1, 1945. Died
December 9, 1975.
Reverend Harry Wardell, S.J. studied
classics at Ignatius College, Guelph,
Ontario and Philosophy and Theology at
Regus College, Toronto. He was posted to
Loyola College (now Concordis University)
in September 1946.

He taught physics and chemistry and joined
the Engineering Department in 1948. He was
with the Faculty of Engineering for 27 years.
In 1966 he became Professor of Mechanical
Engineering at Loyola and latterly Concordia.

Professor Joly, Concordia University's Assist-
ant Dean of Engineering and former Dean of
Engineering at Loyola paid this tribute to
Father Harry Wardell;

..."the contribution that Father Wardell
made to engineering had a singular quality -
it was a giving of his spirit to everyone
with whom he came into contact. It was a
giving of concern without solicitation,
silent, unobtrusive, but for all that,
effective. In the twelve years I have been
associated with Professor Wardell I have
heard others speak of him only in praise.
He gave us all hope and encouragement.

Father Harry Wardell in addition to teaching duties, was
the R.C.Chaplain of the Sailor's Club from 1952 until his
death. He was also National Director for the Apostleship
of the Sea of Canada and Director of the Catholic Sailor's

Club and Mariner's House. He died in Montreal and was
buried in Guelph, Ontario.

FATHER THOMAS J. WARDELL S.J., born
December 6, 1912, Hamilton, Ontario.
Entered the Society of Jesus, January
29, 1933. Ordained July 1. 1945. Died
October 7, 1974.,

Father Tom, as a boy, attended DeLaSalle
"Oaklands" School in Toronto and was for
several years a member of the famous
marching band of that institution.

The years between 1946 and 1974 covered
many fields - teaching at Winnipeg, Assistant Rector at Kingston, Ontario, Teaching
at Loyola High School, Montreal, Chaplain
in the R.C.A.F., Assistant Dean of Students
St. Mary's University, Halifax, Assistant
Pastor St.Ignatius Parish, Montreal and
latterly Chaplain Ontario Reformatory,
Guelph, Ontario.

Father Wickham said this of him --

He was a zealous, active man whose health
was never very strong. But those he lived
and worked with never heard any kind of
complaint from him. Rather he was well
known for his good humour. He had a special
wit all of his own. Above all, he had a
gift of kindness and joyfulness - he was
always so concerned about others that he
forgot about his own troubles --he was
very quiet, very gentle. Perhaps for that
reason we feel his passing away more deeply.
A very personal relationship has been broken.
We have lost such a friendly man, so easy to
approach, so interested in everyone and
gifted with a sense of such practical help.
His life was a quiet witness to an immensely deep faith. Tom's faith brought acceptance of the evils that afflict our existence.
It was shown in the service he gave to others
who were in trouble, as community minister,

looking to the needs of his brothers, as
chaplain in the air force for five years,
as a personal counselor, work he carried
on throughout his life and in these final
years as a prison chaplain where he found
so much happiness in working with prisoners
and their families.

These two brothers who found life service in their church
give a glowing dimension to the family tree. (see ordination photo).

DOROTHY WILMA WARDELL is a quiet, gentle
lady, who does beautiful sculptures and
paintings. In 1944 a 12 by 8 ft. painting
of the Crucifixion she had completed, was
hung in the sanctuary of St.Peter's Church,
Toronto. The photo shows Miss Wardell standing beside her finished work.

Her help in putting together information on the Smith
family through photographs she loaned me, etc., has
been of great value and becoming friends with her has
been a bonus of joy and pleasure.

JOHN LINDSAY WARDELL - R.C.A.F. veteran and
Architectural-Draughtsman, lives in Toronto.
He has three sons and a daughter. He and his
wife, the former Theresa Caroline Roche have
recently become the proud grandparents of
their first grandchild. *

Their children are - Michael Joseph Wardell, Robert John
Wardell, Paul Lindsay Wardell and Mary Catherine Wardell
born January 11, 1963.

Jack Wardell's help and humour have given zest to the
search for contemporary kin.

The great-uncle of Dorothy and John Wardell, John Rose
Smith son of the Rev.John Smith, lived the last five
years of his life in their home. The photos which belonged to him have helped to reconstruct the story of the
Smith family.

*See Genealogical Chart

MARY MATILDA OTTLEY FELLOWES SMITH

born August 12, 1842
died November 23. 1922

The will and codiciles to same, of Mary Matilda are of
interest in that this gives some idea of her travels.
Aunt Tilley's signature shows up at Toronto, Hamilton
and Ottawa. It would seem she was a very kind, lovable
person who willed to special people with sentiment and
love. She remembered her nieces and nephews and their
children. One item recorded in her will gives information of the seal-

> "I do hereby bequeath to my brother
> John Rose Smith the seal given to me
> by my Aunt Ellen, which belonged to
> my father."

The letter of 1822 written by John Smith to his sister
Margaret MacDonald and found among her papers in New
Zealand, was sealed with a seal in the form of a tree
around which were the words "not to be shaken". This may
have had special signifigance because he was a Presbyterian theology student, but the seal has disappeared and no
further information is forthcoming to date.

Aunt Tilley spent her life visiting with kin. Ottly Neame
of England recalls she was often with them at Britannia,
a part of their happy household. However, there is not
much information about her life. She was evidently named
after a cousin. The youngest daughter of Charlotte Morson
Macnab by her first husband, Richard Fellowes, the cousin
married G.B.Lyon Q.C., one-time Mayor of Ottawa and son
of Captain George Byron Lyon of Richmond. The latter was
a friend of John Smith's and was n amed an executor in
the Rev.Smith's will of 1949. However, George Byron Lyon
predeceased his friend by a few months.

Anyway the two Mary Matildas had a very unusual name in
common. Mary Matilda Ottley Lyon Fellowes (her husband
took the name Fellowes on their marriage) lived next
door to her aunt, Jane Morson Smith, when they were both
widows in 1880, on Victoria Street, where the Supreme
Court building now stands.

Mary Matilda Smith, known to her family as "Tilley" is
buried in the Smith/Wyld family plot in Beechwood Cemetery

Ottawa. She died at the Elizabeth Home (for gentlewomen)
on Daly Avenue in 1922 - ten years after the cousin for
whom she was named had died at Toronto, at the age of 90
years.

MARGARET CRAWFORD SMITH born 1844
died April 25, 1920. Ottawa

Margaret was named after her father's favorite sister whom
she greatly resembled. In 1879 she married William Wyld of
Dundas, Ontario, son of James Charles Wyld and Dorothea
Morson Wyld, daughter of Henry Morson, an older brother of
Margaret's mother, Jane Morson Smith.

William Wyld was a lawyer and settled in Ottawa. In 1892
he became an elder of the St.Andrew Presbyterian Church.
He owned property at Britannia Bay, and was the first
president of the Britannia Yacht Club. He sold some property across from his own summer place to John Rose Smith,
his brother-in-law in 1895, and the families spent many
happy times together during the summer months as neighbours.

Margaret Smith Wyld was according to her daughter Ottly,
a fantastic housekeeper and business woman. She was an
intelligent capable woman who on the death of her husband
on March 25, 1905, just when his law firm was beginning
to succeed, took over the business management of family
affairs and with the help of her brother John Rose, assur-
ed her children of secure and happy lives.

There were four children of this marriage--

> GERTRUDE MAY WYLD born 1881 at Dundas,
> was a Nursing sister during WW1, and a
> great favourite at her sister Ottly's
> home in England. She died November 18,
> 1951.

> NAOMI KATE WYLD born 1885, baptized
> St. Andrews Church, Ottawa, October 3,
> 1885. Married Kenneth Done Harris, an
> Ottawa architect in 1910. They had a
> daughter Naomi Jean born 1918, she
> became Mrs. Band and had a daughter.
> It is thought she married several
> times, but no definite facts are
> known regarding her. "Kate" attended
> school in England together with her

116

sister Ottly. She died at Ottawa,
November 24, 1929.

ISOBEL MARION OTTLY WYLD, born in
1887, baptized at St.Andrews Presbyterian
Church, Ottawa, April 27, 1888. Married
1909 Philip Leslie Neame, son of Lawrence Harding Neame and Ada Sant of London, England. They had one son.

SHIRLEY NEAME lives with his mother at Wimbledon, England.
He is an expert on antiques, especially of the regency
period. Mr.Neame has been of great assistance in helping
me identify family photos and recording his mother's memories of people and places. I am very grateful to both
of them for their kind and courteous help on the family
history.

JAMES RAOUL GREIR WYLD, the only son of Margaret and
William, was born at Dundas, Ontario 1883. He married in
1909 Hattie Scott, daughter of Dr.Harry Scott of Gagetown,
New Brunswick. He was employed most of his life by the
Government Dept. of the Interior as Supt. of B.C. Lands.
He died November 21, 1931. Greir and Hattie had one son,
William.

WILLIAM GREIR WYLD, born 1911. This great-grandson of the
Rev. John Smith, is a retired Marine Engineer, and lives
at Chatham, New Brunswick. He was the only Canadian abo-
ard the British ship "S.S.Glairmore" when it was torped-
oed early in World War II. He joined the Canadian Navy
as a Petty Officer.

In 1934, he had married in St.Mary's Roman Catholic Church
Newcastle, New Brunswick, a French-Canadian Acadian girl
named Marie Babineau, daughter of Simon Babineau and his
wife Marie Ann Despres, both of Rogerville, New Brunswick.
William and Marie Wyld have four children and twelve
grandchildren. *   SEE GENEALOGICAL CHART

RODNEY DAWSON WYLD, married Betty Lou
Maher of Craigville, New Brunswick.They
have four children - Gary, Sandra, Gregory and Tanya.

DONALD GREIR WYLD - first marriage at
R.C.Church, Eisborne, Germany, December 3,
1964. - had issue - Mark and Tina. Married

Second wife in 1975, Alice Sonja Jansen
of Koege, Denmark. Their son Jamie Grier
born September 9, 1977.

DIANA ELIZABETH WYLD, married David Garinger, lives in California. They have two
children Lisa and Craig.

JUDITH WYLD married Hugh Anthony Moar.
They have three children. Heather, Troy
and Scott.

It must be recorded here that Mrs. William Wyld, nee
Marie Babineau, owing to her husband recently having
suffered a stroke untertook to answer all my inquiries,
and if it had not been for her k ind help and generosity
in sending family papers and information much of this
branch of the family tree would have gone unrecorded in
the story of the Rev.John Smith. It has been a great
pleasure to have had such friendly correspondence with
her.

JANE MORSON SMITH born Beckwith, September 2, 1847.
died Ottawa, December 28, 1915.

Jane, the youngest daughter of the Rev.John Smith and his
wife Jane, was baptized at Beckwith by a visiting minister from the General Assembly of the Church of Scotland,
Edinburgh, on September 11th, 1847.

She also is buried in the Smith Wyld plot at Beechwood
Cemetery. It would seem there is no real record of her
except in death, apart from the record of baptism, and
mention in the village of Perth census 1851-1852, wherein she is listed as Jennie Smith. scholar, 5 years (next
birthday). She died in St.Luke's Hospital, Ottawa, at
68 years of age.

Her brother John was very devoted to her and his will
left instructions for so much money to be allocated for
flowers for the family plot and - "especially that place
where Jennie is buried".

Jane Morson Smith's photo taken with her mother on the
verandah at Britannia, June 1899 shows a gentle, quiet-
looking woman, who evidently was a lot of fun. A "real
character" as her niece in England recalled looking down
memory lane!

ROBERT SMITH born Beckwith, Aug. 16,
1839. Died - date and place unknown.
Robert, the oldest child of the Smith family, became a
lawyer. He has the reputation in "family tradition"stories
of having squandered the inheritance.

In 1861, when he was 22 years of age, finishing his law
studies in Toronto, his mother on July 31st, through a
Toronto law firm released the property of Lot 14 and part
of 15 on Con.6, Beckwith Township, that his father had acquired, to her eldest son for five shillings. Registered
at Perth, Aug. 21st, 1861, Robert Smith of Toronto sold
the property to his uncle Dr.John James Aitchison of Smiths Falls. This was registered Aug. 22nd, 1861 at Perth.
We find Robert buying back the property in the Spring of
1862 and J.J.Aitchison taking a mortgage on it on which
young Robert defaulted payment. He also had a mortgage on
it with a cousin, Charles D.Morson, which was not discharged. This transaction was executed at Ottawa and witnessed
by Nicholas Sparks and William Horatio Radenhurst. Young
Robert according to the Ottawa Directory of 1863 was an
attorney at that time with the lawyers, Fellowes and Radenhurst, in the Audmonde Bldg. Rideau at Sappers Bridge.

His business maniuplations seem to have caused some confusion. Charles D.Morson put the property up for sale adv-
ertised as belonging to "the heirs of the Rev.John Smith"
but John James Aitchison,M.D., had a "Mortgage Sale" on it
at Perth under Alexander Morris, lawyer, and it was sold
to Jamieson, Saddler, of Perth. Aitchison immediately bought it back from Jamieson and later sold it to James Drummond on 3rd July 1865.

The story goes that Robert's aunt, Charlotte Morson Macnab
encouraged him in extravagant living when he lived in Ottawa in 1863 as a young attorney. He was encouraged to buy
a brewery, a business about which he had no practical knowledge, and it failed. Robert then took off for England and
supposedly practised law there. The photo taken of him by
Notman, Montreal in 1914, shows a dapper gentleman of 75
years. Ottly Neame his niece says she only saw him once,
when her uncle John Rose Smith took she and her sister over
to England to boarding school. Robert met the trio in London. It is thought he spent his life in England, but it
is a long trail unwinding!

119

The missing book of Notman records covers the time when he must have been photographed in Montreal, so no information is possible from that source.

In the appendices are copies of documents pertaining to the property on Concession 6, Beckwith. They tell the story more graphically than mere words. It is possible that Robert or his uncle built the stone house on that property and rented it to P.McLaughlin until the property was sold to Drummond in 1865. It may be Robert had ideas of settling on a country estate in Beckwith. Oh, "the best laid plans of mice and men" or, the saddest words - "it might have been"!

JOHN ROSE SMITH born August, 1849.
died October 18. 1947 at Toronto.

John Rose Smith the youngest son and youngest child of the family, as the order in the will implied, and which fact was verified by census record 1851-1852 Perth, wherein he is recorded as "child- 3 years" (next birthday). His death certificate says he was born August 1844, died 103 years, 2 months of age, and the post office records state his birth date as 1850, which of course is wrong since he was alive at the time of his father's will, Oct. 1849. No record of his birth and baptism has yet been found, and it is possible in later years his date of birth became confused with his sister Margaret's, of which no record has come to light to date. They may have been baptized at Brockville when John Smith's friend the Rev. Cruickshank was minister there but the records are incomplete.

That John Rose Smith lived to be almost a century old is an undisputable fact. He was a man who proved his worth in many ways over the years, and it would seem he did what his older brother failed to do. "John Rose" was a "family" man, though he never married. He looked well after his mother and sisters, and was, we are told of great help to his sister Margaret with financial matters. All his nieces and nephews and their children benefited from his will in some way, and he died leaving quite a sizeable fortune.

At an early age he joined the Ottawa Savings Bank Post Office and worked there until his retirement at the turn of the century.

He was an outdoors man. An ardent oarsman, and a member
of the Ottawa Rowing Club. A grand-nephew told me that
John Rose Smith crossed the Ottawa River above the rapids
at Britannia in a canoe, and also, that he walked fifty
miles to keep an appointment on time, but on arrival,
fell flat on his face with exhaustion!

He had a genius for figuring out the stock market and
made quite a substantial amount of money on his invest-
ments after his retirement. He was especially fond of
the Wardell family and his nephew Lindsay with whom he
lived the last years of his life.

He died October 18, 1947, and was buried from Christ
Church Cathedral - internment Beechwood Cemetery, Ottawa.

The obituary notice of October 20, 1947, in The Evening
Telegram, Toronto, reads, in part -

> Mr. Smith up to the last 18 months was
> keenly interested in current events,
> particularly politics and news of the
> stock exchange. He was born in Perth,
> son of the Rev.John Smith, late Pres-
> byterian minister, and Jane Morson
> Smith. He lived the greater part of his
> life in Ottawa, and during his youth was
> a fine oarsman, a member of the Ottawa
> Rowing Club. Mr.Smith retired 50 years
> ago. He was an Anglican. Funeral services
> will he held in Ottawa.

That he was a responsible, kindly man with a lot of common sense in handling money - possessing a joy of life,
and love of family, attributes not unlike his father's,
is evident.

He well out-lived his brother and sisters, and, setting
forth on his last journey, left warm thoughts among his
kinfolk near and far.

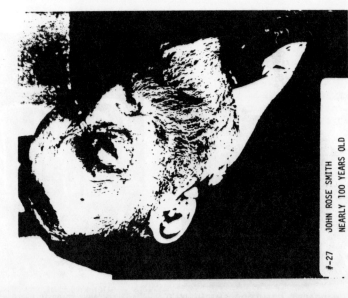

JOHN ROSE SMITH
NEARLY 100 YEARS OLD

#-27

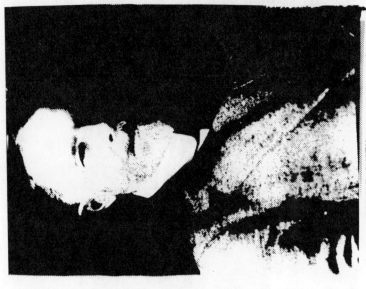

ROBERT SMITH
ELDEST SON OF REV. JOHN SMITH
1914

#-26

#-23   MARGARET CRAWFORD SMITH WYLD
DAUGHTER OF REV. JOHN SMITH

#-24   OTTLY WYLD NEAME AND SON SHIRLEY
ENGLAND, PRIOR TO WORLD WAR II

#-25   WILLIAM WYLD, N.B.
GREAT GRANDSON REV. JOHN SMITH

#-17   ISABELLA ROSE SMITH
        WIFE OF A.R.WARDELL
        DUNDAS, ONT,

#-18   LINDSAY A. WARDELL
        GRANDSON OF REV. JOHN SMITH
              AND FAMILY

JACK WARDELL
PORTRAIT BY HIS SISTER
DOROTHY WARDELL

#-22

FORT STE. MARIE RESTORATION

PHOTO OF PROPOSED PLANS FOR
RESTORATION OF FORT MARIE NEAR
MIDLAND, ONT, BY LINDSAY WARDELL

#-19

Lindsay A. Wardell, architect, 50 Kendal St., Toronto, has prepared plans for proposed restoration of Fort Ste. Marie, banks of Wye River, near Midland, Ont., associated with Jesuit Missionary Martyrs, and it is hoped to have restoration practically completed, if not entirely restored, for Tercentenary of Martyrdom in 1949. Plans were prepared in consultation with Dr. J. F. McIlwraith, assistant curator, Royal Ontario Museum of Archaeology, Toronto, and Professor Kenneth Kidd of that institution, who has been in charge of field work research. (First report, July 8, 1947).

125

OF KIN AND SUCCESSORS

#-20   FATHER HENRY AND FATHER THOMAS
        WARDELL, JULY 1945

"Cattle die, men die;
We all must die,
But, the deeds men do -
Live after them."

From an old Norse saga.

CHAPTER XII

OF KIN AND SUCCESSORS

The trouble with research on a very ordinary name like "Smith" is that one tends to veer off on the track of an unusual name that crops up. In reading in the "Fasti Ecclesiae Scoticanae" that Isabella Smith, the sister of the Rev.John Smith, had married a Rev. George Romanes, I decided to take a detour and concentrate on that name.

Alexander Graham Bell said, "Leave the beaten track occasionally and you will be certain to find something you have never seen before"! How true.

I got tangled up in a delightful way on Romanes and Morsons - wills , pedigrees, and other papers, all giving a lift to the mundane search and adding interesting information on the Smith family.

While the preceeding chapters have told briefly some aspects of the lives of John Smith's family, I expect to later write about the Morsons. There was also an idea in my mind to do a story on each of the ministers of the Manse and to that end I tried to collect information en route.

This chapter is a short record for those interested in John Smith's sisters and what became of them, and of the two ministers who succeeded him from 1851 to 1866.

Like ministers' families everwhere who move from place to place, they did not become permanent pioneer stock of the Beckwith area. None of the third generation were really aware of the Rev.John Smith, their grandfather, or his background. So the road of discovery was a reciprocal adventure.

The maternal family chart of the Rev.John Smith leading to the present generation might be of interest to many people in many places. Marrying in his late 30's and dying comparatively young, his family never really knew him but I believe he was a "family" man.

His sisters Helen and Isabella, who no doubt insisted on
accompanying their bachelor brother to Canada in 1833,
found lives of their own in the years to follow.

ISABELL GAIR ROMANES

The youngest sister of the Rev.John Smith was born to
the Rev.Robert Smith and his wife Isabella Rose Smith
in 18II. She was known to be of a lively personality
and her children and grandchildren returned to her
heritage in Scotland and lived immensely interesting
lives - which, of course, is another story.

Suffice to say she married at Beckwith in 1835. The
Rev. George Romanes the minister of the Presbyterian
Church at Smiths Falls, U.C., who later became a professor at Queen's University. He came into a large inheritance in 1850 and returned to Britain, residing in
London; travelling on the Continent,and spending summers
up at Nigg, Scotland.

Their eldest son James, born at Smiths Falls in 1836,
made frequent trips to Kingston, U. C., his father havng
interests in a lead mine at Sydenham, near Kingston,
which he managed. He later lived with his youngest sister
Charlotte at Dunskeath, near Nigg. His sister Georgina
born at Smiths Falls in 1842, never married and his
brother George John Romanes, born at Kingston, U.C. in
1848 became a professor and scientist. He founded the
chair of biology at Oxford University and did a lot of
research up at Dunskeath, Ross-shire, Scotland.

Professor George John Romanes, married an Ethel Duncan of
Liverpool. His father, Dr.Rev.George Romanes, died at
his London residence, 18 Cornwall Terrace in 1871. His
mother Isabella Smith Romanes died at London on January
2, 1883. Her daughter Georgina having predeceased her
five years earlier.

HELEN SMITH AITCHISON

"Aunt Ellen" is mentioned at various times but it is
difficult to find out any exact information on her life
and times. She was born in 1804 at Cromarty and was 29
years of age when she came to Canada, very much the older
sister to Isabella, no doubt. One can imagine she spent
much time at Smiths Falls with the family there after
Isabella married and went to live at the Smiths Falls'
Manse.

128

She would also be a pillar of the household at the
Manse on the 7th Line and a great help to Jane in raising
the Smith children as was the way of the times for spin-
ster aunts. However, after John Smith died in 1851, his
sister Helen married in October 1852, the Coroner at
Smiths Falls, Dr.John James Atchison. This might well
have been a second marriage for him but research has
turned up little information.

The Atchisons were on the communicants roll of the 7th
Line Church during the Rev.Duncan Morrison's ministry at
Beckwith.

They were involved with the property left by the Rev.
John Smith on Concession 6 and may well have been involved in building the stone house on it or renting the
property out after John Smith's death in1851, when the
census lists a "log house" but by 1861 a McLaughlin is
listed as living in a stone house on Lot 14.

The Aitchisons themselves were recorded as living on the
Brockville Road and he was "of Elmsley" on several papers.

Where and when Helen died is still an unanswered question
but it would seem she was close to her kin - as Isabella
Smith Wardell's son was baptized -- Lindsay Alexander
Aitchison Wardell in 1879, at Dundas.

The ministers succeeding to the Ministry of the Church of
the 7th Line in connection with the Church of Scotland
were:

REV. DUNCAN MORRISON

Duncan Morrison a native of Scotland, came to Canada with
a wife and two children to be educated for the ministry
at Queen's College, Kingston. He studied there 1848-1850
and became a Clerk with the College until his ordination
to the Ministry at Beckwith in October, 1851.
He was minister of the 7th Line Church until 1856 when
he accepted a call to Brockville. From Brockville he was
translated to the church at Owen Sound, October 10th,
1866. He visited Scotland in 1879, when he acted as
Locum Tenens at Penninghame and St.Ninian's, Stirling.
He became a D.D. at Montreal in 1890.

The Rev.Dr.Morrison published a volume called "Great
Hymns" and he died at Owen Sound, May 3, 1894 aged 78 yrs.

He did much to promote the welfare and work of the Presbyterian Church at Owen Sound and in the Knox United Church booklet put out in commemoration of "The First Hundred Years" in 1946, he is respectfully referred to as "Father" of Knox. On page 13 it has been recorded:

> Early in March 1876 Mrs.Morrison, wife of the beloved minister died and a few months after Dr.Morrison requested the Session to take steps to call another minister. It was not until June 6th, 1878 however, that a call was moderated to the Rev. A.H.Scott.

> The part played by Dr.Duncan Morrison in the establishing of Knox Church in those early days cannot be over-estimated. With untiring zeal he travelled over Scotland and Canada seeking financial aid for his congregation in Owen Sound. As a memorial to his work there still peals forth on Sundays the bell that he secured with the aid of friends in Scotland and which for 75 years now has called the faithful to worship. On the bell there is inscribded:

> Erected at Knox Church, Owen Sound, Rev. Duncan Morrison, Minister, John C. Wilson, Glasgow (Founder), Vocco O Cives Vanite in Domini Templum (I call O Citizens, Come into the Temple of the Lord).

REV. WILLIAM MCHUTCHISON

William McHutchison was born in Renfrew, Scotland 1827. He was the eldest son of James McHutchison, merchant, and was educated at Glasgow University and appointed to Banton, Glasgow, 1855.

He came to Canada and was ordained to the ministry at Beckwith in 1856. He was minister of the 7th Line church until 1861. He returned to Scotland on account of ill health. The auction notice of his goods and gear in the local paper indicates he was a bachelor of substance. According to the census of 1861 he had a housekeeper, Mrs.Brown, and hired help, a chap named John King.

He did not stay in Scotland long evidently but went to
New Zealand in 1862 and married at Kilsyth House, Maori
Hill, Dunedin, New Zealand in 1867 but the record from
which this information was extracted does not give the
maiden name of the bride.

The Rev. William McHutchison died at Arrowstown, New
Zealand on February 2nd, 1904. His obituary in the
"Otago Witness", page 31, of February 10th, 1904 reads:

> I have to report the removal from amongst us by death of the Rev.W.McHutchison.
> Deceased had been an invalid for a great
> number of years, being unable to leave
> the house. Mr. McHutcheson arrived in Arrowstown in 1868 and for 13 years acted as
> Headmaster of the local school. Although
> unable through his infirmities to mix
> with his fellowmen, deceased followed very
> closely the trend of the world's politics
> and was very conversant with all questions
> of the day. Deceased is survived by a
> widow, for whom much sympathy is expressed.
> The funeral took place on Thursday afternoon, the Rev.D.E.Fisher conducting the
> service at the grave.

We might mention the REV.WALTER ROSS who succeeded the
Rev. McHutcheson as minister of the Scotch Church of the
7th line, Beckwith. He was a native of Nova Scotia, educated at Queen's College 1856-1861 and ordained to the
Beckwith charge October 15th, 1862 and he ministered to
that congregation until the church closed in 1875.

The census of 1871 records his residence at the old
Manse. During his last years on the 7th Line, he was
also minister for St.Andrews Church, Carleton Place and
simultaneously at Franktown at St.Pauls after it was
built. He spent his latter years at Carleton Place and
his history is no doubt well known to the citizens of
that town.

The church on the 7th Line Beckwith more or less simply
"faded away". Records show that while services there
became few and far between - it must still have been the
center of jurisdiction and management for Beckwith in
connection with the Presbytery.

131

The last item of it's active life was recorded in 1875*
(see appendices) on the occasion of the ordination of
two elders. The item is dated Beckwith, April 25, 1875,
which day the Kirk session met and was constituted by
prayer. Present:The Moderator and Messrs - Robert Bell,
Hugh Robertson, Donald McLaren and Dugald Ferguson, elders and the matter discussed the taking into the eldership of Robert McLaughlin and Hugh George Tait.

The church on the McArthur land, Lot 14, Concession 7,
not being built on Church property, could over the years
have caused problems as generation succeeded generation
and personal involvement in church affairs changed. John
McArthur had died in 1867 and the record in the Church
Minutes pays homage to his eldership and work.* (see
appendices).

James McArthur was one of the workers for the early
Franktown church.

The Manse on the 7th Line being Church property was a
different matter and had to be disposed of in a legal
and orderly manner. Therefore, while the church merely
closed it's doors and fittings and trimmings from the
interior were sold, Robert Bell as head of the Trustees
committee for the church of the 7th Line, had to acquire
permission from the Ottawa Presbytery to sell the Manse.

This was obtained and it was announced for sale in the
local paper and sold in 1878 to a man named Code.

One old timer who died in his 100th year once told me
the Manse was an impressive sight when he was young.
He remembered it as a beautifully kept property.

I often used to imagine how it really looked in it's early
years, circled by a grove of trees. The grey stone solidity of it set at the end of the long driveway, enhanced
by apple trees and lilacs and honeysuckle in bloom.Spring
must have been a delight to the eye, as it still is, in
a different way.

Every season has it's own beauty and trees that flourish,
their own special dignity and strength in all seasons,
till the end of time.

NOTES ON BIBLIOGRAPHY

The author realizes this will seem to some readers a
very unorthodox bibliography.

It must be admitted general sources were used as follows-

Sinclair's Statistical Account of the Parish (Cromarty)
"Inverness Courier" items.
"The Lowland Highlander" by Alan G. Robertson
The Minutes of the General Assembly of the Church of
Scotland (microfilm PAC)
The diaries of the Rev. William Bell, read at the Douglas
Library, Queens University, Kingston, Ontario
But the GLASGOW COLONIAL SOCIETY (GCS) papers helped more
than anything to put flesh on the bones of the Rev. John
Smith, the circumstances and conditions of the times and
his ministry. The GCS papers provided record of informat-
ion invaluable in trying to pin down events and people in
the Presbyterian work in the colonies. Letters have a way
of bringing personalities and character to life as seen
through someone belonging to the committee, or in the
bureaucracy.

In reading through the records one always realized the
magic word was "Gaelic" for the Beckwith congregation,
and John Smith was put through his paces on it very thor-
oughly. He had learned his lessons well and he had also
ofe of the great Gaelic scholars of the day as teacher
and mentor at Dunoon. We read with delight the Rev. Mackay's letter to Robert Burns, Glasgow Colonial Society,
May 25, 1833.

My dear Sir:
        May I beg leave to introduce to you my partic-
ular friend Mr.John Smith, preacher of the Gospel, who, I
am almost sorry to say, is now fixed on going out to Canada. There is no person in the profession to whom I can
with more freedom testify, that he is a true Christian
preacher, and one whom I am convinced will prove himself
worthy of all confidence you can as a Society give him.
I am sorry that leaving town Friday, I am unable to write
anything more but assuredly your Society will be fortunate
in enlisting so excellent a young man in your cause, and I
shall only add, that any favour you can show or do to Mr.
Smith you will have the satisfaction in it.

133

and let me take the liberty of adding I shall feel it a personal favour conferred on myself.

> I am my dear sir,
> Yours respectfully and faithfully
> Wm. Mackay, minr. of Dunoon

AUTHOR'S NOTE

I shall ever be grateful to Dr.Elizabeth McDougall, and to the Dean of Divinity, Glasgow University who recommended I contact her - for helping and advising me regarding the wealth of information in the Glasgow Colonial Society papers!

Much time has been spent in research of various archives, libraries, church and registry papers, and needed information has been compiled in the appendices, but the story of the Rev.John Smith has been made possible through personal contact and help in Canada and Scotland of many people. Of course, such well known books as--

"The Pioneer History of the County of Lanark"Jean S.McGill
"The Story of the Derry" E.H.Kidd
"The Pioneer Pastor" Jessie Buchanan Campbell
and earlier local newspaper articles by J.T.Kirkland and Howard Brown were read with interest in trying to locate the Smith connection to the community, but Mr.Smith turned out to be an unknown quantity to most historians.

Thus, in actual fact this book has made its appearance through information regarding his relatives given by descendants of Mr.Smith. It has generated a colourful mosaic to be added to the discovery of the manse on a country sideroad.

APPENDICES

A-1 Crown Grant of land to Fisher, Lot SE 12, Con.7,
     Beckwith. 1824.
A-2 Documentation of sale of Fisher property to Trustees
     for Established Church of Scotland, Beckwith, 1826.
A-3 Documentation for sale of Glebe (SE 12 Lot 12) on
     7th Line, Beckwith, 1878.
A-4 Records of interest of baptism of children of ELIAS
     CODE who bought the manse from the Church in 1878.
B-1 Some facts about the Presbyterian Church of Scotland,
     covering some fragmentations in same, by D J.Steel.
B-2 Presbyterian Church - Canada. Some facts from The
     Encyclopedia Canadiana.
B-3 The Beckwith split from the records of Knox FREE
     Church Blacks Corner 1946, covering PROTEST May 1843.
B-4 Communion Roll - Free Church, Blacks Corners, 1847
B-5 Some notes of eldership and some elders of the 7th
     Line Presbyterian Church in connexion with the Est.
     Church of Scotland.
C-1 Extracts from Register of Baptisms - Rev.John Smith,
     Minister, 1833-1851, Beckwith 7th Line.
C-2 Extracts of Marriages in the Scotch Church, John
     Smith, Minister.
C-3 List of communicants - the Presbyterian Church.
     Beckwith in connexion with the Established Church of
     Scotland, John Smith, Minister, 1833-1851, with some
     additional listings and record of communion services
     up to 1875.
D   Documentation copies covering property Lot 14 and
     SW Lot 15 Concession 6, Beckwith, covering Crown
     Grant to Marrill of Lot 15, and sale of property to
     Rev.John Smith, transfer to his son, Robert Smith.
     papers involved with Dr.J.J.Aitchison, and subsequent
     "mortgage" sale in 1864, and sale to Drummond of said
     property 1865.

135

Appendix A-1

CROWN GRANT 1824 TO ALEXANDER FISHER
OF PROPERTY LATER SOLD TO CHURCH AS
A GLEBE FOR 7th LINE CHURCH

PROVINCE OF UPPER CANADA

George the Fourth by the Grace of God of the United King-
dom of Great Britain and Ireland, King Defender of the
Faith --- To all to whom these Presents shall come .....
Greetings!

Know Ye, that We, of our special Grace, certain knowledge
and mere notion have given and GRANTED, and by these Presents, do give and Grant, unto -- Alexander Fisher of the
Township of Beckwith in the County of Lanark in the District of Bathurst Yeoman, and Ex Soldier and R by QMG 3:
heirs and assigns for ever ALL that parcel or tract of
LAND, situate in the Township of Beckwith in the County
of Lanark in the District of Bathurst in our said Province, containing by admeasurement One Hundred Acres be the
same more or less, being the North-East half of lot No.
twelve in the Seventh Concession of said Township. Together with all the Woods and Waters thereon lying and being, under the reservations, limitations and conditions,
hereinafter expressed, which said, One Hundred Acres are
butted and bounds, or may be otherwise knows as follows;
that is to say:
Commencing in front of the said concession at the South
East angle of the said lot then North thirty-six degrees
West sixty-six chains seventy links more or less to the
allowance for road in rear of said concession then South
fifty-four degrees West fifteen chains more or less to
the center of the said lot then North thirty-six degrees
East sixty-six chains seventy links more or less to the
allowance for road in front of said concession then North
fifty-four degrees East fifteen chains more or less to
the place of beginning.

Jn. B. Robinson, A.Gen'l.   ....25 June 1824

136

TO HAVE AND TO HOLD the said parcel or tract of Land,
hereby given and granted to the said Alexander Fisher
heirs and assigns for ever,saving nevertheless,to Us,our
Heirs and Successors, all Mixes of Gold and Silver,that
shall or may be hereafter found on any part of said parcel or tract of Land hereby given and granted as aforesaid; and saving and reserving to Us,our Heirs and Successors, all White Pine Trees, that shall or may now or
hereafter grow, or be growing on any part of the said
parcel or thact of Land hereby granted as aforesaid.Prov-
ided always, that no part of the parcel or tract of Land
hereby given and granted to the said Alexander Fisher and
his heirs, be within any reservation heretofore made and
marked for Us, our Heirs and Successors, by our Surveyor
General Woods, or his lawful Deputy, in which case, this
our grant for such part of the Land hereby given and
granted to the said Alexander Fisher and his heirs for
ever, as aforesaid, and which shall upon a survey thereof
being made, be found within any such reservation, shall
be null and void and of none effect, any thing herein
contained to the contrary actwithstanding. Provided also,
that the said ALEXANDER FISHER and his heirs and assigns,
shall and do within three years, erect and build or cause
to be erected and built, in and upon some part of the siad
parcel or tract of Land, a good and sufficient dwelling
house the said Alexander Fisher or his assigns, not having
built, or not being his or their own right, lawfully possessed of a house in our said Province, and be therein or
cause some person to be therein resident, for and during
the space of three years, then next ensuing the building
of same. Provided also, that if at any time or times hereafter, the Land so hereby given and granted to the said
Alexander Fisher and his heirs shall come into the possession and tenure of any person or persons whomsoever
either by virtue of any Deed of sale, conveyance, enfeoffment and or exchange; or by gift, inheritance, descent,
devise or marriage, such person or persons shall within
twelve months next after his, her or their entry into and
possession of the same, take the oaths prescribed by Law,
before some one of the Magistrates of our said Province,
and a cerfificate of such oath having been so taken shall
cause to be recorded in the Secretary's

Office of the said Province. Indefault of all or any of
which conditions, limitations, and restirctions, this
said Grant and everything herein contained, shall be and
We hereby declare the same to be null and void, to all intents and purposes whatsoever; and the Land hereby granted
and every part and parcel thereof shall revert to and
become vested in Us, our Heirs and Successors, in like
manner as if the same, had never been granted, any thing
herein contained to the contrary thereof in any wise notwithstanding.

AND WHEREAS by an Act of the Parliament of Great Britain
passed in the tirty-first year of the Reign of His late
Majesty King George the Third, entitled "An Act to repeal
certain parts of an Act, passed in the fourteenth year of
His Majesty's Reign, entitled "An Act for making more
effectual provision for the Government of The Province
of Quebec, in North America, and to make further provision
for the Government of said Province". It is declared
"that no grant of lands hereafter made, shall be valid
or effectual, unless the same shall contain a specification of the lands to be allotted and appropriated solely
to the maintenance of a Protestant Clergy within the said
Province in respect of the Lands to be thereby granted".
..NOW KNOW YE, That We have caused an allotment or appropriation of....
Fourteen acres and two sevenths to be made on lot No.
Twenty-four in the Third Concession of the said Township
of Beckwith.
Given under the Great Seal of our Province of Upper Canada:
Witness our trusty and well-beloved
    Sir Perigrine Maitland, K.C.B.and Gn. for our said
Province and Major General Commanding our forces therein
this NINETEENTH-day of MAY in the year of our LORD one
thousand eight hundred and twenty-four and the fifth of
our Reign   (initials) PM
BY COMMAND of His Excellency in Council D.Commonfy (?)
Entered with 4 February 1824 under the Adm. of Sir P.
Mait land K. C.B.
..........fees suspd. Settlement Duty Performed.

                            24 June 1824

DOCUMENTATION OF SALE OF FISHER PROPERTY
TO TRUSTEES FOR ESTABLISHED CHURCH OF SCOTLAND
BECKWITH 1826

A MEMORIAL to be registered pursuant to the statutes in
such case made and provided of an indenture of Bargain
and Sale made the first day of November in the year of
our Lord 1826 Between Alexander Fisher of Beckwith in the
District of Bathurst in the Province of Upper Canada Yeoman of the one part and John McTavish and Alexander
Dewar of the same place Yeomen TRUSTEES OF THE ES-
TABLISHED CHURCH OF SCOTLAND in BECKWITH aforesaid where
by the said Alexander Fisher in consideration of thirty
pounds did grant unto the said John McTavish and Alexander Dewar and their successors in office forever, all and
singular, that certain piece of land situated in the Township of Beckwith, in the County of Lanark, in the District
of Bathurst in said province being composed of the North
East half of lot number twelve in the seventh concession
of the said Township of Beckwith, containing one hundred
acres of land more or less which land is buten and bounded
or may be other wise known as follows that is say, commencing in front of the said concession at the South East
angle of the said lot then North thirty-six degrees West
sixty-six chains seventy links more or less to the allowance for road in rear of the said concession then South
fifty-four degrees West fifteen chains more or less to
the center of the said lot then South thirty-six degrees
East sixty-six chains seventy links more or less to the
allowance for road in front of the said concession. Then
South fifty-four degrees East fifteen chains more or less
to the place of beginning containing one hundred acres of
land more or less TOGETHER WITH ALL HOUSES, OUTHOUSES,
WOODS and WATER thereon erected, lying and being. To
have and to hold the same with appurtenances freed and
discharged from all encumbrances whatsoever, unto the
said John McTavish and Alexander Dewar, Trustees aforesaid (and their successors in office) forever, and which
said deed is witnessed by JAMES BOULTON OF PERTH, in the

139

A-2

District......Esquire and is hereby agreed to be registered by me the grantor herein named in witness whereof
I have hereunto set and put my hand and seal this first
day of November, 1826.

(Signed) Alexander Fisher.

Signed and sealed in
presence of
J. Boulton.

(Signed)
Nicholas Anderson

Registered on Tuesday, the twenty-sixth day of June in
the year one thousand, eight hundred and twenty-seven at
two of the clock in the afternoon.

(Signed) Alex. McMillan,
Reg'r. County Lanark.

#-21   DOROTHY WARDELL STANDING BESIDE
HER PAINTING "THE CRUCIFIXION"
1944

140

DOCUMENTATION OF SALE OF GLEBE
ON 7TH LINE BECKWITH 1878

THIS INDENTURE made in duplicate the twelfth day of
February One thousand eight hundred and seventy eight in
pursuance of the Act respecting short forms of conveyances.

BETWEEN - ROBERT BELL of the Village of Carleton Place in
the County of Lanark, Esquire JAMES GILLIES of the same
place, Lumber Merchant PETER McARTHUR of the Township of
Beckwith in the County of Lanark, Yeoman, Dugald Ferguson
of the said Township of Beckwith, Yeoman, DONALD CARMICH-
AEL of the said Township of Beckwith, Yeoman, GEORGE
COMRIE of the said Township of Beckwith, Yeoman and JOHN
CAMPBELL of the same place Yeoman, TRUSTEES OF THE PRES-
BYTERAIN CONGREGATION OF ST.ANDREWS CHURCH AT CARLETON
PLACE AND ST PAUL'S CHURCH AT FRANKTOWN in connection
with the Presbyterian Church in Canada, hereafter called
the TRUSTEES of the FIRST PART, and ELIAS CODE of the
same township of Beckwith, Yeoman, of the SECOND PART.

WHEREAS by an Act of the Legislature of Ontario passed in
the thirty six year of the reign of Her Majesty Queen
Victoria and instituted an act respecting the property of
Religious Institutions it is provided that where land held
by trustees for the use of a congregation as a religious
body becomes unnecessary to be retained for such use and
that it is desired advantageous to sell the land the
trustee for the time being m ay give public notice of an
intended sale, specifying the premises to be sold and the
time and terms of the sale, and after publication of the
notice for four successive weeks in a weekly paper published in or near the place where the lands are situated
they may sell the lands at public auction according to
the notice.

AND WHEREAS the lands and premises hereinafter particularly described and held by the congregation of St.Andrew
Church at Carleton Place and St. Paul's Church at

Franktown in connection with the Presbyterian Church in
Canada for the use and purpose of a Glebe and a residence
for a minister had become unnecessary to be retained for
such purposes and they deemed it advantageous to sell
said lands.

AND WHEREAS by the Act of Legislature of Ontario passed
the thirty-six year of the reign of Her Majesty Queen
Victoria and instituted an act respecting the union of
certain Presbyterian Churches therein named it is provided amongst other things that before any of the promises
of leasing if for a period exceeding seven years or sel-
ling, exchanging, or mortgaging be exercised by any congregation or trustees thereof the sanction of the Presbytery within those bounds such congregation is placed shall
be allowed.

AND WHEREAS the trustees of said congregation on the Sixth day of February one thousand eight hundred and seventy
seven presented such a request to the Ottawa Presbytery
being the presbytery within whose bounds such congregation is placed and therein requested leave to dispose of
the lands and premises hereinafter described.

AND WHEREAS the said Ottawa Presbytery did on the said
sixth day of February authorize and empower the said congregation to sell and dispose of the lands and premises
hereinafter mentioned.

AND WHEREAS the said trustees caused a notice to be published for four successive weeks in a weekly newspaper
published at the said village of Carleton Place, called
"The Central Canadian" that the premises hereinafter particularly described would be put up for sale at public
auction at Joseph Wilson's Hotel in the said village on
Saturday the tenth day of March one thousand eight hundred and seventy seven at the hour of three o'clock in
the afternoon.

AND WHEREAS at the time and place last aforesaid the
premises hereinafter particularly described were put up
for sale at public auction and the said party here of

the second part became the purchaser thereof, being the
highest bidder therefore for the sum of one thousand four
hundred and fifty dollars lawful money of Canada.

AND WHEREAS after said sale and before the execution of
these presents the said trustees duly notified the said
congregation of a meeting to be held of the same for the
purpose of ratifying and signifying their assent to said
sale.

AND WHEREAS at said meeting the said ROBERT BELL (one of
the parties of the first part) was chosen Chairman of the
same by the votes of majority of the members of said congregation present at said meeting.

AND WHEREAS the members of said congregation present at
said meeting unanimously resolved that said sales be confirmed and that said Chairman signify their assent to such sale by being a party to and executing these presents
- from this INDENTURE WITNESSETH that in consideration of
the said sum of one thousand four hundred and fifty dollars of lawful money of Canada now paid by the said party of the second part to the said trustees (the receipt
whereof is hereby by them acknowledged) they, the said
trustees (the parties of the first part) do grant unto
the said party of the second part his heirs and assigns
forever all and singular that certain parcel or tract of
land and premises situate in the Township of Beckwith in
the County of Lanark and Province of Ontario containing
one hundred acres more or less and being composed of the
North East half of lot number twelve in the seventh concession of the said Township of Beckwith To Have and To
Hold unto the said party of the second part his heirs and
assigns to and for his and their sale and only use forever. Subject nonetheless to the usual laws and limitations, promises and conditions expressed in the original
grant thereof from the crown.

The said Trustees (the said parties of the first part)
covenant with the said party of the second part that they
have the right to convey the said lands to the said party of the second part and that the said party of the se-

cond part shall have quiet possession of the said lands
free from all encumbrances and the said trustees covenant
with the said party of the second part that they will execute such further assurances of the said lands as may be
requested.

AND the said trustees covenant with the said party of the
second part that the said party of the second part that
they have done no act to encumber the said lands and the
said trustees release to the said party of the second
part all their claims upon said lands.

In witness whereof the said parties hereto have hereunder
set their hands and seals -

signed and sealed and
delivered
In presence of

Thos. Greig.

> R. Bell
> James Gillies
> Peter McArthur
> Dugald Ferguson
> Robert Scott
> Donald Carmichael
> George Comrie
> John Campbell

BAPTISMS RECORDED IN CHURCH MINUTES OF SESSION

	FATHER	MOTHER	BAPTIZED

John Boyd
born   Beckwith
Oct. 10. 1876   Elias Code Elizabeth McCuan Feb. 14. 1877

Duncan
born   Beckwith
Aug. 26. 1878   Elias Code Elizabeth McCuan Mar. 10. 1879

                                                 Beckwith
Elias   Elias Code Elizabeth McCuan Dec. 7. 1880

NOTE

Beckwith here no doubt referred to the Church at Blacks
Corners as AFTER 1875 all Presbyterian Churches (Free and
Church of Scotland) of the Township were under the um-
brella of The Presbyterian Church in Canada.

THE PRESBYTERIAN CHURCH OF SCOTLAND

The following from D.J.Steel's book "Sources for
Scottish Genealogy and Family History XII - National
Index of Parish Records" pages 190-193, covering the
fragmentations in the Church of Scotland - is quoted
here with the kind permission of D.J.Steel.

SECEDING PRESBYTERIAN CHURCHES

Until 1690, Presbyterianism in Scotland was
involved in constant struggles against repeated
attempts to impose episcopacy on the Scottish
Church, and internal differences were insignifi-
cant. With its final victory, however, these
rapidly became apparent. The Cameronians, the
followers of the militant Covenanter Richard
Cameron, were opposed to the acceptance of non-
Presbyterian and non Covenanting sovereigns,
or political association with a Prelatic country
and the acceptance in the Church of Episcopal
ministers willing to conform to Presbyterianism.
They therefore refused to take the Oath of Alle-
giance or to exercise any civil function. They
were, however, few in number and influence, and
the majority of later secessions from the Established Church sprang directly or indirectly from
the question of patronage. Patronage (i.e. the
right of a layman to appoint a minister even
against the wishes of the kirk session) was decreed
by Parliament in 1567, abolished in 1640, restored
in 1661, abolished in 1690 and finally restored by
the Act of Toleration of 1712.

THE ASSOCIATE SYNODS

The first secession arose not through direct
opposition to patronage but because the Assembly in
1732 abolished the last remnant of popular election
by enacting that in cases where patrons neglected

or declined to exercise their right of presentation the minister was to be chosen, not by the congregation, but only by the elders and Protestant heritors. A number of ministers led by Ebenezer Erskine, Minister of Stirling and his brother Ralph, protested vigorously and were ejected. In December 1733 they constituted themselves into the Associate Presbytery, disowning the authority of the General Assembly. The following year they refused concessions made by the General Assembly and were finally ejected in 1740. Meanwhile their numbers had grown, until in 1745 there were 45 congregations under the Presbytery's jurisdiction and it was reconstituted into an Associate Synod. In 1746, the Synod split over the question of the religious clause of the oath taken by burgesses in Edinburgh, Glasgow and Perth, and in April 1747 two bodies were formed, each claiming to be the Associate Synod. Those who condemned the swearing of the burgess oath as sinful came to be popularly known as "anti-burghers"while those who contended that the abstinence from it should not be made a term of communion were designated "Burghers". The Associate (Anti-Burgher) Synod held its first meeting in Edinburgh on April 10th, 1747. It grew with considerable rapidity, and for purposes of organization was formed into four provincial synods and took the name of The General Associate Synod. That associate (Burgher) Synod held its first meeting at Stirling on June 16, 1747. The number of congregations under its charge also increased. In 1799 there was controversy within the Burgher synod concerning the role of the secular authorities. The Old Lights held that it was the duty of the secular authorities to uphold true religion. The New Lights, the majority, believed that the secular authorities had no power in matters of religion. The Old Lights withdrew and in 1805 formed themselves into a synod with three Presbyteries (Glasgow, Edinburgh, Perth and Dunfermline) and called themselves the Original Associate (Burgher) Synod. In 1839, they rejoined the Church of Scotland, except for a few ministers who constituted themselves into the remnant Burgher Synod.

Meanwhile the Antiburghers were split over the same issue. Here too, New Lights or Voluntaries formed the majority. In 1806, the Old Lights formed the Constitutional Presbytery.

In 1820, the two groups of New Lights came together: 120 congregations of the General Associate or Anti-Burgher Synod united with 154 congregations of the Associate or Burgher Synod to form the United Secession Church, which by 1847 had increased to 400 congregations. However, a number of Anti-Burgher ministers refused to accept the union and formed the Synod of Protesters. In 1827, this united with the Old Light Constitutional Presbytery to form the Associate Synod of Original Seceders or Original Secession Synod, which in 1842 united with the Remanent Burgher Synod to form the United Original Secession Church, which in turn united with the Free Church in 1852. Two Ministers, Wright of Edinburgh and Lambie of Pitcairngreen who refused to accept the 1842 union formed with a congregation at Dundee the Associate Presbytery of Original Seceders. The minority who refused to accept the 1852 union continued as the United Original Secession Synod.

THE REFORMED PRESBYTERIANS
In 1689 when there was the first General Meeting of the "Society Men" there were allegedly 9,000 belonging to Cameronian Societies*through this figure is probably an excessive estimate. Their three ministers all joined the Church of Scotland in 1690 and until 1706 they had no minister. In that year they joined by Rev. John McMillan who was pastor of the United Societies from 1707 to 1751 and soon there were others. In 1743 their first Presbytery was constituted at Braehead, and they took the title of the Reformed Presbyterians. Rev. W. McMillan estimates their total strength at this time as between eight hundred and a thousand.**Apart from the United Societies there were between 1690 and 1720 small separated sects of Covenanters-Harlites (or Cotmoor Folks) Howdenites, Russelites, Adamites and others. After McMillan's marriage by Church

of Scotland minister, a larger broke off, led by
William Wilson, a schoolmaster in Douglas. They
are sometimes called "The Active Testimony Bearers".
Another party, led by Robert Smith broke off about
1715.

THE RELIEF PRESBYTERY
In the first half of the eighteenth Century,
Presbyteries not infrequently disregarded the presentations of lay patrons and settled ministers desired by the congregation, but legal decisions showed
that their nominee, though legally minister of the
parish, could not claim his stipend. The Church was
divided over the patronage question into a Moderate
Party and a Popular Party. Both objected to patronage but believed in the enforcement of the existing
law. By the new policy inaugurated by Dr. William
Robertson the Assembly compelled Presbyterians to
give effect to presentations and in a long series
of disputed settlements, the "Call" was finally disregarded and it was declared that the Church courts
must induct any qualified presentee. The result was
that frequently when unpopular presentee was settled,
the people quietly left the Established Church and
erected a meeting house. In 1761, Thomas Gillespie
was deposed for refusing to assist at the ordination
of an unpopular presentee and formed with Thomas
Boston and Thomas Collier the Presbytery of Relief.
Unlike the Associate Synods, the Relief Presbytery
never regarded its secession as final and sought
reconciliation, though without success. Indeed many
of the Relievers never ceased to regard themselves
as members of the Church of Scotland. In 1764 there
were 120 Relief meeting houses and by 1770 when a
presentee was unpopular, secession had become more
frequent than submission.

THE FREE CHURCH
Within the Established Church the Patronage
Question came to a head in the years 1833-1843. In
1834 the General Assembly passed the "veto" Act by
which it was declared to be a fundamental law of the

church that no pastor should be intruded on a congregation contrary to the will of the people, and by which it was provided that the simple dissent of a majority of heads of families in a parish should be enough to justify a presbytery in rejecting a presentee. The question of the legality of this measure soon came to be tried in the Civil courts and it was ultimately answered by the decisions of the Court of Session in 1838 that a presbytery had no right to reject a presentee simply because the parishioners protested against his settlement, but was bound to disregard the veto. This decision was confirmed by the House of Lords in 1839, but Assembly decided to press the matter and open negotiations with the Government. However, a petition to the Queen in 1842 praying for abolition of patronage met with no redress, and in March 1843 by a majority of 135 the House of Commons declined to alter the law. At the Assembly of 1843, Thomas Chalmers and 451 ministers (over a third of the total) left the Established Church and formed the Free Church of Scotland. Within four years there were more than 700 Free Churches.

RE*-UNION

In 1847 a union was formed between all the congregations of the United Secession Church and 118 out of 136 of the Relief Churches, forming the United Presbyterian Church. In 1900 this was united with the Free Church to form the United Free Church of Scotland. A small minority of the Free Church consisting of 25 ministers and 63 congregations for the most part in the Highlands and Islands, held aloof from the Union and laid claim to the property of the Church. This Claim was upheld by the House of Lords, but the Churches (Scotland) Act of 1905 decided it was entitled only to the churches and manses which it could effectively use, the others being awarded to the United Free Church. Meanwhile, patronage had been abolished by an Act of 1874 which granted to the congregation the right of electing parish ministers. Intermittent negotiations bet-

ween the Church of Scotland and the United Free Church finally bore fruit in 1929 when the two churches
were re-united.

APPENDIX B-2

PRESBYTERIAN CHURCH - CANADA

The Encyclopedia Canadiana gives a concise description of the background of the Presbyterian Church on the Canadian scene from its early days, and for the reader interested in the religious background of the Beckwith community, some easily understood extracts are given as follows:

The early history of Canadian Presbyterianism is one of considerable complexity. Although this denomination was the first to achieve national unification, there were at one time no fewer than eleven distinct self governing Presbyterian organizations. Almost all of these groups had the same doctrine and polity, their separateness being due mainly to factors that originated outside of Canada and were largely alien to the Canadian religious scene. Geographical influences played a part since, prior to Confederation in 1867, all of the Canadian denominations naturally tended to organize along regional rather than national lines. Until political unity was achieved it was almost inevitable that the Maritime Provinces and the Canadas should maintain separate religious organizations. Other divisions stemmed from the fact that Presbyterianism especially in Upper Canada entered the country in two streams, one from United States and one from Scotland, and organizations were formed having ties with one or other of these parent bodies. By far the most prolific source of division however was the fact that during the 18th and 19th centuries, Scottish Presbyterianism itself was a prey to constant fragmentation. Most of these Scottish divisions were reproduced in Canada; the different branches of Scottish Presbyterianism sending ministers and forming organizations here, while Scottish immigrants on their arrival in Canada attached

themselves to the group with which they had been
associated at home. While nearly all of the secessions from the Established Church of Scotland were
occasioned by the controversy over lay patronage and
the intrusion of the State into what was regarded as
the sphere of the Church, and although these were not
relevant issues in Canada, old world divisions were
perpetrated here through the loyalty of Scottish
clergy and people to their own history and traditions.
In time, however, and in the new land, memories of
historic conflicts faded, and the unification of the
denomination resulted.

We further learn from the Encyclopedia:

Most of the clergy in the Colony were from one or
other of the Secession churches, the Established
Church being slow to follow its migrating members
overseas. The situation was changed however in
1825 with the formation within the Church of Scotland of the Glasgow Colonial Society "for promoting
the moral and religious interests of the Scottish
settlers in British North America".

During the 15 years of its existence the Society
sent to Canada nearly 50 ordained clergymen.

The first Presbyterian congregation in Canada was
organized at Quebec about 1765 and the second at
Montreal in 1786. In Upper Canada Presbyterianism
owed its beginnings to missionary effort from the
United States, the first systematic attempt to serve
this area being made by the American Dutch Reform
Church.

After about 1817, clergy were sent by the Associate
or Burgher Synod of Scotland, and after 1825 by the
Church of Scotland. The first permanent organization in Upper or Lower Canada was the Presbytery of

the Canadas, constituted in Montreal in 1818, and
becoming a synod two years later. Owing to the difficulties of a few men meeting regularly when scattered over a wide area and dependent upon primitive
methods of communication the Synod had a precarious
existence until it was ultimately organized as the
United Synod of Upper Canada in 1831.

In the same year was established a Synod "in connection with the Church of Scotland". Nine years of
negotiations resulted in 1840, in a union of the two
synods. The United body retaining the name of the
synod in "Connection with the Church of Scotland".
One of its first actions was to secure in 1841 a Royal Charter for establishment of Queen's College,
Kingston, which was opened in 1842.

Meanwhile three other smaller Presbyterian groups
organized themselves in Upper Canada in 1833, the
Presbytery of Niagara, which survived until about
1850. In 1834 the missionary Presbytery of Canada
in connection with the United Associate Secession
Church in Scotland, later to become the Synod of the
United Presbyterian Church in Canada and in 1836 the
Presbytery of Stamford of the Associate Synod of
North America. In the Canadas therefore, as in the
Maritime Provinces, there were in 1840 four separate
Presbyterian organizations.

The Scottish Disruption of 1843 vitally affected
these Canadian bodies connected with the Church of
Scotland. Although they were not an integral part
of the church, and while grievances that led to the
formation of the Free Church of Scotland were not
live issues in Canada, the events of Scottish ecclesiastical history were once more reproduced here.

Canadian Presbyterians of the period thought of themselves less as independent entities than as offshoots
of the Scottish Churches, at a time when feelings
were intense. Many were in entire sympathy with the
Scottish Free Church - its struggle for spiritual
autonomy and felt that to maintain even a nominal
connection with the Church of Scotland represented
a betrayal of principle.

Consequently, no sooner had the Disruption occurred
in Scotland than all the Canadian synods in connection with the Church of Scotland were threatened
with division.

In 1844 a majority withdrew from the Synod of Nova
Scotia in connection with the Church of Scotland to
form the (FREE) Synod of Nova Scotia, adhering to
the Westminster Standards. Similarly New Brunswick
in connection with the Church of Scotland resulted
in the formation of the (FREE) Synod of New Brunswick adhering to the Standards of the Westminster
Confession.

A similar pattern developed in the Canadas, where in
1844 a minority seceded from the Synod of the Presbyterian Church of Canada in connection with the
Church of Scotland to organize the Synod of the
(FREE) Presbyterian Church of Canada. This Free
Church Synod experienced very rapid growth, the
number of ministers on its rolls increasing from 23
to 158 between 1844 and 1861. In this latter year
it united with the Synod of the United Presbyterian
Church in Canada to become the Synod of the Canada
Presbyterian Church.

Since Queen's College, Kingston, remained in the
hands of the Synod in Connection with the Church of
Scotland, steps were taken immediately by the Free

Church Synod to establish a theological seminary which opened at Toronto late 1844.

Although the year 1844 thus saw Canadian Presbyterianism seriously divided, the current then began to move in the direction of unification. By 1868 a series of regional unions had reduced the number of organizations to four, two in connection with the Church of Scotland, and two without any such connection - two in the Maritime Provinces and two in the Canadas.

After confederation in 1867 sentiment in favour of a national union of all Canadian Presbyterians developed rapidly. It seemed desirable to leaders in all groups that churches sharing the same doctrinal standards and polity should pool their efforts and resources in evangelizing the newly formed Dominion.

Formal union was consumated in Montreal in 1875, the united body adopting the name of the PRESBYTERIAN CHURCH IN CANADA. The Rev. John Cook minister of St. Andrews Church, Quebec (City) was elected as first moderator.

A few ministers and congregations, most of them connected with one of the Church of Scotland synods, declined to enter the union. Some of these maintained a separate existence for several years; but were gradually absorbed into the main Presbyterian body.

The General Assembly of the unified church was divided into 4 Synods and 33 Presbyteries having on their rolls the names of some 600 ministers and approximately 88,000 communicant members.

156

The Presbyterian union of 1875 was followed by a
half-century of unprecedented growth by 1925 had given this denomination the largest Protestant consti-
tuency in Canada.

THE BECKWITH SPLIT FROM THE RECORDS OF KNOX
(FREE) CHURCH OF
BLACKS CORNERS' BECKWITH TOWNSHIP, COUNTY OF LANARK,
DISTRICT OF BATHURST 1844

Kept at United Church Archives, Toronto.

PROTEST - May 1843

At Edinburgh, within a large Hall at Canonville the
18th day of May 1843 years, by Commissioners of the
General Assembly of the Church of Scotland appointed
to meet on 18th day of May 1843. This Protest was
afterwards signed by all the ministers who resigned
their connexion with the State - and appointed Rev.
Dr. Chalmers to be their Moderator.

Closer to home - in the records of the Knox Church,
Blacks Corners - the Protest is recorded as follows:

Protest of:
Certain Ministers or Elders belonging to the Synod
of Canada in connexion with the Church of Scotland.

At Kingston, the 10th day
of July, 1844 years
Whereas the Church is divinely constituted deposi-
tary and guardian of revealed truth, is specially
bound to lift up her testimony for those particular
truths which are at any time endangered or overborne
by the antagonist powers of this world. AND whereas
those great and fundamental truths which respect
the supremacy of Christ in his Church, - the spiritual independence of her rulers, their exclusive
responsibility to her great Head, the rights and
privileges of his people, and the proper relation
which should subsist between the Church and the
State - are at the present day endangered and

have actually been overborne in the Established
Church of Scotland, through recent encroachments
of the State upon the spiritual province, and
submitted to by her; AND whereas in righteous
testimony against these encroachments great numbers
of office bearers and members of said Church
have solemnly and deliberately come out, and
are now formally constituted into the Free Protesting Church of Scotland, a church which has, during
the last twelve months, enjoyed many unrequivocal
token of the approbation of her great Head; AND
whereas the Synod of the Presbyterian Church of
Canada in connexion with the Church of Scotland,
apart from all consideration of a general kind,
which should have led them to testify against the
defections and corruptions of the said Established
Church, were specially bound to do so, because of
their connection with said Church, and because also,
of reiterated testimonies solemnly and deliberately
lifted up by the Synod in former years in behalf of
the contendings of those who have been compelled
to secede; AND whereas the due and proper testimony against the defections and corruptions of the
Established Church of Scotland was a termination
of the peculiarly close and intimate connection
in which the Synod stood to her. AND whereas it
has been in an orderly and constitutional way,
proposed to the Synod, having been made the subject
of petitions and overtures of congregations and
Presbyteries whilst it has been advocated by many
of the members, that the Synod, should terminate
its connection with said Church and alter its
designation accordingly; AND whereas this Synod,
by the vote of a majority of its members came to
the decision, that is shall not terminate said
connection, nor take other such actions, as was
required. Therefore, we, the undersigned ministers
and elders, members of the Synod in connection,
with the Church of Scotland, do in our name, as
well as in the name of all who adhere to us, hereby
Dissent and Protest against such decision, for the

following reason. First, that in our conscientious conviction, this Synod and thereby giving their virtual sanction to the procedure of the Established Church of Scotland, in the great questions at issue between that Church and the Free Protesting Church of Scotland and lending the weight of their influence as a church, to the support of principles which are incompatible with the purity and the liberty of any church by which they are allowed, and which are fitted, at the same time, to do grievous injury to the cause of the Redeemer throughout the world. Second: that in a cause relating to a church in which they have many and obvious reasons for feeling a very deep and special interest; a cause too, in which the honour of Christ's Crown, and the interests of his kingdom are intimately concerned. They have refused to discharge the obvious duty of lifting up a full and unambiguous testimony for the truth, and thereby strengthening the hands of those who are witnessing for Christ and suffering for his sake. Third: that after solemnly pledging themselves in various forms, and at different times, to maintain the great principles for which the Free-Protesting Church is now contending and which the Established Church of Scotland has practically repudiated, - and especially after the import and sincerity of such pledges had been brought into question by the acting of various ministers and even of one of the inferior church courts, they have virtually receded from their solemn pledges, and destroyed the weight of every expression of the aforesaid principles embodied in their records. Fourth: that by leaving an open door for the admission of ministers and elders from the Established Church of Scotland holding unsound views on the great principles aforesaid, they have most seriously endangered the purity of the Church, and brought even her independence into peril through the probable introduction of office bearers prepared to submit to the same encroachments of the civil power by which the Church of Scotland has

been enslaved. _Fifth_: that they have rendered
the relation in which they stood toward the
Established Church of Scotland so doubtful and
Equivocal, that even their declaration of spiritual
independence is necessarily deprived of all significance and weight, that the terms in which their
endowments are held have een, in effect, declared
to be such as are incompatible with the proper
regulation of their interwith other churches, and
even with free action in many other matters, of
greater importance, and that, morever, they have
cast away the opportunity of placing the church on
a basis which might have gathered around her all
the sound hearted Presbyterianism of the province.
Sixth: that they have given additional weight to
be the practical argument against Establishments,
furnished by the present position of the Established
Church of Scotland - strengthened the hands of those
who, in this province, are denying the lawfulness
and expediency of all national endowments for
religious purposes and rejected the opportunity
which God in his providence had afforded them of
proving to the World, that entire freedom of action,
and a jealous deterioration to guard against the
encroachments of the civil powers, were perfectly
compatible with the enjoyment of the countenance
and support of the State. _Seventh_: that in a
matter in which the consciences of many of their
brethren were aggrieved and for refusing relief
in regard to which no moral necessity could be
pleaded on their part, such relief has nevertheless
been refused, wherefore. For all these and other
reasons which might be stated, we dissent from the
decision to which this venerable court yesterday
came, and while feeling painfully the solemnity of
our position, and deeply distressed in the view of
the possible results, we solemnly protest to this
venerable Court, before God, the Church of Christ,
and the World, that it is our conscientious belief,
that, in respect of the premises, sin, in matters

fundamental, has been done by this court, and that while at the same time, we continue to adhere, to the confession of Faith, and other standards of this Church, we can yet no longer, with a conscience hold office in the Presbyterian Church of Canada in connection with the Church of Scotland, and further, we Protest, that, the guilt of schism lies not with us but with those who have acted in a way which compels us to depart, and further, also, we protest in behalf of ourselves and those of the people of this Church who may now or hereafter adhere to us, that we hold ourselves entitled to all the property and emoluments of whatever kind, now in our possession.

Duncan B. Blair, Minister
John McEwen,   Elder.

COMMUNION ROLL - KNOX (FREE) CHURCH - BLACKS CORNERS 1847

John McDonald, Elder
Mrs. John McDonald
Neil Stewart, Elder
Mrs. Neil Stewart
John McEwen, Elder
Mrs. John McEwen
Catherine McEwen(widow)
Jane Stewart
Mrs. Jas. Stewart
Alexander Stewart
Christian Stewart
Allan Cameron
Mrs. Allan Cameron
Duncan MacNee
Janet MacNee(widow)
Catherine MacNee
Mrs. Finlay(widow)
Mrs. Campbell
Ewen MacEwen(postmaster)
Mrs. Ewen MacEwen
John MacEwen
Mrs. John MacEwen
Hugh MacEwen
Mrs. Hugh MacEwen
Alex Stewart
Mrs. Alex Stewart
Mrs. D. Stewart(widow)
William Duff
Mrs. W. Duff
Jannet Duff
James Duncan
Mrs. John Black
Allan MacDonald
Mrs. Allan MacDonald
Colin King
Mrs. Colin King
Colin Sinclair

Charles Stewart
John McTavish, Jr.
Mrs. John McTavish
Peter McTavish
Mrs. Peter McTavish
Elizabeth McTavish
John Robertson
Donald Robertson
Alexander Dewar
Mrs. A. Dewar
Margaret Dewar
Catherine Dewar
George Dewar
Margaret Dewar
Anne Dewar
Donald MacDougald
Mrs. Donald MacDougald
John MacDougald
Jannet MacDougald
Margaret MacDougald
Christian MacDougald
Mrs. Catherine MacDougall(widow)
Elizabeth MacDougall
Jannet MacDougall
Duncan MacEwen
Mrs. Duncan MacEwen
John MacEwen
Mrs. John MacEwen
Findlay MacEwen
Mrs. Finlay MacEwen
Alexander MacEwen
Mrs. R. MacEwen
James MacEwen
Mrs. Peter Dewar(widow)
John MacDougall
Mrs. John MacDougall
Duncan McIallum

Mrs. Colin Sinclair
John Sinclair
Mrs. John Sinclair
John Miller
Mrs. John Miller
William MacDonald
Mrs. Wm. MacDonald

John Macnab Sr.
William Murehead
Alex. MacLaren
Ann MacLaren
John Stewart
Archibald McArthur
Mrs. McArthur.

B-5

SOME NOTES OF ELDERSHIP AND SOME ELDERS
OF 7th LINE CHURCH, BECKWITH

FORMULA FOR ELDERS

I do sincerely own and declare the Scriptures of the Old
and New Testaments to be the word of the Lord and the Westminster Shorter Catechism to contain the true doctrine
to which I will constantly adhere; as likewise that I own
and acknowledge the Presbyterian Church Government of this
Church by Sessions, Presbyteries, Synods and General As-
semblies to be the only Government of this Church; and
that I will submit thereto, concur therewith and never endeavour directly or indirectly the prejudice or subversion
thereof; and that I shall observe all public ordinances
within this church as the same are authorized.

Beckwith, 1st June 1834
This day, immediately after divine service in the
forenoon, public intimation was given, that Peter Campbell, John Campbell and John McDonald, the persons above
named have been elected to fill the office of Eldership
by a committee of the Presbytery of Bathurst assembled
with the heads of families connected with the Scotch Presbyterian congregation in this place and that if no objections against the life and conversation of said individual
should be brought forward within ten days from this date,
their Ordination to the Office of the Eldership in the
Church shall take place according to the rules of the
Church of Scotland.

Township of Beckwith
15 June 1834.
This day after divine service in the forenoon the
minister presented to the congregation the following persons had been elected to and accepted of the Office of
Eldership in this Church, viz: Peter Campbell, John Campbell, and John McDonald - their edit had been duly
sound and no objections offered to their life and conversation and that these persons were therefore by authority
of the Presbytery of Bathurst to be set apart to the of-

165

fice of Elders. The minister then calling upon the persons chosen and having put to them the questions appointed by Act of Assembly and they having formally given satisfactory answers to the same, the said individuals were by solemn prayer ordained and set apart to the office of Eldership in this Church and congregation as Elders in the Church of Scotland. The Elders and people were then reminded of dedication to their respective duties.

John Smith, Moderator.

Page 105 of the Minutes of Session of the Scotch Church 7th Line, Beckwith, records:

Beckwith, 30th June, 1867.
Which day the Kirk Session met and was constituted by prayer. Present Rev. W. Ross, Moderator, Messrs. James Ferguson, Donald McLaren, Dugald Ferguson and Hugh Robertson, Elders.

Since last meeting of Session it has pleased Almighty God to remove by death, Mr. John McArthur, who had been an office bearer of this Church for 21 years. The Session express their profound sorrow for the loss they have sustained and record their deep sense of christian character and great worth of their departed brother. He was a kind neighbour, a sincere friend and a faithful disciple of the Lord Jesus Christ. The Session will long deplore his loss.
The Session do also record their deep sympathy with Mrs. McArthur and her family and commend them to the protection of Him who has promised to be the Father of the fatherless and the Husband of the widow. It is the Session's desire that this their testimony to the worth of their departed brother and their sympathy with his sorrowing family, may be communicated to Mrs. McArthur.

W. Ross, Moderator and Session
Clerk.

On page 114 of the Minutes Beckwith, it is recorded:

Beckwith, 14 December 1869
The Kirk Session met this day and was constituted
with prayer. Present: Rev. W. Ross, Moderator, Messrs.
James Ferguson and Dugald Ferguson, Elders. The session
having taken into consideration the propriety of adding
to the number of elders in this congregation made choice
of MR. ROBERT BELL, presently residing within their
bounds to be a member of this Kirk Session. And the
said Mr. Robert Bell having been ordained an elder of
the Church of Scotland in Canada in the congregation of
Ramsay and his resignation to the Eldership in that congregation having been accepted by the Kirk Session of
Ramsay the Session appoint his admission to take place
in presence of the congregation on the Sabbath 9th day
of January 1870, and an edict to this effect to be served
on the sabbath to the people, this is if they have an
objection to state why the above named person should not
be admitted to the Eldership they will have an opportunity of doing so, to any of the members of Session within
ten days after the Edict is serviced. Closed with
prayer.
W. Ross, Moderator and Session Clerk.

Beckwith, 26 December 1869
This day immediately after divine service both in
the forenoon and afternoon the following intimation was
made: The Session having made choice of Mr. Robert
Bell, formerly an elder within the congregation of
Ramsay to act along with them in the Eldership of this
congregation having appointed his admission to take
place on Sabbath the 9th January 1870, and it is hereby
intimated that if no objection against the admission of
the said Mr. Robert Bell shall be brought before the
Session within ten days from this date his admission to
the Eldership in the congregation shall take place on
the 9th day of January 1870.

Beckwith, 9th January 1870
This Kirk Session met this day and was constituted
with prayer. Present: Rev. W. Ross, Mod., Messrs Dugald
Ferguson and Hugh Robertson, Elders. The Session having
promised for the purpose of ascertaining whether any objections were brought forward against the admission of

Mr. Robert Bell to the eldership in this congregation the
Rev. W. Ross having reported that his Edict was duly served; no person brought any objection forward; whereupon
it was agreed, in terms of the former resolution that the
admission of the said Mr. Robert Bell be proceeded with
this day immediately after divine service. Adjourned to
meet today after divine service.
W. Ross, Moderator.

Beckwith, 9th January 1870
Which day the Kirk Session met according to agree-
ment. Present: Rev. W. Ross, Messers Dugald Ferguson and
Hugh Robertson, Elders. In accordance with the former
resolution the Moderator did this day, after Divine Service put to Mr. Robert Bell the question appointed to be
put to persons before their admission to the Eldership
and he having given satisfactory answers to the same, he
did admit Mr. Robert Bell, to the Office of the same, in
this congregation after which he and the people were admonished on their respective duties. Mr. Robert Bell now
present received the right hand of fellowship from the
other members of Sessions and his name was ordered to be
added to the Roll.

Page 116 records:

It is agreed that the Sacrament of the Lord's Supper
should be dispensed in the Church of the 7th Line of
Township on the last sabbath of January being 30th January of the month.
W. Ross, Moderator and Session Clerk.

Beckwith, 9th May 1875
Which day the Kirk Session met and was constituted
by prayer. Present: The Moderator, Messrs. R. Bell, H.
Robertson, Donald McLaren, James Ferguson and Dugald Ferguson, Elders. The Session having commenced the purpose
of ascertaining whether any objections were brought forward against the admission of Mr. George Tait and the or-

B-5

dination of Mr. Robert McLaughlin to the Eldership in this
congregation, the Moderator having reported that their e-
dict was duly secured, no person brought any objection
forward whereupon it was agreed in terms of former resolution that the ordination of the said Mr. Robert McLaughlin
be proceeded with this day immediately after divine service. Adjourned to meet today after divine service.

W. Ross, Mod., and Session Clerk.

Beckwith, 9th May, 1875

Which day the Kirk Session met according to adjourn-
ment. Present: The Moderator, Messrs, R. Bell, H. Robertson, D. McLaren, J. Ferguson and D. Ferguson, Elders, in
accordance with the former resolutions the Moderator did
this day after divine service put to Messrs. Geo. Tait
and Robt. McLaughlin, the questions appointed to be put
to the Eldership and they having given satisfactory answers to the same he did admit Mr. Geo. Tait and ordain
Mr. Robt. McLaughlin to the office of the eldership in
this congregation, after which all the people were admonished on their respective duties.

Messrs. Geo. Tait and Robt. McLaughlin being now present,
received the right hand of fellowship from the other members of the Session and their names were ordered to be
added to the Roll.

(See Appendix C-3 July 7, 1878).

169

EXTRACTS FROM - REGISTER OF BAPTISMS

THE SCOTCH CHURCH, BECKWITH

JOHN SMITH, MINISTER

COMMENCED LABOURS NOV. 3. 1833

	FATHER	MOTHER	PLACE	BORN	BAPTIZED
JANE	DUNCAN FERGUSON	ANN MCLAREN	BECKWITH	OCT. 27. 1833	NOV. 23. 1833
JANE	PETER SCOTT	MARG. MCINTOSH	BECKWITH	APR. 14. 1833	NOV. 23. 1833
JANE	WM. WATSON	ELIZ. HUMES	GOULBOURNE	JNE. 16. 1833	NOV. 24. 1833
JOHN	JOHN STEWART	HELEN LAMMOND	BECKWITH	JLY. 27. 1833	NOV. 25. 1833
JOHN SMITH	DUNCAN MCLAREN	MARGT. MCNEE	BECKWITH	JNE. 14. 1833	NOV. 25. 1833
MARY	JOHN THORN	MARGT. MILLER	BECKWITH	AUG. 20. 1833	NOV. 25. 1833
DONALD	DONALD MALLOCH	JANE MCGREGOR	BECKWITH	SEP. 19. 1833	DEC. 19. 1833
PETER	JHN. MCDIARMID	MARY STEWART	BECKWITH	JLY. 3. 1833	DEC. 24. 1833
MARY ELIZABETH	SIMON ROCHE	- - -	BECKWITH	OCT. 8. 1833	DEC. 29. 1833
CATHERINE	PETER ROBINSON	SARAH MOORE	BECKWITH	DEC. 9. 1833	JAN. 1. 1834
MARY ESTHER	CALEB STRONG BELLOWS	ESTHER MANSEL	BECKWITH	APR. 15. 1833	JAN. 1. 1834
CATHERINE	JOHN MCEWEN	JANE MCEWEN	BECKWITH	JAN. 4. 1834	JAN. 31. 1834
FINLAY	JOHN MCEWEN	JANE MCEWEN	BECKWITH	- - -	- - -
JANET	HUGH MCEWEN	CATH MCEWEN	BECKWITH	FEB. 6. 1834	FEB. 20. 1834
HELEN	JAMES DAZEL	ANN WALL	BECKWITH	FEB. 12. 1834	FEB. 25. 1834
PETER	JOHN McARTHUR	GRACE ANDERSON	BECKWITH	JAN. 25. 1834	FEB. 6. 1834

ABBREVIATION "CHRIS."--CHRISTIAN   "ELIS."--ELIZABETH

170

APPENDIX C - 1.

	FATHER	MOTHER	PLACE	BORN	BAPTIZED
JOHN	JOHN KING	ANN McLAREN	BECKWITH	JAN. 12. 1834	FEB. 16. 1834
JAMES	ROBT. McCORKLE	ELIZ. DOWNIE	GOULBOURNE	JAN. 10. 1834	MAR. 16. 1834
DANIEL	DUNCAN McLAREN	CATH. KING	GOULBOURNE	JAN. 2. 1834	MAR. 16. 1834
ANN	JOHN McLAREN	ELIZ. McCUAN	BECKWITH	MAR. 1. 1834	MAR. 16. 1834
JAMES	JOHN CRAM	ELIZ. STALKER	BECKWITH	JAN. 29. 1834	MAR. 31. 1834
WILLIAM	JAMES McFARLANE	GRACE McLAREN	BECKWITH	MAR. 6. 1834	MAR. 31. 1834
JANE	DUNCAN ROBERTSON	JANE MOOR	BECKWITH	JAN. 25. 1834	MAR. 31. 1834
DANIEL	DUNCAN McCUAN	CATH. CARMICHAEL	BECKWITH	FEB. 2. 1834	MAR. 31. 1834
ARCHIBALD	JOHN SINCLAIR	SARAH BLACK	BECKWITH	MAY. 7. 1834	JNE. 23. 1834
MARGARET	JAMES FERGUSON	CHRIS. McLAREN	BECKWITH	MAY. 27. 1834	JNE. 29. 1834
MARGARET	ALEX SCOTT	ELIS McDIARMID	BECKWITH	JNE. 5. 1834	AUG. 3. 1834
ARCHIBALD	PETER DEWAR	JANET McGREGOR	BECKWITH	APR. 21. 1834	JNE. 29. 1834
THOMAS	WM. McDONALD	CLEM McINTYRE	BECKWITH	JLY. 11. 1834	AUG. 31. 1834
JOHN	ROBT. McLACHLIN	ELIZ. FERGUSON	BECKWITH	AUG. 11. 1834	OCT. 19. 1834
ALEXANDER	ALEX. DEWAR	JANET KENNEDY	BECKWITH	SEP. 8. 1834	OCT. 26. 1834
MARGARET	ALEX. McTAVISH	JANE McEWEN	BECKWITH	SEP. 24. 1834	NOV. 30. 1834
CATHERINE	JOHN McEWEN	CHRIS. McEWEN	BECKWITH	OCT. 26. 1834	DEC. 22. 1834
ELISABETH	JOHN CAMPBELL	ELLISON DENHAM	BECKWITH	NOV. 20. 1834	DEC. 8. 1834
DUNCAN	MALC. DEWAR	ANN CORRIE	BECKWITH	OCT. 13. 1834	DEC. 21. 1834
JAMES	DUNCAN McEWEN	CATH. McEWEN	BECKWITH	OCT. 12. 1834	DEC. 21. 1834

APPENDIX C-1

	FATHER	MOTHER	PLACE	BORN	BAPTIZED
CHRISTIAN	JOHN FERGUSON	MARY FERGUSON	BECKWITH	APR.24.1835	APR.28.1835
PETER	PETER McGREGOR	CATH. FERGUSON	BECKWITH	APR.22.1835	MAY.10.1835
DONALD	PETER McLAREN	MARGT. McNEE	BECKWITH	JAN.11.1835	MAY.25.1835
ISABELLA	ROBT. STEWART	HELEN STEWART	BECKWITH	FEB.25.1835	MAR. 9.1835
CHRISTIAN	THOMAS WHYTE	HELEN DRUMMOND	BECKWITH	DEC.30.1834	MAR. 9.1835
ISABELLA	DONALD McDONALD	JANET SCOTT	BECKWITH	MAR. 3.1835	APR. 5.1835
DONALD	ANGUS McDIARMID	ANN LIVINGSTONE	BECKWITH	MAR.23.1835	APR. 5.1835
MARGARET	ALEX. STEWART	ELIZ. DOUGLAS	BECKWITH	JNE.25.1835	JLY.26.1835
CATHERINE	ROBT. KENNEDY	CHRIS. McDIARMID	BECKWITH	MAR. 4.1835	MAR. 1835
HELEN	JAMES STEWART	ISABELLE STEWART	BECKWITH	JNE.14.1835	JLY. 1835
MARGARET	DUNCAN McLAREN	MARGT. McNEE	BECKWITH	SEP.15.1835	- - -
PETER	JAMES DUNCAN	CATH. McLAREN	BECKWITH	NOV. 1.1835	- - -
ANN	FINDLAY McNAUGHTON	CHRIS. ANDERSON	BECKWITH	NOV.10.1835	DEC.25.1835
ARCHIBALD	JOHN DEWAR	MARGT. BUCHANAN	BECKWITH	AUG.27.1835	DEC.28.1835
JOHN	JAMES McLAREN	CATH. McLAREN	McNAB TWP.	DEC.25.1835	JAN. 8.1836
JOHN	JOHN McEWEN	JANET McEWEN	BECKWITH	- - -	AUG.31.1836
MARY ANN	JOHN CAMPBELL	-- BROWN	GOULBOURNE	APR.14.1835	FEB. 7.1836
ROBERT	ROBT. McCORKLE	ELIS. DOWNIE	GOULBOURNE	SEP.23.1835	MAR.20.1836
JOHN	JOHN McEWEN	CHRIS. McEWEN	BECKWITH	- - -	MAR.23.1836
ALEXANDER	ALEX. McKENZIE	ANN CAMERON	BECKWITH	- - -	MAR.27.1836

	FATHER	MOTHER	PLACE	BORN	BAPTIZED
MARY	JAMES FERGUSON	CHRIS. McLAREN	BECKWITH	APR. 7.1836	APR.10.1836
FINLAY	HUGH McEWEN	CATH. McEWEN	BECKWITH	MAR.20.1836	APR.17.1836
JAMES	JAMES McFARLANE	GRACE McLAREN	BECKWITH	MAR.20.1836	MAY.15.1836
JANET	ALEX. SCOTT	ELIS. McDIARMID	BECKWITH	APR. 6.1836	MAY.15.1836
MARGARET	JOHN MILLIGAN DAVIES	AGNES KIRKWOOD	GOULBOURNE	FEB.29.1836	JNE.15.1836
JAMES	WM. GILLESPIE	CATH. McDONALD	FITZROY	APR.22.1836	JNE.15.1836
DUNCAN	JOHN CRAM	ISAB. STALKER	BECKWITH	JAN.29.1836	JNE.15.1836
FINLAY	JOHN CAMERON	ANN McNAUGHTON	BECKWITH	NOV. 2.1835	JNE.15.1836
JOHN	JOHN McGREGOR	MARY McINTYRE	BECKWITH	JLY. 1.1836	- - -
MARY	THOMAS WHYTE	HELEN DRUMMOND	BECKWITH	JLY.19.1836	1836
ALEXANDER	DUNCAN McEWEN	CATH. McEWEN	BECKWITH	SEP.11.1836	1836
DUGALD	JOHN SINCLAIR	SARAH BLACK	BECKWITH	APR. 5.1836	DEC.11.1836
JOHN	WM. McDONALD	CLEM. McINTYRE	BECKWITH	JNE.10.1836	DEC.25.1836
JOHN	PETER McLAREN	MARGT. McNEE	BECKWITH	NOV. 4.1836	JAN.29.1837
JANET	DUNCAN McCALLUM	HELEN SLOANE	BECKWITH	FEB.10.1837	MAR. 1837
MARGARET	ROBT. KENNEDY	CHRIS. McDIARMID	BECKWITH	DEC.30.1836	MAR. 1837
JOHN	JOHN CARMICHAEL	MARY McGREGOR	BECKWITH	MAY 1.1837	MAY.28.1837
ANDREW	WM. McKAY	AGNES MOOR	GOULBOURNE	JNE. 5.1837	JNE.21.1837
ANDREW	THOS. HERON	ANN GORDON	GOULBOURNE	MAR. 8.1837	JNE.21.1837
JOHN	JOHN DEWAR	MARGT.BUCHANAN	BECKWITH	MAY.20.1837	JLY.23.1837
JAMES	PETER McGREGOR	CATH. McGREGOR	BECKWITH	JNE.18.1837	OCT. 8.1837

173

	FATHER	MOTHER	PLACE	BORN	BAPTIZED
JANET	JOHN McEWAN	ANN McEWAN	BECKWITH	SEP. 7.1837	OCT. 8.1837
ANDREW BUCHANAN	WM. ROGERSON	SARAH S.ADAMSON	FITZROY HRBR.	JNE.26.1837	OCT.22.1837
DONALD	JOHN ROBERTSON	CATH. DOUGLAS	BECKWITH	SEP. 3.1837	- - -
CHRISTIAN	DUNCAN McLAREN	MARGT. McNEE	BECKWITH	OCT. 2.1837	NOV.10.1837
PETER	JOHN McDONALD	CATH. McNEE	BECKWITH	FEB.24.1836	NOV.10.1837
CATH'R	JOHN McEWAN	JANET McEWAN	BECKWITH	FEB.28.1837	MAR. 1837
JOHN	JOHN GORDON	MARGT. MOORHEAD	GOULBOURNE	JLY.26.1837	DEC.14.1837
MARY	PETER McGREGOR	MARY McGREGOR	BECKWITH	NOV. 3.1837	
WILLIAM	JOHN McKENZIE	CATH. ANDERSON	BECKWITH	JAN.25.1838	
WILLIAM	THOMAS WHYTE	HELEN DRUMMOND	BECKWITH	JAN.19.1838	MAR.11.1838
PETER	JOHN McGREGOR	MARY McINTYRE	BECKWITH	MAR.18.1838	AUG. 8.1838
ROBINSON	ROBINSON LYON	MARY ANN BANKS	GOULBOURNE	FEB.28.1838	APR.23.1838
MALCOLM	ALEX DEWAR	JANET KENNEDY	BECKWITH	APR. 9.1838	MAY.13.1838
MARY	ALEX SCOTT	ELIZ. McDIARMID	BECKWITH	APR. 4.1838	MAY.13.1838
ISABELLA	JOHN McEWAN	CHRIS. McEWAN	BECKWITH	APR.13.1838	MAY.20.1838
JAMES	JOHN CRAM	ISABELLA STALKER	BECKWITH	FEB.11.1838	- - -
PETER	ANGUS McDIARMID	ANN LIVINGSTONE	BECKWITH	DEC.28.1836	JLY. 1838
DUNCAN	ALEX. McKENZIE	ANN CAMERON	BECKWITH	OCT.10.1838	OCT.11.1838
ROBERT	JAMES FERGUSON	CHRIS. McLAREN	BECKWITH	APR.15.1838	OCT.11.1838
FINLAY	PETER DEWAR	JANET McEWAN	BECKWITH	JNE.25.1838	OCT.11.1838

	FATHER	MOTHER	PLACE	BORN	BAPTIZED
JAMES	JOHN McDONALD	MARY McDONALD	BECKWITH	MAR.31.1838	--
PETER	DUNCAN McEWAN	CATH. McEWAN	BECKWITH	OCT.12.1838	--
THOMAS	ALEX. McEWAN	CATH. McEWAN	OSGOOD	JAN.28.1838	JAN. 9.1839
MARY JANE	DONALD CAMPBELL	ISABELLA McEWAN	OSGOOD	DEC.28.1838	JAN. 9.1839
- - -	JOHN McNAB	CATH. McDONALD	OSGOOD	MAY.13.1838	JAN. 9.1839
JOSEPH	HAZLETT ANDERSON	ELIZ. NEWTON	OSGOOD	JAN.26.1838	JAN. 9.1839
WILLIAM	WM. HERMAN	ELIZ. KENNEDY	OSGOOD	NOV.11.1838	JAN. 9.1839
ANN	DONALD McRAE	ISABELLA RUSSELL	RICHMOND	APR. 3.1836	JAN. 6.1839
ISABELLA	DONALD McRAE	ISABELLA RUSSELL	RICHMOND	APR. 4.1838	JAN. 6.1839
MARY JANE	JOHN H. CRAWFORD	MARY JANE BURKE	RICHMOND	JLY.11.1838	JAN. 6.1839
MARGARET	THOMAS ANGUS	JANE SWAN	(not known)	NOV. 7.1838	JAN. 3.1839
SARAH ANDERSON	ROBINSON HARPER	AGNES MARTIN	(not known)	DEC.23.1837	JAN. 3.1839
MARY JANE	THOMAS ALEXANDER	ELIZ. DOHERTY	HUNTLY	SEP.18.1838	JAN. 5.1839
MARGARET	PATRICK MARTIN	MARGT. McKINLAY	HUNTLY	FEB.16.1832	JAN. 5.1839
HELEN	PATRICK MARTIN	MARGT. McKINLAY	HUNTLY	AUG.19.1836	JAN. 5.1839
JANET	PATRICK MARTIN	MARGT. McKINLAY	HUNTLY	MAY.13.1838	JAN. 5.1839
MARY	JAMES McINNES	MARG. McEWAN	BECKWITH	JNE.20.1838	MAR.13.1839
DAVIE	JOHN DEWAR	MARG. BUCHANAN	BECKWITH	JAN.22.1839	MAR.17.1839
JOHN	ANGUS McDIARMID	ANN LIVINGSTONE	BECKWITH	DEC.22.1838	MAR.24.1839
GRACE	ALEX STEWART	ELIZ. DOUGLAS	BECKWITH	FEB. 2.1839	MAR.17.1839
ELIZABETH	PETER McLAREN	MARGT. McNEE	BECKWITH	JAN.11.1839	MAR.31.1839

175

APPENDIX C-1

	FATHER	MOTHER	PLACE	BORN	BAPTIZED
MARGARET	JOHN McKENZIE	CATH ANDERSON	BECKWITH	- - -	- - -
JOHN	JOHN McDONALD	ISABELLA McNEE	BECKWITH	FEB.25.1839	APR.14.1839
MARGARET	JOHN STEWART	GRACE STEWART	BECKWITH	- - -	APR.28.1839
HUGH	JOHN CAMERON	ANN McNAUGHTON	BECKWITH	DEC.26.1838	APR.14.1839
ISABELLA	JOHN McEWAN	ANN McEWAN	BECKWITH	APR.25.1839	MAY.26.1839
DANIEL	ALEX McTAVISH	ANN McEWAN	BECKWITH	MAR. 8.1839	JNE.16.1839
JAMES	PETER McARTHUR	ANN ANDERSON	BECKWITH	MAY. 6.1839	JNE.26.1839
JOHN	JAMES McKAY	JANE MURRAY	GOULBOURNE	JNE. 1.1839	JLY. 2.1839
DAVID	ROBT. McCORKLE	ELIZ. DOWNIE	GOULBOURNE	DEC.16.1838	JLY. 2.1839
MARY	ALEX McEWAN	JANET McNAB	BECKWITH	JNE. 4.1839	- - -
ISABELLA	PETER McGREGOR	MARY McGREGOR	BECKWITH	MAY.18.1838	MAY.17.1839
MARY	HUGH McGREGOR	CATH. McEWAN	BECKWITH	JLY.12.1839	JLY.15.1839
MARY	DUNCAN McCALLUM	HELEN SLOANE	BECKWITH	JLY. 5.1839	JLY.19.1839
WILLIAM	PETER ROBERTSON	SARAH MOOR	BECKWITH	JLY.15.1839	JLY.19.1839
WILLIAM M.	WILLIAM FERGUSON	MARY ANDERSON	BECKWITH	DEC. 9.1838	JLY.19.1839
- - -	THOMAS WHYTE	HELEN DRUMMOND	BECKWITH	- - -	- - -
JANET	ROBT. KENNEDY	CHRLS. McDIARMID	BECKWITH	JLY.21.1839	SEP.26.1839
JANET	JAS. STEWART	ISABELLA STEWART	BECKWITH	JAN.27.1839	FEB. 7.1839
ARCHIBALD	PETER McGREGOR	CATH. FERGUSON	BECKWITH	JAN. 5.1840	JAN.17.1840
JOHN	PETER McGREGOR	MARGT. McINTYRE	BECKWITH	JAN. 8.1840	FEB.24.1840
DUNCAN	JOHN McGREGOR	MARY McINTYRE	BECKWITH	JAN.26.1840	FEB.24.1840

176

	FATHER	MOTHER	PLACE	BORN	BAPTIZED
SARAH ANN	JAMES LOURIE	SARAH RONAN	FITZROY	JAN.31.1840	FEB.28.1840
JANET	ADAM McCROSTY	JANET SHARPE	OSGOOD	JAN.23.1840	MAR. 4.1840
MARGARET	JAMES ANDREWS	JANE THOMPSON	OSGOOD	JAN.11.1840	MAR. 4.1840
JOHN	JAMES KING	ANN McARTHUR	BECKWITH	NOV. 3.1839	MAR.15.1840
ROBERT	ALEX SCOTT	ELIS. McDIARMID	BECKWITH	FEB. 9.1840	MAR.18.1840
PETER	ALEX DEWAR	JANET KENNEDY	BECKWITH	MAR. 5.1840	MAR.18.1840
JOHN	DUGOLD STEWART	JANET FERGUSON	BECKWITH	JAN.26.1840	MAR.22.1840
MARY	ALEX FERGUSON	ANN McDIARMID	BECKWITH	DEC.12.1839	MAR.22.1840
JANET	PETER McDIARMID	JANET LIVINGSTONE	BECKWITH	JAN.18.1840	MAR.23.1840
DUNCAN	JAS. McARTHUR	CATH. FISHER	BECKWITH	MAY.29.1839	APR. 2.1840
MARY	HUGH McEWAN	MARION McNEIL	BECKWITH	JAN. 3.1840	APR.12.1840
JANET	DUNCAN McLAREN	MARGT. McNEE	BECKWITH	APR. 1.1840	MAY.11.1840
ELIZABETH	HUGH McEWAN	CATH. McEWAN	BECKWITH	JLY. 1.1840	JLY.19.1840
JANET M.	JOHN McDONALD	MARG. McDONALD	BECKWITH	MAY.31.1840	AUG. 2.1840
CATHERINE	ROBERT LAIDLAW	CHIS. McMILLAN	BECKWITH	MAY.24.1840	AUG. 9.1840
MARY	COLIN FERGUSON	CATH. McGILLIS	BECKWITH	JNE. 8.1840	AUG.16.1840
CHRISTIAN	JOHN McEWAN	CHRIS. McEWAN	BECKWITH	JNE.29.1840	AUG.30.1840
MARY	DUNCAN McEWAN	CATH. McEWAN	BECKWITH	AUG. 5.1840	SEP.17.1840
PETER	JOHN McLAREN	- - -	BECKWITH	AUG. 7.1840	SEP.27.1840
JOHN	JOHN McEWAN	JANET McEWAN	BECKWITH	SEP.14.1840	SEP.27.1840

	FATHER	MOTHER	PLACE	BORN	BAPTIZED
DONALD COMRIE	PETER McARTHUR	ANN ANDERSON	BECKWITH	SEP.17.1840	NOV. 8.1840
DUNCAN	JOHN ROBINSON	CATH. DOUGLAS	BECKWITH	DEC. 1.1840	JAN. 3.1841
ELIZABETH	ROBT.McLACHLAN	---	BECKWITH	APR. 3.1840	JAN. 3.1841
MARGARET	DUNCAN McCALLUM	HELEN SLOANE	BECKWITH	NOV. 9.1840	FEB.28.1841
AGNES	THOMAS WHYTE	HELEN DRUMMOND	BECKWITH	FEB.10.1841	FEB.28.1841
ELSABETH	DUNCAN McCUAN	CATH. CARMICHAEL	BECKWITH	MAR. 7.1841	MAY.28.1841
CHARLOTTE	REV.JOHN CRUIKSHANK	CATH. FELLOWS	BYTOWN	MAR.20.1841	MAY.28.1841
JOHN	JOHN McEWAN	ANN McEWAN	BECKWITH	MAR. 7.1841	JNE.13.1841
MARY	JOHN SINCLAIR	SARAH BLACK	BECKWITH	OCT.11.1841	JNE.13.1841
ELISA JANE	WM. McEWAN	ELIS. CAMPBELL	BEDFORD	FEB.16.1841	JNE.27.1841
---	JAS. STEWART	ISABELLA STEWART	BECKWITH	APR. 6.1841	JNE.27.1841
DUNCAN	PETER McLAREN	MARGT. McNEE	BECKWITH	MAR.21.1841	JLY. 4.1841
JANET	JOHN McDONALD	ISABELLA McNEE	BECKWITH	MAY. 9.1841	JLY. 4.1841
DUNCAN	JOHN CAMPBELL	ALLISON --	BECKWITH	---	JLY. 9.1841
FINLAY	ALEX. McEWAN	JANET McNAB	BECKWITH	APR. 6.1841	JLY.25.1841
ELIZABETH	ALEX. FERGUSON	ANN WILLIAMS	BECKWITH	MAY.10.1841	JLY.25.1841
MARY	ROBT. KENNEDY	CHRIS. McDIARMID	BECKWITH	JNE.28.1841	JLY.25.1841
ALEX.	NEIL STEWART	ISABELLA STEWART	BECKWITH	JLY. 8.1841	AUG. 8.1841
MARY	HUGH McGREGOR	CATH. McEWAN	BECKWITH	JNE. 7.1841	AUG. 8.1841
DUNCAN	DONALD CAMERON	JANE McMILLAN	BECKWITH	MAY. 1.1841	AUG.19.1841

178

	FATHER	MOTHER	PLACE	BORN	BAPTIZED
CHRISTIAN	ALEX. McTAVISH	ANN McEWAN	BECKWITH	JLY. 4,1841	SEP.12.1841
JANET	PETER McGREGOR	MARY McGREGOR	BECKWITH	---	AUG.14.1841
FINLAY	HUGH McEWAN	MARION McNEIL	BECKWITH	---	AUG.19.1841
HELEN	ALLAN CAMERON	HELEN STEWART	BECKWITH	OCT. 4,1841	OCT.24.1841
DOUGLAS	JAMES McTAVISH	ANN McFARLANE	BECKWITH	OCT.28.1841	NOV.25.1841
ANN	ALEX. McLAREN	MARIA STEWART	BECKWITH	OCT.29.1841	NOV.28.1841
JOHN A. RAMSAY	REV.ALEX MANN	MARY LESLIE BEATTIE PACKENHAM		MAY.21,1841	JNE. 5.1841
JOHN	EWEN CAMERON	RACHAEL STEWART	BECKWITH	NOV.11,1840	JNE. 5.1841
JANE	ROBERT WHYTE	SARAH McVICAR	BECKWITH	APR.30.1841	JNE. 5.1841
MARGARET	ANGUS McDIARMID	ANN LIVINGSTONE	BECKWITH	MAY.13,1841	JAN. 2.1842
CHRISTIAN	JOHN McTAVISH	ISABELLA STEWART	BECKWITH	JAN.22.1842	FEB. 1.1842
ALEXANDER	JOHN DEWAR	MARGT. BUCHANAN	BECKWITH	OCT. 6,1841	FEB. 6.1842
MARGARET	JOHN FERGUSON	CATH. McGILLIS	BECKWITH	FEB. 6,1842	FEB.14.1842
---	ALEX STEWART	ELIZ. DOUGLAS	BECKWITH	DEC.21.1841	JAN.27.1842
ROBERT	ALEX McGREGOR	ISABELLA FERGUSON	BECKWITH	FEB.27,1842	APR. 3.1842
ARCHIBALD	ALEX McKENZIE	ANN CAMERON	BECKWITH	FEB.16,1842	APR.10.1842
MARY	JOHN McGREGOR	MARY McINTYRE	BECKWITH	MAY. 3,1842	APR.17.1842
JOHN	ALEX. DEWAR	JANET KENNEDY	BECKWITH	APR. 2.1842	MAY.15.1842
MARGARET	DUNCAN McLAREN	MARY McLAREN	BECKWITH	APR.17,1842	MAY.29.1842
MARY	JAS. McARTHUR	CATH. FISHER	BECKWITH	MAY.27.1842	JLY. 1.1842

179

APPENDIX C-1

	FATHER	MOTHER	PLACE	BORN	BAPTIZED
JAMES COLLIN	JAS. McCAUL	ANN McDOUGALD	CUMBERLAND	JAN.21.1842	JLY.14.1842
ARCHIBALD	ARCH'D McCALLUM	MARY CAMERON	CUMBERLAND	DEC.23.1841	JLY.14.1842
CHRISTIAN	ROBT. McLACHLAN	MARY McDONALD	CUMBERLAND	FEB. 7.1842	JLY.14.1842
WILLIAM	SAMUEL LOUGH	ELIS. DALE	CUMBERLAND	SEP.24.1842	JLY.14.1842
ANN	DUNCAN McEACHANAN	MARION McDOUGALD	LOCABER	FEB.24.1842	JLY.14.1842
ANN	ROBT. McARTHUR	ANN ANDERSON	BECKWITH	JNE.15.1842	JLY.24.1842
WILLIAM	DUNCAN McEWAN	CATH. McEWAN	BECKWITH	JNE.14.1842	AUG.14.1842
MALCOLM	THOMAS WHYTE	HELEN DRUMMOND	BECKWITH	APR. 1.1842	AUG.10.1842
JOHN	JOHN McDOUGALD	MARGT. McDUGALD	BECKWITH	---	AUG.15.1842
EWEN	JOHN McEWEN	JANET McEWEN	BECKWITH	---	SEP. 6.1842
JAMES	PETER SCOTT	MARGT. DOUGLAS	MONTAGUE	APR.22.1842	SEP.25.1842
DUNCAN	DUNCAN McLAREN	CATH. KING	BECKWITH	AUG.23.1842	SEP.25.1842
ROBERT	JAMES SCOTT	JANET DOUGLAS	BECKWITH	MAY.25.1842	SEP.26.1842
MARY	JOHN McEWEN	CHRISTIAN McEWEN	BECKWITH	AUG.19.1842	--
JANE	JAMES STEWART	ISABELLA STEWART	BECKWITH	OCT.11.1842	NOV.13.1842
HELEN	NEIL STEWART	ISABELLA STEWART	BECKWITH	OCT.12.1842	NOV.13.1842
JAMES	JOHN ROBERTSON	CATH. DOUGLAS	BECKWITH	SEP. 7.1842	--
ISABELLA GEORGINA	REV.GEO.ROMANES	ISABELLA SMITH	SMITH FALLS	OCT.17.1842	JAN. 6.1843
ROBERT	ALEX. FERGUSON	ANN McDIARMID	BECKWITH	JAN. 1.1843	APR. 9.1843
MARY	DUNCAN McLAREN	MARY McNEE	BECKWITH	FEB. 6.1843	APR. 9.1843

	FATHER	MOTHER	PLACE	BORN	BAPTIZED
MARY	JOHN ANDERSON	JESSIE COMRIE	BECKWITH	DEC.29.1842	APR. 6.1843
CATHERINE	JOHN CAMPBELL	ELIZ. McNAUGHTON	BECKWITH	FEB.28.1843	MAY. 3.1843
PETER	JOHN STEWART	GRACE STEWART	BECKWITH	- - -	MAY. 7.1843
JOHN	ALEX. MILLER	AGNES MOOR	BECKWITH	JAN.31.1843	MAY.24.1843
ELIS.	JOHN McEWEN	ANN McEWEN	BECKWITH	FEB.22.1843	MAY.21.1843
PETER	PETER McLAREN	MARIA STEWART	BECKWITH	APR. 6.1843	MAY.28.1843
CATHERINE	HUGH McGREGOR	CATH. McEWAN	BECKWITH	MAY. 4.1843	JLY.16.1843
MARGARET	PETER McNAB	CATH. KENNEDY	BECKWITH	APR.12.1843	JLY.23.1843
ELISABETH	ROBERT KENNEDY	CHRIS. McDIARMID	BECKWITH	MAY. 8.1843	JLY.23.1843
ALEX. HUNTER	WM. COCHRANE	JANET WILLIAMS	BECKWITH	JNE. 1.1843	JLY.30.1843
WILLIAM	ALEX. McGREGOR	ISABELLA FERGUSON	BECKWITH	JLY. 7.1843	SEP.10.1843
JOHN	JOHN McLAREN	ELIZ. McEWEN	BECKWITH	JNE. 5.1843	SEP.17.1843
ALEXANDER	PETER McLAREN	MARGT. McNEE	BECKWITH	MAY. 3.1843	SEP.26.1843
CATHERINE	JOHN DEWAR	MARGT. BUCHANAN	BECKWITH	AUG. 6.1843	OCT.13.1843
MARGT. HOBBIE	JAMES CALDWELL	JANE BOYD	BECKWITH	AUG. 3.1843	OCT.13.1843
JANET	JOHN McEWEN	JANET McEWEN	BECKWITH	SEP.22.1843	OCT.22.1843
ELISABETH	JOHN McDONALD	ISABELLA McNEE	BECKWITH	AUG.26.1843	OCT.29.1843
JANET	DUNCAN McLAREN	MARY McLAREN	BECKWITH	AUG.22.1843	OCT.29.1843
PETER	WM. COMRIE	REBECCA GRIER	BECKWITH	AUG. 9.1843	OCT.29.1843
WILLIAM	HUGH JOHNSON	JANE SHANNON	BECKWITH	MAY.22.1843	NOV. 5.1843

181

APPENDIX C-1

	FATHER	MOTHER	PLACE	BORN	BAPTIZED
JAMES	ALEX THOMPSON	CECILIA ROBERTSON	BECKWITH	SEP. 1.1843	NOV. 8.1843
PETER) twins	PETER McGREGOR	MARGT. McINTYRE	BECKWITH	JLY.29.1843	NOV. 8.1843
MARGARET)	PETER McGREGOR	MARGT. McINTYRE	BECKWITH	JLY.29.1843	NOV. 8.1843
PETER	JAMES ANDERSON	MARGT. McINTYRE	BECKWITH	---	---
MARGARET	PETER McGREGOR	MARY McGREGOR	BECKWITH	AUG. 8.1843	JAN. 7.1844
JOHN	JOHN McTAVISH	ISABELLA STEWART	BECKWITH	OCT.10.1843	JAN. 9.1844
BARBARA	HUGH McEWAN	MARION McNEIL	BECKWITH	SEP.19.1843	FEB.18.1844
ALEXANDER	ALEX. McEWAN	JANET McNAB	BECKWITH	NOV.17.1843	FEB. 8.1844
NICHOL	JOHN McNICHOL	HELEN HUNTER	DALHOUSIE	APR.17.1843	MAR. 5.1844
JOSEPH	JOHN McINTYRE	AGNES HETHERINGTON	DALHOUSIE	OCT. 1.1843	MAR. 5.1844
JOHN	JOHN McINTYRE	AGNES HETHERINGTON	DALHOUSIE	SEP. 9.1841	MAR. 5.1844
MARGARET	ALEX. STEWART	MARGT. McLAREN	BECKWITH	NOV.25.1843	MAR.26.1844
JANE	ALLAN CAMERON	HELEN STEWART	BECKWITH	MAR. 4.1843	MAR.26.1844
CATHERINE	PETER McARTHUR	ANN ANDERSON	BECKWITH	APR.20.1844	MAY.16.1844
MARGARET	PETER McLAREN	CATH. McLAREN	BECKWITH	APR.23.1844	MAY.16.1844
JOHN	PETER McTAVISH	JANET CARMICHAEL	BECKWITH	MAR. 7.1844	MAY.16.1844
MARY ANNABELLA	REV.J.CRUIKSHANK	CATH. FELLOWS	BROCKVILLE	MAY.12.1844	JLY.14.1844
JAMES	JAMES SCOTT	JANET DOUGLAS	BECKWITH	MAY. 1.1844	AUG.25.1844
RACHEL	JOHN McGREGOR	MARY McINTYRE	BECKWITH	JLY.19.1844	SEP. 8.1844
PETER	JOHN ANDERSON	JANET COMRIE	BECKWITH	SEP. 9.1844	---

182

APPENDIX C-1

	FATHER	MOTHER	PLACE	BORN	BAPTIZED
ANN	ALEX. DEWAR	JANET KENNEDY	BECKWITH	JNE.14.1844	NOV.17.1844
ISABELLA	JOHN CAMPBELL	ELIZ.McNAUGHTON	BECKWITH	MAR.22.1844	JAN. 2.1845
JOHN	JAMES BOYD	AGNES NEXTON	BECKWITH	JLY.10.1844	MAR.30.1845
JOHN	ROBT. DRENNAN	ELIS. BROTON	BECKWITH	FEB. 6.1844	MAR.30.1845
MARY	ALEX. McGREGOR	ISABELLA FERGUSON	BECKWITH	---	MAY.11.1845
JESSIE	HUGH McGREGOR	CATH. McEWAN	BECKWITH	JAN.21.1845	MAY.25.1845
JAMES	WILLIAM COCHRANE	JANET WILLIAMS	BECKWITH	APR. 4.1844	JNE. 1845
DANIEL	DUNCAN McLAREN	MARY McLAREN	BECKWITH	MAY.18.1844	JLY.20.1845
JOHN	PETER McLAREN	CATH. McLAREN	BECKWITH	MAY.14.1845	JLY.20.1845
MARY	ALEX. STEWART	MARGT. McLAREN	BECKWITH	OCT.22.1845	FEB. 1.1846
MARGARET	PETER McARTHUR	ANN ANDERSON	BECKWITH	JAN. 1.1846	FEB.15.1846
DUNCAN	JAMES ANDERSON	MARGT. McINTYRE	BECKWITH	FEB.27.1846	MAR.17.1846
ISABELLA	WM. FERGUSON	CATH. ANDERSON	BECKWITH	NOV.23.1845	APR.19.1846
MARGARET	JOHN CAMPBELL	ELIZ. McNAUGHTON	BECKWITH	MAR.19.1845	APR.27.1846
ISABELLA	JOHN SCOTT	ELIZA FERGUSON	BECKWITH	SEP.30.1845	MAY. 2.1846
CHRISTIAN	COLIN FERGUSON	CATH. McGILLIS	BECKWITH	FEB.29.1843	NOV.27.1846
ANN	COLIN FERGUSON	CATH. McGILLIS	BECKWITH	APR.21.1846	NOV.27.1846
CHRISTY ANN	JOHN ANDERSON	JANET COMRIE	BECKWITH	NOV.12.1846	NOV.27.1846
JOHN	DUNCAN McLAREN	MARY McLAREN	BECKWITH	NOV.24.1846	JAN. 8.1847
JANET	PETER McLAREN	CATH. McLAREN	BECKWITH	SEP. 3.1846	JAN. 8.1847

APPENDIX C-1

	FATHER	MOTHER	PLACE	BORN	BAPTIZED
ELISABETH	JAMES SCOTT	JANET DOUGLAS	BECKWITH	JNE.18.1846	MAR.17.1847
JAMES	JOHN SCOTT	ELIZ. FERGUSON	BECKWITH	APR. 4.1847	JNE.13.1847
ANN	HUGH McGREGOR	CATH. McEWAN	BECKWITH	FEB.18.1847	JNE.20.1847
JANE MORSON	REV.JOHN SMITH	JANE MORSON	BECKWITH	SEP. 2.1847	SEP.11.1847
NOTE:	(Baptized by Rev.J. Stevenson of the Assembly's Deputation from Scotland)				
PETER	JOHN CROSSE(?)	CHRISTIAN ANDERSON	BECKWITH	OCT.23.1846	SEP.21.1847
PETER	PETER McARTHUR	ANN ANDERSON	BECKWITH	AUG.26.1847	SEP.26.1847
MARY	DUNCAN McLAREN	MARGT. McNEE	BECKWITH	JNE.21.1847	FEB.15.1848
ELISABETH	DUNCAN FERGUSON	JANET FERGUSON	BECKWITH	JAN.11.1848	MAR. 5.1848
AGNES	JOHN ROMINES	HANNAH ARMSTRONG	ELMSLEY	OCT.30.1847	MAR. 7.1848
DAVID	JAMES PAISLEY	MARY GIBSON	ELMSLEY	JAN.13.1848	MAR. 7.1848
MARGARET	PETER McLAREN	CATH. McLAREN	BECKWITH	APR.27.1848	MAY. 4.1848
JANET	ALEX STEWART	MARGT. McLAREN	BECKWITH	FEB.13.1848	MAY.14.1848
PETER) twins	WILLIAM FERGUSON	CATH. ANDERSON	BECKWITH	JNE. 8.1848	JNE.12.1848
DUNCAN)	WILLIAM FERGUSON	CATH. ANDERSON	BECKWITH	JNE. 8.1848	JNE.12.1848
ROBERT	ALEX. GRAHAM	MARY WATSON	BECKWITH	DEC.29.1847	JNE.27.1848
DUNCAN	JOHN CAMPBELL	ELIZ. McNAUGHTON	BECKWITH	APR.24.1848	OCT.13.1848
JANE	JOHN ANDERSON	JANET COMRIE	BECKWITH	OCT.17.1848	NOV.19.1848
PHILIP FRASER	COUS. COLTER	ELIZA FRASER	SMITH FALLS	AUG.21.1848	DEC.24.1848
ISABELLA	WILLIAM McNEY	ELIZA SCOTT	ELMSLEY	APR. 5.1846	DEC.24.1848
CHARLOTTE	JOHN SMITH	MARY SHEPHERD	ELMSLEY	OCT.20.1848	DEC.24.1848

184

APPENDIX C-1

	FATHER	MOTHER	PLACE	BORN	BAPTIZED
JAMES	JOHN McRAE	GRACE STEWART	BECKWITH	FEB.20.1847	DEC.26.1848
MARTHA JANE	JOHN BENLMAN	NANCY CHARTERS	BECKWITH	OCT.12.1848	JAN.14.1849
PETER	DUNCAN McLAREN	MARY McLAREN	BECKWITH	JAN.21.1849	FEB.20.1849
CHRISTIAN	JOHN SCOTT	ELIZABETH FERGUSON	BECKWITH	FEB.1.1849	MAR.4.1849
ALEXANDER	HUGH McGREGOR	CATH. McEWEN	BECKWITH	FEB.21.1849	MAR.7.1849
JOHN	PETER McARTHUR	ANN ANDERSON	BECKWITH	MAR.31.1849	APR.29.1849
ROBERT	DUNCAN FERGUSON	JANET FERGUSON	BECKWITH	OCT.15.1849	DEC.23.1849
JOHN	DAVID BELL	MARGT. NELSON	BECKWITH	FEB.1.1847	JAN.23.1850
WILLIAM	DAVID BELL	MARGT. NELSON	BECKWITH	AUG.31.1849	JAN.23.1850
JOHN	ALEX GRAHAM	MARY WATSON	BECKWITH	NOV.21.1849	JAN.24.1850
DONALD	PETER McLAREN	CATH. McLAREN	BECKWITH	JAN.16.1850	FEB.27.1850
JOHN	FRANCIS HUNTER	BARBARA WARWICK	SMITH FALLS	MAR.22.1850	JNE.10.1850
GRACE	ALEX. STEWART	MARGT. McLAREN	BECKWITH	APR.11.1850	AUG.11.1850
HUGH	JOHN McEWAN	CHRISTIAN McEWAN	BECKWITH	JNE.17.1850	NOV.10.1850
PETER	JOHN CAMPBELL	ELIS. McNAUGHTON	BECKWITH	APR.17.1850	NOV.20.1850
MARGARET	JOHN McRAE	GRACE STEWART	BECKWITH	MAY.27.1849	NOV.20.1850
DUNCAN	DUNCAN McLAREN	MARY McLAREN	BECKWITH	NOV.24.1850	JAN.30.1851
ROBERT	JOHN SCOTT	ELIS. FERGUSON	BECKWITH	DEC.14.1850	MAR.23.1851

APPENDIX C-1

FATHER	MOTHER	PLACE	BORN	BAPTIZED
JOHN FERGUSON	JAMES MAXWELL	MARY FERGUSON	BECKWITH	MAR.24,1851	JNE.14,1851
MARGARET	JOHN ANDERSON	JANET COMRIE	BECKWITH	MAY.10.1851	JNE.14.1851

NOTE: The Rev. John Smith died April 18, 1851. The Rev. William Bell was Moderator pro tem until the Rev. Duncan Morrison was ordained as minister of The Scotch Church, Beckwith, in October 1851.

Two baptisms are recorded in June.

The foregoing is recorded from the written records of The Scotch Church, Beckwith, at the United Church Archives, Toronto, Ontario.

186

REGISTER OF MARRIAGES
IN
THE SCOTCH CHURCH
BECKWITH

JOHN SMITH, MINISTER

By License:

18 Jan. 1834	Duncan McKenzie to Annabella McGregor
29 Jan. 1834	Colin Sinclair to Margaret MacNab of Drummond
20 Feb. 1834	Robert Kennedy to Christian McDiarmid
1 Aug. 1834	Archibald McGregor to Catherine Stewart

By Proclamation:

10 Jan. 1834	John McEwan to Christian McEwen
7 Mar. 1834	John McDonald to Janet Condie of Montague
14 Mar. 1834	Thomas Whyte to Helen Drummond
21 Mar. 1834	Peter McLaren to Margaret McNee
20 May. 1834	John Campbell to Sarah Brown both of Gouldbourne
22 Sep. 1834	Francis Edwards to Margaret Campbell of Goulbourne
5 Dec. 1834	John Robertson to Catherine Douglas of Montague
20 Mar. 1835	John McDonald to Isabella McNee
12 Jne. 1835	John Miller to Mary Campbell of Drummond
12 Aug. 1835	Rev. Geo. Romanes to Isabella Smith
27 Nov. 1835	James Orr Ramsay to Catherine Stewart

By License:

29 Jan. 1836	Samuel Smith to Nancy Simpson both of Goulbourne
3 Nov. 1836	Peter McGregor to Mary McGregor

By Proclamation:

18 Feb. 1836	Donald Gunn of Ramsay to Catherine MacNab of Goulbourne
26 Apr. 1836	Robert Hannan to Mary Campbell

By Licence:

10 Aug. 1837   Duncan McIntosh Millar of Perth and Martha Galbraith of Ramsay
Witnesses: Peter Anderson, John McArthur

By Proclamation:

17 May. 1837   Patrick McHatterick and Mary Simpson of Goulbourne Witnesses Geo.Railey,Thos.Simpson
2 May. 1837   Duncan McCallum and Helen Sloane
Witnesses: Thos. Ferguson, Jas. McArthur.
2 May. 1837   John McDougall and Margaret McDonald
Witnesses: John McTavish, Peter Robertson

By Licence:

19 Jan. 1838   Donald Anderson and Janet Stewart
Witnesses: Peter Anderson, John McGregor.
26 Jan. 1838   James McDiarmid and Susanna McDonald (widow) of Drummond
Witnesses: Doug. McTavish, Alex McTavish.
23 Feb. 1838   William Forbes of Fitzroy and Elizabeth Benois of Packenham
Witnesses: Andrew Dickson, Wm. Dickson.
31 Mar. 1838   Donald McLean and Margaret Galbraith both of Ramsay
Witnesses: Dugald Stewart, Peter Comrie.
30 Jly. 1838   Peter McArthur and Ann Anderson both of Beckwith
Witnesses: John McArthur, Peter Anderson.
1 Aug. 1838   Rev. John Cruikshank of Bytown and Cath. Fellows of Rockcliffe, Ottawa District
Witnesses: Thomas and Charles Morson.
21 Sep. 1838   Hugh McGregor and Catherine McEwen both of Beckwith

	Witnesses: John McEwen, Peter McGregor.
28 Sep. 1838	John McQuasey and Catherine Dewar both of Beckwith
	Witnesses: Arch. McPhail, Peter Comrie
13 Oct. 1838	James King of Drummond and Ann McArthur of Beckwith
	Witnesses: John McArthur, Colin King.
16 Oct. 1838	Donald McGregor of Drummond and Elis. McLaren of Beckwith
	Witnesses: Arch. McGregor, Jas. King.
9 Nov. 1838	Dugald Stewart Sadler and Janet Ferguson both of Beckwith
	Witnesses: John Ferguson, Robt.Dickson.

By Proclamation:

9 Mar. 1838	James Duff and Margaret Rattery both of Beckwith
	Witnesses: Alex Thompson, Hugh McEwan
13 Mar. 1838	Alex McEwan of Beckwith and Janet McNab of Osgood
	Witnesses: Finlay and Duncan McEwan.
15 Jne. 1838	John Buckham of Torbolton and Catherine Ferguson of Beckwith
	Witnesses: Robt. McLachlan, Alex Ferguson

By License:

18 Jan. 1839	Robert Laidlaw (Tailor) Beckwith and Christian McMillan of Ramsay
	Witnesses: James Duncan, Alex. McGregor.
9 Apr. 1839	James McArthur and Catherine Fisher both of Beckwith
	Witnesses: James McInnes, John McArthur.
9 Jne. 1839	Robt. McGregor and Grace Scott both of Beckwith
	Witnesses: John Scott, John Stewart.
18 Jly. 1839	William McCrumb Yonge Johnson District and Jane Dalzielle of Ramsay
	Witnesses: Hugh McEwen, New Year Watson.
26 Jly. 1839	John McLachlan and Frances Comboy, both of Ramsay

C-2

	Witnesses: Wm.Wilson, Alex Anderson.
14 Oct. 1839	Peter Anderson and Cath. York both of Goulbourne
	Witnesses: Joseph Little, David Mitchell.
7 Feb. 1840	John Dowdel, Yeoman, Beckwith and Elis Shannon of Drummond
	Witnesses: Graham Codd, John Shannon,
12 Mar. 1840	Neil Stewart, both of Beckwith
	Witnesses: John Scott, Jas. Stewart

By Proclamation:

11 Sep. 1840	Thomas Crozier, Yeoman of Drummond and Margaret Moffat, spinstress of Beckwith
	Witnesses: John Allan, Robt. Moffat.

By License:

12 Mar. 1841	John McTavish Yeoman, and Isabella Stewart, both of Beckwith
26 Mar. 1841	Duncan McLaren and Mary McLaren both of Beckwith
	Witnesses: Peter McLaren, John King.
30 Apr. 1841	Alex McGregor and Isabella Ferguson both of Beckwith
	Witnesses: John Campbell, Duncan Ferguson.
2 July 1841	Thomas Ferguson, Schoolmaster, and Mary Comrie, spinstress, both of Beckwith
	Witnesses: Peter Comrie, Alex McGregor,
24 Dec. 1841	Donald Buchanan, Weaver, of Drummond and Grace Stewart spinstress of Beckwith
	Witnesses: John Campbell, Neil Stewart
4 Mar. 1842	John McNab, Yeoman and Ann Kennedy, both of Beckwith
	Witnesses; Neil Stewart, Donald Kennedy
11 Mar. 1842	Hamilton Lowrie, Yeoman of Huntley and Mary Gordon of Goulbourne, spinstress
	Witnesses: Wm. and John McArthur
21 Apr. 1842	William Comrie, Yeoman of Beckwith and

	Rebecca Grier, spinstress of Carleton Place Witnesses: John Anderson, Thos. Ferguson.
22 Apr. 1842	Peter McDiarmid, Yeoman, of Beckwith and Janet McIntosh, spinstress of Goulbourne Witnesses: Robt. Dickson, Robt. Kennedy.

By Proclamation:

27 Oct. 1843	WM. Rattery, Yeoman, to Ann Duff, spinstress, both of Beckwith Witnesses: Donald Campbell, John McTavish
7 Dec. 1843	James Moffat, Yeoman, to Rosanna Reid, spinstress both of Beckwith Witnesses: Wm. and Robt. Moffat.

By License:

2 Feb. 1844	Duncan McLaren of Drummond, Yeoman, to Janet Moor of Ramsay, spinstress, Witnesses: John A. Gammill, John McLaren.
29 Mar. 1844	Jonathan McDonald of Bromley to Sarah Bain of Ramsay, spinstress, Witnesses: John Nicholson, Robt. Lowrie.
9 Aug. 1844	WM. Mair, Shoemaker of Beckwith to Susanna Thompson of same place, spinstress. Witnesses: Alex Anderson, Nath. McCaffrey.
25 Sep. 1844	Cornelius Haring, Yeoman of Goulbourne to Caroline Sanders of Smith Falls, spinstress, Witnesses: Daniel Spiarman, Sam'l Gordon.

By Proclamation:

6 May. 1844	WM. Gilmore, Yeoman of Ramsay, to Hellen Burns, spinstress of same place, Witnesses: Allan Gilmore, Wm. Slater.

By License

18 Mar. 1845   Robt. Laurin, Yeoman of Ramsay, to Mary
               Nicholson of same place, spinstress,
               Witnesses: Alex Nicholson, John
                           Sutherland.
19 Mar. 1845   John Alex. Gemmill, Gentleman, of
               Beckwith to Janet Cannon of Ramsay,
               spinstress,
               Witnesses: Andrew Dickson, Napoleon
                           Lavelley.
27 Jne. 1845   William Ferguson of Beckwith to Cath.
               Tillotson Anderson spinstress to same
               place,
               Witnesses: Dun. Ferguson, Peter McArthur
 4 Jly. 1845   John Scott, Yeoman of Beckwith to
               Eliza Ferguson, of same place, spinster,
               Witnesses: John and Jas. Ferguson.
14 Aug. 1845   William Harper, Gentleman of Huntley
               Township to Jane Evans spinstress of
               Richmond town,
               Witnesses: David Evans, Anth. Phillips.

By Proclamation

28 Feb. 1845   James Nelson, Yeoman of Ramsay to Marion
               McFarland spinstress of same place,
               Witnesses: George Nelson, John McFarlane.
15 Apr. 1845   Alex Gillon, Yeoman, of Ramsay to Chris.
               Sutherland, spinstress of same place,
               Witnesses: John Gillon, Angus Sutherland

By License

14 Feb. 1846   Hugh Johnson, Yeoman of Carleton Place
               to Louise Stansell, spinster of same
               place,
               Witnesses: James Boyd, Thos. Murphy.
 5 May. 1846   Robt. Ferguson, Yeoman of Beckwith to
               Cath. Campbell, spinstress of same place,
               Witnesses: John Ferguson, John Campbell.

C-2

6 Nov. 1846   Donald Stewart, Yeoman of Beckwith to
               Elison Stewart, spinstress of same place,
               Witnesses: John Scott, Geo. McLaurin.

By Proclamation

19 Jan. 1847   James Tomlinson, Yeoman, of Goulbourne
               to Sarah Rennie spinstress of the same
               place,
               Witnesses: Sam'l Tomlinson, James Flood.
5 Mar. 1847   Thomas La ng, Carpenter of Ramsay to
               Margaret Neilson, spinstress of same
               place,
               Witnesses: James Neilson, Arthur Lang.
12 May. 1847   Robt. Moffat, Yeoman of Ramsay to Jane
               Mary Ann Sanders spinstress of Beckwith
               Witnesses: Thos. and Geo. Burges.

By License

11 Mar. 1847   John McGregor, Yeoman, of McNab to Janet
               Fisher, spinstress of Beckwith,
               Witnesses: Peter McArthur, James McInnes.
25 Nov. 1847   Alex Graham, Farm servant of Beckwith to
               Mary Watson, spinstress of same place,
               Witnesses: Thos. Watson, Alex Stewart.

By Proclamation

20 Jan. 1848   Francis Hunter, Yeoman of Elmsley to
               Barbara Warwick, spinstress of same place,
               Witnesses: Duncan King, Robt. Hunter.

By License

28 Mar. 1848   John McDougall, Schoolmaster, of Beckwith
               to Elisabeth McTavish, spinstress of
               same place,
               Witnesses: James and Peter McArthur.
28 Sep. 1848   John Brown, Merchant of White Lake,
               Township of McNab, to Maria Evans,

spinstress of Richmond.
Witnesses: William Byres, Wm. Evans.

29 Sep. 1848 David Evans, Clergyman of Richmond to
Martha Gordon of Goulbourne, spinstress,
Witnesses: Robt. Wm. Evan, John Gordon.

By Proclamation

15 Feb. 1848 James Rattrary, Yeoman, of Beckwith to
Catherine Thompson, spinstress of same
place.
Witnesses: Peter Carmichael, John
McGregor.

By License

30 Mar. 1849 James McEwen, Carpenter of Beckwith to
Catherine McCuan spinstress of same place.
Witnesses: John McEwan, John McCuan.

4 Oct. 1849 James Maxwell, Weaver of Beckwith to
Mary Ferguson, spinstress of same place.
Witnesses: Robt. Ferguson, John Scott.

By Proclamation

6 Aug. 1849 James Simpson, Yeoman of Goulbourne, to
Margt. McGregor of Ramsay, spinstress.
Witnesses: John McKay, Robt. Scott.

By License

22 Apr. 1850 Donald Campbell, Yeoman, of Beckwith to
Jane Duff, spinstress of same place,
Witnesses: Robt. Ferguson, John Campbell.

26 Mar. 1850 George McDougall, Yeoman of Beckwith to
Mary McEwan, spinstress of same place,
Witnesses: Duncan Stewart, Peter
McArthur.

11 Feb. 1851 Archibald Campbell, Yeoman, of Beckwith
to Sarah Gillies, spinstress of same
place,

Witnesses: John Campbell, Robt.
            Ferguson.

LIST OF COMMUNICANTS

of

THE PRESBYTERIAN CHURCH IN TOWNSHIP OF BECKWITH

IN CONNEXION WITH THE ESTABLISHED CHURCH OF SCOTLAND

7th LINE BECKWITH

(Extracted from the Minutes of the Kirk Session PAO)

Beckwith, 7 Feb. 1835

    The session met and was constituted by prayer, Sederunt. Rev. John Smith, Moderator, Peter Campbell, John Campbell and John McDonald, elders.

    The following list of those desirous of admission to the Ordinance of the Lord's Supper was produced, and the session being satisfied with the claims of those undermentioned, it was agreed that they should be admitted:

DUNCAN McLAREN	JAMES FERGUSON	CATHERINE McEWAN
MARGARET McLAREN	CHRISTIAN FERGUSON	JOHN McEWAN sr.
DUNCAN FERGUSON	JOHN SCOTT	ANNE McEWAN
CHRISTIAN FERGUSON	MARGARET SCOTT	CATHERINE McEWAN
ANNE ANDERSON	DONALD McDONALD	PETER McFARLANE
JOHN ANDERSON	CHRIS. McDOUGALL	HUGH McEWAN
ALEX McTAVISH	ALEX SCOTT	CATHERINE McEWAN
ANNE McTAVISH	ELIZABETH SCOTT	PETER DEWAR
MARGARET FISHER	ALEX McGREGOR	JANET DEWAR
JOHN McTAVISH	MARY McGREGOR	DONALD KENNEDY
PETER McTAVISH	DUNCAN McGREGOR	ROBERT KENNEDY
ALEX McTAVISH	CATH. McDOUGALL	JOHN KENNEDY
JOHN McGREGOR	MARY McGREGOR	CATHERINE KENNEDY
MARY McGREGOR	PETER SCOTT	ANNE KENNEDY
CATHERINE McNEE	MARGARET SCOTT	MALCOLM DEWAR

JOHN McARTHUR	DONALD LIVINGSTON	ANN DEWAR
GRACE McARTHUR	JOHN McDIARMID	JOHN McTAVISH
ANNE McARTHUR	MARY McDIARMID	MRS. McTAVISH
JAMES DUNCAN	ALEX STEWART	DUNCAN McLAREN
MRS. J. DUNCAN	ELIZABETH STEWART	DANIEL McLAREN
COLIN McLAREN	JOHN McEWAN	ALEX. McLAREN
MRS. McLAREN	JANET McEWAN	DANIEL McLAREN
JAMES McINNES	JOHN McEWAN	WILLIAM MUIRHEAD
MARGARET McINNES	CHRIS. McEWAN	AGNES McLAREN
DUNCAN FERGUSON	JOHN McEWAN sr.	MARY McLAREN
JAMES STEWART	JANET ROBERTSON	CATHERINE McLAREN
ISABELLA STEWART	CATHRINE FISHER	ANNE WILSON
DONALD ANDERSON	JOHN DAVIDSON	PETER COMRIE
MRS. ANDERSON	JANET COMRIE	DONALD McLAREN
DONALD McINTOSH	MARGARET McLAREN	MRS. FERGUSON
JOHN CAMPBELL,eld.	JANET LIVINGSTON	JANET LIVINGSTON
MRS. CAMPBELL	JOHN STEWART	HELEN STEWART
FINLAY McEWAN	ROBERT McLARIN	DAVID STEWART
MARY McEWAN	AGNES STEWART	CATHERINE STEWART
HUGH McEWAN	JOHN STEWART	JOHN McKENZIE
CHRISTIAN McLAREN	ANNE McARTHUR	JAMES McARTHUR sr.
PETER McLAREN	JAMES McARTHUR Jr.	COLIN KIRY
MARGARET McLAREN	ANNE KIRY	MRS. FISHER
ROBERT FERGUSON	CHRISTIAN FISHER	ELIZABETH SCOTT
DUNCAN McEWAN	JOHN McDONALD eld.	PETER CAMPBELL eld.
CATHERINE McEWAN	PETER ANDERSON	CHRISTIAN ANDERSON
GEORGE McLAREN	JOHN ANDERSON	MARGARET ANDERSON
CATHER. ANDERSON	WM. McKENZIE	CATHER. McKENZIE
PETER CARMICAIL	MARG. CARMICAIL	JOHN CARMICAIL
MARY CARMICAIL	PETER McGREGOR	MARG. McGREGOR
ALEX. DEWAR	JANET DEWAR	ROBERT STEWART
HELEN STEWART	JOHN FERGUSON	MARY FERGUSON
DOUGLAS McTAVISH	ELIZA. McTAVISH	ROBERT SCOTT
ISABELLA SCOTT	DONALD ANDERSON	DUNCAN McKEE
JANET McKEE	ISABELLA McKEE	DUNCAN McCUAN
MRS. CATH. McCUAN	JOHN McLAREN	PETER McGREGOR
DAVID THOMSON	MRS. THOMSON	DONALD ROBERTSON
MRS. ROBERTSON	ISABELLA GAIR SMITH (sister of Rev. John Smith)	

C-3

NAMES ADDED TO COMMUNION ROLL -- JOHN SMITH, MODERATOR

Beckwith, 12 February, 1836.

ROBERT DICKSON
ROBERT DICKSON
JAMES McGLASHAN
JANET McGLASHAN
PAULANE McFARLANE
CATHERINE McFARLAND
PETER McDIARMID
HELEN SMITH
(sister of Rev. John Smith)
AGNES DICKSON

ALEX McFARLANE
PETER McLAREN
ANNE McFARLANE
DUNCAN FERGUSON
ISABELLA FERGUSON
MARY COMRIE
SIMON ROCHE

JOHN SMITH, Moderator.

Beckwith, 12 February, 1837.

ALEX STEWART
JANET CARMICAEL
ANNE DICKSON
JULIA BUCHANAN
JESSIE BUCHANAN
GEORGE BUCHANAN

JOHN CRAM
MRS. CRAM
JOHN DEWAR
MRS. DEWAR
(Margaret Buchanan)

JOHN SMITH - Moderator.

Beckwith, 12 July, 1837.

MARGARET McLAREN
ALEX McEWAN
JAMES McEWAN
THOS. WHYTE
DONALD CLARKE
MRS. ANNE McKENZIE
JOHN CAMERON
RS. ANNE CAMERON
HERINE McLAREN
McKENZIE

ANGUS McDIARMID
DUGALD STEWART
JOHN ROBERTSON
CLEMINTINE McDONALD
MRS. BUCHANAN
(widow of Rev. George)

JOHN SMITH - Moderator

C-3

Beckwith, 11 February, 1838.

PETER McLAREN
JAMES DUFF
GRACE SCOTT
JANET STEWART
ELIZ. STEWART
ISABELLA STEWART
JOHN McGREGOR

JOHN STEWART
GRACE STEWART
JOHN CAMPBELL

JOHN SMITH - Moderator.

Beckwith, 1 July, 1838.

MRS. McLAREN
JOHN GORDON
MRS. GORDON

MRS. STEWART

JOHN SMITH - Moderator.

Beckwith, 17 February, 1839.

CATHERINE CRAM
JANET CRAM
MARGARET McLAREN
JOHN BROWN
MRS. MARY BROWN
ALLAN CAMERON
PETER ANDERSON
ALEXANDER McGREGOR
MRS. DUGLAD STEWART
MRS. WHYTE

PETER McARTHUR
MRS. CAMERON
ROBERT GIBSON
MOSES GIBSON
MRS. SMITH
(wife of the Rev. John)

JOHN SMITH - Moderator.

Beckwith, 16 June, 1839.

PETER McGREGOR
WILLIAM COMRIE
PETER ROBERTSON
ISABELLA STEWART

DANIEL CAMPBELL

JOHN SMITH - Moderator.

Beckwith, 13 February, 1841.

JOHN M. DOUGALD   ALEXANDER STEWART
JAMES McFARLANE   JOHN McLAREN
MARY CARMICAIL   (school master)
MRS. HUGH McEWAN
COLIN FERGUSON   JOHN SMITH - Moderator.
MARGARET GILLIES

Beckwith, 11 July, 1841.

MARGARET DRUMMOND   ALEXANDER FERGUSON
ELIZABETH McTAVISH
ALEXANDER MILLER   JOHN SMITH - Moderator.
MRS. A. MILLER

Beckwith, 12 February, 1842.

JOHN McNAB
CHRISTIAN McNAB
DUNCAN McLAREN
THOMAS FERGUSON   JOHN SMITH - Moderator.

Beckwith, 1 July 1843.

CATHERINE DUNCAN   JOHN McCUAN
MRS. JOHN ANDERSON   DUNCAN McCUAN
CHRISTIAN FISHER   JOHN SMITH - Moderator.

Beckwith, 24 February, 1844.

ALEXANDER GRAHAM
JANE THOMSON
WILLIAM COCHRANE   JOHN SMITH - Moderator.

C-3

January 22, 1846.

This note is recorded.

> The effect of the unhappy disruption which on 9th
> July, 1844 took place in the Presbyterian Church
> of Canada in connexion with the Church of Scotland
> extended more or less to all Churches under the
> Spiritual charge of the synod. The Beckwith order
> and discipline were for a time nearly suspended,
> the elders without exception ceasing to officiate.
> A necessity of course arose to re-organize the
> Session.
>
> JOHN SMITH - Moderator.

Beckwith, 27 June, 1846.

ROBERT CARMICAIL
JANET CARMICAIL
JOHN KING, Jr.
CATHERINE McCUAN
DONALD FERGUSON
DUGALD FERGUSON
WILLIAM FERGUSON
MARY FERGUSON
ISABELLA SCOTT

John King, Sr.
MRS. KING
JOHN SCOTT
MRS. JOHN SCOTT
MRS. WM. FERGUSON

JOHN SMITH - Moderator.

Beckwith, 27 February, 1847.

PETER JOSEF CARMICAIL
ISABELLA KING
JOHN STEWART

MRS. JOHN STEWART

JOHN SMITH - Moderator.

Beckwith, 3 July, 1847.

Name of - MARY WATSON - added.

Beckwith, 6 February, 1848.

Decided that -
    Surplus collection from Sacramental occasion
    service (27th) be sent in aid of the French
    Canadian Mission.
                       JOHN SMITH - Moderator.

Beckwith, 26 February, 1848.

JANET KING
DUNCAN FERGUSON
MRS. DUNCAN FERGUSON   JOHN SMITH - Moderator.

Beckwith, 24 June, 1848.

JAMES CARMICAIL   WILLIAM McKENZIE
DANIEL McLAREN   McGREGOR by confirmation.
JANET FERGUSON
JANET McFARLANE   JOHN SMITH - Moderator.

Beckwith, 17 February 1849.

MARGARET ANDERSON
JOHN BENIMAN
MRS. JOHN BENIMAN   JOHN SMITH - Moderator.

Beckwith, 23 June, 1849.

ANNE CARMICAIL
MARY CARMICAIL
    (and it was decided surplus collection to go to
    Synod fund).
                       JOHN SMITH - Moderator.

C-3

Beckwith, 16 February, 1850.

JAMES MAXWELL   CATHERINE FERGUSON
JOHN FERGUSON   CATHERINE McLAREN
MARY McLAREN
ELIZABETH McLAREN   JOHN SMITH - Moderator.
PETER McLAREN

Beckwith, 28 September, 1850.

DONALD CARMICAIL   ANNE McTAVISH
GEORGE COMRIE
JANE COMRIE   JOHN SMITH - Moderator.
     (number of communicants on this occasion was 100).

REV. JOHN SMITH died 18th day of April, 1851.

Beckwith, 14 June, 1851.

     On which day, after public worship the Session met
     and was constituted by prayer. Present: Rev. Wm.
     Bell, Moderator pro tem. Messrs. John McArthur,
     James Ferguson, McDonald, McLaren, elders. Tokens
     of admission to Lord's table were given out to the
     members of the church present after which the
     Session adjourned till the following day.

June 15, 1851.

     Sacrament of Lord's Supper was administered -
     94 members partook. WM. BELL, Moderator, pro tem.

NOTE:

     The Presbytery of Bathurst ordained the Rev. Duncan
     Morrison to the pastoral charge of Beckwith on the
     22nd day of October, 1851, year.

Beckwith, 27 February, 1852.

ARCHIBALD CAMPBELL
MRS. CAMPBELL   - were added to the
                                       communion roll.

                          DUNCAN MORRISON, Moderator.

Beckwith, 1 March, 1852.

        90 members sat down to communion.

Beckwith, 25 June, 1852.

PATRICH McLAUGHLIN
MRS. McLAUGHLIN (his wife)
JOHN McRAE and his wife
MRS. McRAE
ROBERT SCOTT
JAS. McCUAN
HELEN FERGUSON
ANN McFARLANE
DONALD STEWART
JAMES STEWART
DONALD McLAREN
ELIZABETH THOMPSON
CATHERINE CAMPBELL

DUNCAN MORRISON, Moderator.

June 28, 1852.

112 members partook of the Sacrament.

February 11, 1853.

26 names added - included Robt. McLaughlin and Mrs.
McLaughlin his wife.

Beckwith, 14 February 1853.

There were 150 communicants on this occasion, six
of whom were from other congregations.
MRS. AITCHISON (nee HELEN SMITH) congregation of Smith
Falls.
PATRICK CAMPBELL, Perth (Mr. Bell's congregation).
JOHN CAMPBELL, Perth (Mr. Bain's congregation).
GEORGE BROWN and his wife and
DAVID BROWN from the congregation at Richmond.

March 1856.

14 names added to Communion Roll among which were
JAMES AITCHISON M.D. and HELEN SMITH AITCHISON,
his wife.

Beckwith, 17 August, 1856.

Rev. Duncan Morrison advised he had accepted call to
Brockville Church. The Presbytery of Bathurst ordained
the REV. WM. McHUTCHESON.

Beckwith, 4 July, 1857.

Names added to Communion Roll -

JANE McLAUGHLIN	MARGARET McTAVISH
ROSE McLAUGHLIN	DUNCAN McLAREN
ANN McLAUGHLIN	MRS. PETER FERGUSON
ESTER McLAUGHLIN	
ROBERT McGREGOR	

NOTE: The foregoing brief excerpts are given to show
the ongoing life of The Scotch Church of the 7th
line Beckwith.

Some further excerpts from the Minutes of Session
during the Ministry of the Rev. Walter Ross are
being included in this appendix which might be
of interest regarding how the Church on the 7th
line was phased out of action. JOHN McARTHUR,
an elder of the Scotch Church in connexion with
the Church of Scotland since 1846, died in 1867,
aged 66 years. (see Appendix B-4).

Extracts showing the rotation of services between
Beckwith, Carleton Place and Franktown under
REV. WALTER ROSS' ministry.

Beckwith, July 7, 1864.

Added to Communion Roll by certificate. MRS. WALTER
ROSS.

Beckwith, 29 January, 1870.

The Kirk Session met this day and was constituted with
prayer. Present: REV. W. ROSS, Moderator. Messrs.
Dugald Ferguson, James Ferguson, Donald McLAREN and
Robert Bell, Elders.* (*Robert Bell - Eldership. See
appendix B4). Tokens of admission to Lord's table were
distributed to the members present. Adjourned to meet
on Sabbath after communion. W. ROSS, Moderator.

C-3

Beckwith, 30 January, 1870.

Which day the Kirk Session met according to adjourment.
Present: Rev. W. Ross. Messrs. D. Ferguson, R. Bell,
J. Ferguson, D. McLaren, H. Robertson, elders. About
80 communicants on this occasion. Agreed that the
Sacrament of the Lord's Supper be dispensed in the
Church at Carleton Place on the third sabbath of Februa-
ry 20th day of the month.. W. ROSS, Moderator.

Beckwith, 19 February, 1870.

        Names added to communion Roll by certificate:
PATRICK STRUTHERS
MRS. PAT STRUTHERS   MRS. ROBERT ANDERSON
JAMES CAMPBELL   JAMES GILLIES
MRS. JAMES CAMPBELL   MRS. JAMES GILLIES
GEORGE LOWE   MRS. ROBERT FERGUSON
MRS. GEORGE LOWE   MRS. WM. MURPHY
MRS. JAMES POOLE   MRS. ALEX. LANG.
JOSIAH J. BELL
MARY BELL (his wife)

Beckwith, 12 June, 1870.

Session met. Agreed the Sacrament of Lord's Supper be
dispensed in the Church of the 7th Line, on 4th sabbath
of the month being 26th instant. It was also agreed
that the Session meet on Friday the 24th instant at
1 o'clock in the forenoon to purge the Communion Roll.
                        W. ROSS, Moderator.

On the 26th it was noted there were 84 communicants at
the 7th line Church.

September 18, 1870.

Agreed Sacrament be dispensed in Church at Carleton
Place 4th sabbath in October 23rd of month.

October 22, 1870.

    Names added to Communion Roll -
GEORGE McPHERSON   MRS. ISABELLA BELL
MRS. GEORGE McPHERSON   ANDREW SMITH
MR. WILSON (Dr. Wilson)
MRS. DANIEL McCUAN
    About 62 communicants partook of the Lord's Supper
    October 23, 1870 at Carleton Place.

Beckwith, 25 December, 1870.

Session met. Sacrament to be dispensed in the Church of
the 7th Line, 5th Sabbath of the month, 29th day of
January.   W. ROSS, Moderator.

Beckwith, 29 January, 1871.

Session met, W. ROSS, Moderator. Messrs. Robert Bell,
Donald McLaren, James Ferguson, Hugh Robertson and
Dugald Ferguson, elders.

There were 70 communicants.
Agreed, Sacrament to be dispensed at Church at Carleton
Place, May 28th.

Carleton Place, 21 May, 1871.

Session met. 62 communicants. Agreed to dispense
communion at the Church at Franktown 2nd July.
                                W. ROSS, Moderator.
NOTE:
From Page 124 Kirk Session Minutes it is recorded:
ROBERT BELL was re-elected to represent the Session and
congregation in Presbytery and Synod for current syn-
docial year.

Franktown, 2 July, 1871.

Session met. 59 communicants.

The records are written in a regular rhythm from then on.

December 1871 - Franktown - 69 Communicants.
May 3, 1872 - Carleton Place
June 30, 1872 - Franktown. etc. etc.

Seemingly the Scotch Church of the 7th Line was phased out of action as far as services, but not as the center of church jurisdiction. The following items verify this for we find these entries in the Kirk Minutes of 1874-1875.

Beckwith, 7th Line
12 July, 1874

Which day the Kirk Session met and was constituted by prayer. Present: The Moderator. Messrs. James Ferguson, Donald McLaren and Dugald Ferguson, elders. Robert Bell Esq. was unanimously re-elected to represent the Session and congregation in Presbytery and Synod for the current synodical year. Closed with prayer.
W. ROSS, Moderator and
Session Clerk.

St. Andrews Church, Perth,
May 11, 1875.

The Presbytery upon the report of the Committee appointed to examine the Records of the Kirk Session of Beckwith, instruct the clerk to attest the same as carefully and correctly kept.   WM. BAIN, D.D.
Presbytery Clerk.

Beckwith, 25 April, 1875.

Which day the Kirk Session met and was constituted by Prayer. Present: The Moderator, Messrs. Robert Bell, Hugh Robertson, Donald McLaren, and Dugald Ferguson, elders. The Session having taken into consideration the prospect of adding to the number of its Elders in the

congregations and being persuaded that Hugh George Tait,
and Robert McLaughlin are fit and proper persons for
holding the sacred office of the Eldership, they unanimously made choice of the said Messrs. George Tait and
Robt. McLaughlin to be members of the Kirk Session and
appointed the admission. Mr. George Tait on ordained
Elder of the Church of Scotland and the ordination of
Mr. Robt. McLaughlin to take place in presence of the
congregation on Sabbath the 9th day of May. They likewise appoint an edict to this effect to be served on
Sabbath the 25th day of April and intimation to be made
to the people that if they have any objection to state
why the above named persons should not be admitted and
received to the Eldership, they will have an opportunity
of doing so to the moderator of the Session within ten
days after the edict is served. Closed with prayer.
                    W. ROSS, Moderator,
                    and Session Clerk.

Beckwith, 25 April, 1875.

This day immediately after divine service public intimation was given that Messrs. George Tait and Robert
McLaughlin the persons named in the foregoing minutes
of Session had been elected as fit and proper persons
to fill the office of Eldership by the Session, and that
if no objection against the life and conversation of
said individuals should be brought forward within 10
days from this date the admission of the said Mr. George
Tait and Mr. Robt. McLaughlin to the office of the
Eldership in this church shall take place on the 9th
day of May.* WALTER ROSS, Moderator.

(*see Appendix B-4 for Ordination of above Elders at
Beckwith).

Beckwith, 9 May, 1875.

It was agreed that the Sacrament of the Lord's Supper
should be dispensed in St. Andrews Church, Carleton

Place, on the first Sabbath in June, being the sixth
day of the month.

The Kirk Session met on two occasions in private homes
in Beckwith according to page 150, of the Minutes, May
30, 1876, and on page 153, on June 1876; but to all
intents and purposes the Church on the 7th Line had
closed its doors, and the Communion Services continued
to be held alternately between Carleton Place and Franktown.

It is recorded that on Sunday the 9th July 1876, 75
partook of communion at St. Paul's Church, Franktown;
and on 24th September 1876 there were 50 who partook
of Communion at Carleton Place.

An item of the 7th July 1878, under St. Paul's Church,
Franktown, reads:

> It has pleased Almighty God to remove by death
> Mr. Robert McLaughlin, who had been an office
> hearer of this church for three years. The
> Kirk Session expresses their deep sense of the
> Christian character and great worth of their
> dear departed brother. Mr. McLaughlin was a
> kind husband and father, a good neighbour, a
> sincere friend and an exemplary disciple of
> the Lord.

This no doubt was the Robert McLaughlin who with his
wife was admitted to Communion, February 11, 1853,
when Rev. Duncan Morrison was minister of the Scotch
Church and whose children later became members of the
Kirk of the 7th Line, in connexion with the Church of
Scotland.

APPENDIX D

Copy of Crown Grant issued to Reverend George Buchanan, 1831.

J. Colborne
PROVINCE OF UPPER CANADA

WILLIAM THE FOURTH by the Grace of God of the United Kingdom of Great Britain and Ireland, King Defender of the Faith -- To all to whom these Presents shall come ----- Greeting:

Know ye, That We, of our special Grace, certain Knowledge, and mere Motion, have given and GRANTED, and by these Presents, do Give and GRANT, unto The Reverend George Buchanan of the Township of Beckwith of the County of Lanark in the District of Bathurst, clergyman of the Church of Scotland located by the Qr. Mr. Gen'ls Dept. Heirs and assigns forever; ALL that parcel or tract of LAND, situate in the Township of Beckwith in the County of Lanark in the District of Bathurst in our said Province: containing by admeasurement Four Hundred Acres. Lots number Nine and Fourteen in the Sixth Concession of said Township of Beckwith be the same more or less, being TOGETHER with all the Woods and Waters thereon lying and being, under the reservations, limitations and conditions, hereinafter expressed: which said Four Hundred Acres and - butted and bounded, or may be otherwise known as follows: that is to say; Commencing on front of said concession at the southeast angle of each of the said lots respectively then, north thirty six degrees west sixty six chains seventy links more or less to the allowance for Road in rear of said concession then south fifty four degrees west thirty chains more or less to the western limit of each lot then south thirty six degrees east sixty six chain seventy links more or less to the allowance for Road in front of said concession then north fifty four degree east thirty chains more or less to the place of beginning of each lot.

K.J.Boulton, Atty. Genl.   Recorded 20 October 1831

TO HAVE AND TO HOLD, the said parcel or tract of

213

land, hereby given and granted him the said REVERAND
GEORGE BUCHANAN his heirs and assigns forever; saving
nevertheless to Us, our Heirs and Successors, all Mines
of Gold and Silver that shall or may be hereafter found
on any part of the said parcel or tract of Land hereby
given and granted as aforesaid; and saving and reserving
to Us, our Heirs and Successors all White Pine Trees,
that shall or may now or hereafter grow, or be growing
on any part of the said parcel or tract of Land hereby
granted as aforesaid, PROVIDED ALWAYS that no part of
the parcel or tract of land hereby given and granted to
the said George Buchanan and his heirs, be within any
reservation heretofore made and marked by Us, our
heirs and successors, by our Surveyor General of
Woods, or his lawful Deputy, in which case, this our
grant for each part of the Land hereby given and granted
to the said George Buchanan and his heirs forever, as
aforesaid; and which shall upon a survey thereof being
made, be found within any such reservation, shall be
null and void and and of none effect, any thing herein
contained to the contrary notwithstanding. PROVIDED
ALSO that the said George Buchanan, his heirs or assigns,
shall and do within three years, erect and built, or
cause to be erected and built, in and upon some part of
the said parcel or tract of Land, a good and sufficient
dwelling house the said George Buchanan or his assigns
not having built, or not being in his or their own
right, lawfully possessed of a house in our said Province, and be therein, or cause some person to be therein
resident, for and during the space of three years, then
next ensuing the building of the same. PROVIDED ALSO,
that if at any time or time hereafter the Land so hereby
given and granted to the said George Buchanan and his
heirs shall come into the possession and tenure of any
person or persons whomsoever, either by virtue of any
Deed of sale, conveyance, enfeoffment, or exchange:
or by gift, inheritance, descent, devise, or marriage, such person or persons shall within twelve
months next after his, her, or their entry into,
and possession of the same, take the oaths prescribed by Law, before some one of the Magistrates of our said Province, and a certificate

of such oath having been so taken shall cause to be
recorded in the Secretary's Office of the said Province. IN DEFAULT of all or any of which conditions,
limitations this said Grant and very thing herein
contained, shall be and We hereby declare the same
to be null and void, to all intents and purposes
whatsoever; and the Land hereby granted and every
part and parcel thereof, shall revert to, and become
vested in Us, our Heirs and Successors, in like manner as if the same, had never been granted, any thing
herein contained to the contrary thereof in any wise
notwithstanding.

AND WHEREAS by an Act of the Parliament of Great Britain passed in the thirty-first year of the Reign of
His late Majesty King George the Third, entitled,
"An Act to repeal certain parts of an Act, passed in
the Fourteenth year of His Majesty's Reign, entitled
"An Act for making effectual provision for the Government of the Province of Quebec, in North America and
and to make further provision for the Government of
the said Province". It is declared "that no grants
of Lands hereafter made, shall be valid or effectual,
unless same shall contain a specification of the
Lands to be alloted and appropriated solely to the
maintenance of a Protestant Clergy within the said
Province in respect of the Lands to be thereby granted" -- NOW KNOW YE, that We have caused an allotment or appropriation of Fifty-seven acres and One
Seventh to be made in lot Number Twenty-One in the
Eighth Concession of said Township fo Beckwith.

GIVEN under the Great Seal of our Province of Upper
Canada: Witness our trusty and well-beloved Sir John
Colburne KCB lt. Governor of our said Province and
Major General Commanding our forces therein this
Eleventh day of October in the year of our Lord one
thousand eight hundred and thirty one and second of
our Reign. By Command His Excellency in Council D.
Cameron J.C. U.C. 21 January 1824 under the Adm. of
Sir P. Maitland KCB lt. Gov. entered with the Sudr.
18 October 1831 for 400 acres, fees suspended.
Settlement duly performed. D. Boulton. Andr. Gen.

215

Rev. George Buchanan to Alexander McLaren

I hereby certify that the within named Robert Grant
upon his oath before me proved the signing and sealing of this Memorial and the execution of the Deed
to which the said Memorial relates.

Alex. McMillan Dy
Reg. C. of Lanark

A Memorial to be registered pursuant to the Statute
in such case made and provided: Of an Indenture dated Seventh day of March in the year of our Lord,
one thousand eight hundred and thirty four. Made
between The Reverend George Buchanan of the Township
of Beckwith in the County of Lanark in the District
of Bathurst and Province of Upper Canada, Clergyman,
of the Church of Scotland of the one part, and Alexander McLaren of the said Township, County, District
and Province, Yeoman, of the other part, purporting
to be a Deed of Bargain and Sale, whereby the said
Reverend George Buchanan for and in consideration of
the sum of One hundred pounds of lawful money of
Upper Canada did grant, bargain, sell, alien, transfer, convey and confirm unto the said Alexander Mc-
Laren his heirs and assigns forever, all and singular that certain parcel or tract of land and premises, situate, lying and being in the Township of Beckwith in the County of Lanark, in the District of
Bathurst and Province of Upper Canada, being composed of Lot No. Fourteen in the Sixth Concession of
the said Township of Beckwith, containing by admeasurement two hundred acres be the same more or less;
which said two hundred acres butted and bounded or
may be known as follows that is to say commencing
in front of the Sixth Concession at the South East

216

Angle of the said lot. Then north thirty six degrees
west sixty six chains seventy links more or less to
the allowance for road in rear of the said concession. Then south fifty four degrees west thirty chains more or less to the limit of the said lot. Th-
en south thirty six degrees east sixty six chains
seventy links more or less to the allowance for road
in front of the said concession. Then north fifty
four degrees east thirty chains more or less to the
place of beginning. Together with all houses, outhouses, woods and waters thereon, erected, lying and
being. And all and singular the hereditaments and
appurtenances to the said premises in any wise belonging - to have and to hold the aforesaid premises
unto the said Alexander McLaren, his heirs and assigns forever. Which said indenture or Bargain and
Sale is witnessed by Robert Grant of the Town of Perth, Clerk, and James Young of the same place, Yeoman.
And this Memorial thereof is hereby required to be
registered by me the said Alexander McLaren the Grantee therein named. As witness my hand and seal this
seventh day of March in the year of our Lord one
thousand eight hundred and thirty four.

                    (signed) Alexander McLaren.

Signed and Sealed
In the Presence of
The obliteration on the
second page being first made.

Robert Grant
James Young

REGISTERED ON SATURDAY THE EIGHTH DAY OF MARCH IN
THE YEAR OF OUR LORD ONE THOUSAND EIGHT HUNDRED AND
THIRTY FOUR AT HALF PAST TEN OF THE CLOCK IN THE
FORENOON.

                    (signed) Alex. McMillan
                             Reg. C. of Lanark

217

A Memorial to be registered pursuant to the statue
in such case made and provided:-

Of an Indenture dated Seventh day of March in the year of our Lord one thousand eight hundred and thirty
four. Made between
      The Reverend George Buchanan of the Township of
      Beckwith in the County of Lanark in the District
      of Bathurst, and the Province of Upper Canada,
      Clergyman of Church of Scotland of the one part
      - and -
      Alexander McLaren of the said township County,
      District and Province, yeoman, of the other pa-
      rt purporting to be a Deed of Bargain and Sale,
      whereby the said -
Reverend George Buchanan for and in consideration of
the sum of one hundred pounds of lawful money of Upper Canada did grant, bargain, sell, alien transfer
and convey and confirm unto the said Alexander McLaren his heirs and assigns forever all and singular
that certain parcel or tract of land and premises,
situate lying and being in Township of Beckwith, in
the County of Lanark, in the District of Bathurst,
and Province of Upper Canada being composed of Lot
No. fourteen in Sixth Concession of the said Township of Beckwith, containing by admeasurement two
hundred acres more or less which said two hundred
acres are butted and bounded or may be otherwise known as follows (that is to say) commencing in front
of said concession at the south east angle of the
said lot, then north thirty six degrees west sixty-
six chains seventy links, more or less to the allowance for road in rear of the said concession. Then
south fifty-four degrees west thirty chains more or
less to the limit of the said lot. Then south thirty-six degrees east sixty-six chains seventy links
more or less to the allowance for road in front of
said concession. Then north fifty-four degrees east thirty chains more or less to the place of beginning. Together with all houses, outhouses, woods
and waters thereon erected lying and being. And all
and singular the hereditaments and appurtenances to
the said premise in anywise belonging. To have and

to hold the aforesaid premises unto the said Alexander McLaren, his heirs and assigns forever. Which said Indenture or Bargain and Sale is witnessed by Robert P. Grant of the Town of Perth, Clerk, and James Young of the same place, yeoman.

And this Memorial thereof is hereby required to be registered by me the said Alexander McLaren the Grantee therein named. As witness my hand and seal this seventh day of March in the year of our Lord one thousand eight hundred and thirty-four.
                    (signed) Alexander McLaren.

Signed and sealed in the presence of
The Obliteration on the second page
being first made.

Robert P. Grant
James Young.

REGISTERED ON SATURDAY THE EIGHTH DAY OF MARCH IN THE YEAR OF OUR LORD ONE THOUSAND AND EIGHT HUNDRED AND THIRTY-FOUR AT HALF PAST TEN OF THE CLOCK IN THE FORENOON.

                    Alex. McMillan, Reg. Co. of Lanark.

Rev. George Buchanan to
Alexander McLaren.

I hereby witness that the within named Robert Grant upon his oath before me proved the signing and sealing of the memorial and the execution of the Deed to which the said Memorial relates.

                    Alex. McMillan, Reg. Co. of Lanark.

219

Libre D Folio 48 Memorial No. 48.

ALEXANDER McLAREN TO JOHN SMITH

I hereby certify that the within named Colin
McLaren upon his oath before me proved the signing
and sealing of this Memorial and the Execution of
the Deed to which the said Memorial relates.

Alexr. McMillian Dy.
Reg. C. of Lanark.

A Memorial to be registered pursuant to the stat-
uate in that case mad and provided - of an indenture, dated the eleventh day of June in the year
of our Lord one thousand eight hundred and thirty
four made between Alexander McLaren of the Township of Beckwith in the County of Lanark in the
District of Bathurst, and Province of Upper Canada
Yeoman, of the one part, and the Reverend John
Smith of the said Township, County, District and
Province, Clergyman of the Established Church
of Scotland of the other part, purporting to be a
Deed of Bargain and Sale, whereby the said
Alexander McLaren for and in consideration of the
sum of One hundred pounds of lawful money of Upper
Canada, hath granted, bargained, sold, aliened,
transferred, conveyed and confirmed unto the said
Reverend John Smith, his heirs and assigns forever,
all and singular, the certain parcel or tract of
land and Premises, situated, lying and being in
the Township of Beckwith in the County of Lanark
in the District of Bathurst and Province of Upper
Canada, being composed of Lot No. Fourteen in the
Sixth Concession of said Township of Beckwith
containing by admeasurement two hundred acres be
the same more or less; which said two hundred
acres are butted and bounded or may be otherwise
known as follows, that is to say Commencing in
front of the said concession at the south east
angle of the said lot. Then North thirty-six
degrees West Sixty-six chains seventy links more

220

or less to the allowance for road in rear of the
said concession. Then south fifty-four degrees
West, thirty chains more or less to the limit of
the said lot, then South thirty-six degrees east,
sixty-six chains seventy links more or less to
the allowance for road in front of the said concession north fifty-four degrees east, thirty
chains more or less to the place of beginning.

Together with all houses, out-houses, woods and
waters thereon erected lying and being, and all
and singular, the hereditaments and appurtenances
to the said premises in any wise belonging: To
Have and to Hold the same unto the said Reverend
John Smith, his heirs and assigns, to the sole and
proper use, benefit and behoof of the Reverend
John Smith, his heirs and assigns, forever. Which
said Indenture of Bargain and Sale is witnessed
by Colin McLaren and John McArthur both of Beckwith, yeoman, and this Memorial is hereby required
to be registered by me the said Reverend John
Smith, the grantee therein named. As witness my
hand and seal, this twelfth day of June in the
year of our Lord One thousand eight hundred and
thirty-four.

                    (signed)   JOHN SMITH

Signed and sealed in presence
of
Colin McLaren
Robert McLaren.

REGISTERED ON THURSDAY THE TWELFTH DAY OF JUNE IN
THE YEAR OF OUR LORD ONE THOUSAND EIGHT HUNDRED
AND THIRTY-FOUR AT TWO OF THE CLOCK IN THE AFTER-
NOON.

                    Alex. McMillan Dy.
                    Reg. Co. of Lanark.

Copy of Crown Grant issued to William Marrill of South
West lot 15, Sixth Concession, Township of Beckwith,
in 1840 --- this property sold to the Rev. John Smith
in 1844.

Geo. Arthur.

PROVINCE OF UPPER CANADA

VICTORIA, by the Grace of GOD, of the United Kingdom of Great Britain and Ireland, Queen Defender
of the Faith - To all to whom these Presents shall
come -- GREETING:

KNOW YE, that We, of our special Grace, certain,
Knowledge, and mere Motion, have given and GRANTED
and by these Presents do give and GRANT to WILLIAM
MARRILL of the Township of Beckwith, in the County
of Lanark in the District of Bathurst his heirs
and assigns forever; ALL that parcel or tract of
LAND, situate in the Township of Beckwith in the
County of Lanark in the District of Bathurst in
our said Province by admeasurement One Hundred
Acres be the same more or less, being composed of
SOUTH WEST HALF OF LOT NUMBER FIFTEEN in the Sixth
Concession of the said Township of Beckwith.

TOGETHER with all the woods and waters thereon
lying and being, under the reservations, limitations and conditions, hereinafter expresses:

WM. H. DRAPER   Recorded 26th December 1840.
        A.G.

TO HAVE AND TO HOLD, the said parcel or tract of
Land, hereby given and granted to him the said
William Marrill, his heirs and assigns forever,
saving, nevertheless to Us, our Heirs and Successors, all Mines of Gold and Silver that shall
or may be hereafter found on any part of the said

parcel or tract of Land hereby given and granted
as aforesaid; and saving and deserving to Us,
our Heirs and Successors, all White Pine Trees,
that shall or may now or hereafter grow, or be
growing on any part of the said parcel or tract
of land hereby granted as aforesaid. PROVIDED
ALWAYS, that no part of the parcel or tract of
land hereby given and granted to the said William
Marrill and his heirs, be within any reservation
heretofore made, and marked for Us, our Heirs, and
Successors, by our Surveyor General of Woods, or
his lawful Deputy, in which case, this our grant
for such part of the Land hereby given and granted
to the said William Marrill and his heirs forever,
as aforesaid; and which shall, upon a survey thereof being made, be found within any such reservation, shall be null and void, and of no effect,
anything herein contained to the contrary notwithstanding. AND WHEREAS, by an Act of the Parliament of Great Britain, passed in the thirty-
first year of the reign of His late Majesty King
George the Third, entitled "An Act to repeal
certain parts of an Act passed in the fourteenth
year of His Majesty's Reign, entitled "An Act for
making more effectual provision for the Government
of the Province of Quebec, North America", and to
make further provision for the Government of the
said Province, it is declared "that no grant of
Lands thereafter made, should be valid or effectual,
unless the same should contains a specifications
of the Lands to be allotted and appropriated solely
to the maintenance of a Protestant Clergy within
the said Province, in respect of the Lands to be
thereby granted". -- NOW KNOW YE, We have caused
an allotment or appropriation of
>   fourteen acres and two sevenths to be made in
>   lot number nine in the Nineth Concession of
>   the said Township of Beckwith.
Given under the Great Seal of our said Province of
Upper Canada. Witness our trusty and well-beloved
Sir George Arthur, KCB, Lt. Gov. of our said
Province and Mjor.Genl.Comm. of our forces therein
at Toronto, this eighteenth day of December in the
year of our Lord one thousand eight hundred and

and forty and in the fourth year of our Reign.
By Command of His Excellency in Council   G.A.

Order Land Board Dist. of Bathurst
12 December 1825 Adminst. Sir. P. Maitland
K.C.B. Regd. 6 July 1804 - Patent
fee and survey paid - Settlement duties
performed.

                        R.A. Tucker
                        Sect'y.

Libr. H. Fol. 366
Memorial - No. 28a

    DUNCAN CAMPBELL to
    The
    REV. JOHN SMITH

    I hereby certify that the within named John
    Campbell upon his oath before me proved the
    signing and sealing of this Memorial and the
    Execution of the Deed to which the said Memorial
    relates.
                        Alexr. McMillan, Dy.
                        Regr. Co. of Lanark.

    A MEMORIAL to be registered pursuant to the Sta-
    tute in that case made and provided, of an
    INDENTURE of Bargain and Sale, dated the Eighth
    day of March in the year of our Lord, One Thousand
    Eight Hundred Forty-four made between DUNCAN
    CAMPBELL of the Township of Beckwith in the County
    of Lanark in the District of Bathurst in the
    Province of Upper Canada, yeoman, of the one part,
    and JOHN SMITH, MINISTER OF THE SCOTCH PRESBYTE ·
    RIAN CHURCH in Connexion with the Church of Scot-
    land, of the same place - of the other part,
    purporting to be a Deed of Bargain and Sale, where-
    by the said DUNCAN CAMPBELL for and in considera-
    tion of fifty pounds of Lawful money of the
    Province of Canada, hath granted, bargained, sold,
    aliened, transferred, conveyed and confirmed unto
    the said JOHN SMITH, his heirs and assigns forever,
    ALL AND SINGULAR that certain parcel or tract of
    Land premises situate lying and being in the
    Township of Beckwith, in the County of Lanark,
    and in the District and Province aforesaid, being
    composed of the SOUTH WEST HALF OF LOT NUMBER
    FIFTEEN in the Sixth Concession of the Township of
    Beckwith, containing by admeasurement ONE HUNDRED

ACRES more or less, which said One Hundred Acres
may be known by the original GRANT from the
Crown.

Together with all houses, outhouses, woods and
waters thereon erected lying and being, and all
and singular the hereditaments and appurentenances
to the said premises in any wise belonging: TO
HAVE AND TO HOLD THE SAME unto the said John Smith,
his heirs and assigns, to the sale and proper use,
benefit and behood of the said John Smith, his
heirs and assigns FOREVER. And which said Indenture, or Bargain and Sale is witnessed by JOHN
CAMPBELL and ARCHIBALD CAMPBELL both of the Township of Beckwith, yeomen, and this Memorial thereof is hereby required to be registered by me the
said John Smith --- Grantee, therein named.

As WITNESS my hand and Seal, this Eighth day of
January in the year of our Lord One Thousand
Eight Hundred and Forty-five.

Signed and Sealed in the presence of
John Campbell
Maria McWilliams
                    (signed) JOHN SMITH

REGISTERED ON WEDNESDAY THE EIGHTH DAY OF JANUARY
IN THE YEAR OF OUR LORD, ONE THOUSAND EIGHT
HUNDRED AND FORTY-FIVE AT ELEVEN OF THE CLOCK IN
THE FORENOON

                    Alex McMillan Dy.
                    Regr. Co. of Lanark.

```
Liber B. Beckwith
Folio 488
Memorial No. 321.
------------------
```

Of <u>Indenture of RELEASE</u>

Jane Smith
to
Robert Smith

Paterson Harrison Hodgins - Toronto

County of York)	I, David Hastings McAdam of

County of York   )   I, David Hastings McAdam of
One of the United)   the City of Toronto in the
Counties of York)   County of York Gentleman
and Peel   )   make oath and say
)
        To Wit)   1) That I was present and did
)   the Indenture to which the
                               within Memorial relates duly
                               signed sealed and delivered
                               by the therein named Jane
                               Smith and that I am a subs-
                               cribing witness to the exe-
                               cution of the said Indenture.

                               2) That I the Deponent also
                               saw the said Memorial duly
                               signed and sealed by the the-
                               ein named Robert Smith which
                               said Memorial was attested
                               by me this Deponent and a-
                               nother subscribing witness
                               and that both said Instru-
                               ments were executed at the
                               City of Toronto aforesaid.

Sworn before me at the City of   (Signed)
                                                      D.H. MAcAdam

Toronto in the County of York this first
day of August AD 1861.
     (signed) Clarkson Jones

A Court in QB for York and Peel.

A MEMORIAL to be registered of an Indentures of
Release made the first day of July in the year of
our Lord one thousand eight hundred and sixty-one
and made between JANE SMITH of the City of Ottawa
in the County of Carleton and Province of Canada
WIDOW of the first part and Robert Smith formerly
of the same place but now of the City of Toronto
in the County of York and Province aforesaid
Gentleman of the second part.

WHEREBY after reciting that "Whereas John Smith
late of the Township of Beckwith in the County of
Lanark, Clerk now deceased did on or about the
twenty-first day of October in the year of our Lord
one thousand eight hundred and forty-nine duly
make and publish his last will and testament whereby he did devise and bequeath unto the said party
of the first part for and during her lifetime all
the Real and Personal estate of which he was then
possessed or thereafter might become possessed of;
and did then direct that on the demise of the said
party of the first part he the second party of the
second part should have hold and become possessed
of all the said Real Estate in fee simple and
further reciting".

"AND WHEREAS it has been agreed by the said party
of the first part that she shall release unto the
said party of the second part the said life estate
hereinbefore devised to her by the said testator
John Smith."

IT WAS WITNESSED that the said party of the first
for and in consideration of the sum of five shillings to her in hand paid by the said party of
the second part (the receipt whereof is thereby
acknowledged) did grant bargain sell, alien, assign,
and convey unto the said party of the second part
his heirs and assigns forever all the life estate
of her the said party of the first part in the
lands to her by the said in part received will
devised.

229

TO HAVE AND TO HOLD the same unto the said party
of the second part his heirs and assigns forever.

WHICH said Indenture is witnessed by David Hastings
MacAdam of the City of Toronto in the County of
York, Gentleman.

AND the Memorial therein is hereby required to be
registered by me Robert Smith the said grantee
therein named.

AS WITNESS my hand and seal this first day of
August in the year of our Lord one thousand eight
hundred and sixty-one.

Signed, Sealed and Delivered
in presence of   (signed) ROBERT SMITH.
D. H. MacAdam
John Kennedy.

```
Liber B. Beckwith
Folio 487
Memorial No. 320.


                    Memorial
                       of
                Probate of Will of
             The Reverend John Smith
             ------------------------

             Paterson Harrison Hodgins
                      Totonto
             ------------------------


  County of York  )  I, David Hastings MacAdam of the
  one of the      )  City of Toronto in the County
  United Counties )  of York, Gentleman, make oath
  of York and Peel)  and say that;
                  )
                  )  1) I with another subscribing
          To Wit)   witness were present and did
                  )  see Jane Smith within the Memo-
                     rial named duly sign and seal
                     the said Memorial in the day of
                     which the same bears date.

                     2) That the said Memorial was
                     executed at the City of Toronto
                     in the County of York aforesaid.

  Sworn before me at the
  City of Toronto in the
  County of York this 1st    (signed) D.H. MacAdam.
  day of August AD 1861.

  Clarkson Jones

  A court for taking affidavits
  in the Queens Bench for York
  and Peel.
```

MEMORIAL to be registered of Probate of the Will of
the Reverend John Smith, late of the Township of
Beckwith in the County of Lanark and Province of
Canada Clerk dated the twenty-fourth day of September in the year of our Lord, one thousand eight
hundred and fifty-one.

WHEREBY the said John Smith did devise all his
Real and Personal property at the time of the
making of the said will possessed or thereafter
to be acquired by him the said John Smith to his
wife Jane Smith or Morson for her life time and
after her death to their son Robert Smith.

AND WHICH said will is dated the twenty-first day
of October in the year of our Lord one thousand
eight hundred and forty-nine and was executed in
Upper Canada and is witnesses by Peter Comrie of
the Township of Beckwith aforesaid School Teacher
and Thomas Hawkins of the same place, labourer.

AND THIS Memorial hereof is hereby required to be
registered by me the said Jane Smith, one of the
Devisees therein named.

Witness my hand and seal this thirty-first day of
July AD 1861.

                    (signed) JANE SMITH

Signed, sealed and
delivered in presence
of
D.H.MacAdam
J.M.Parris

REGISTERED on Thursday the fifteenth day of August
AD 1861, at one of the clock in the afternoon
Liber B Beckwith Folio 487 Memorial No. 320.
    (signed) A.C.Sinclair, Dy. Regr. South Riding
            Lanark.

Memorial No. 322.
Folio 489.

Robert Smith to
James Atcheson

MEMORIAL - Sale on twentieth day of August 1861
and made between Robert Smith of the City of
Toronto in the County of York and James Atcheson
of the Village of Smiths Falls in the County of
Lanark - Physician, whereby the sum of 396 pounds
of lawful money given to the said party, his heirs
and assigns --- those parcels of land in Township
of Beckwith in the County of Lanark, containing by
admeasurement three hundred acres be the same more
or less being composed of Lot Number 14 and the
south west half of lot Number 15, both in the
sixth concession of the Township of Beckwith.

Witnessed by Robert Moffat of Town of Perth.

Registered Aug. 20th, 1861.

Liber B. Beckwith
Folios 480 & 491
Memorial No. 323.

Memorial of MORTGAGE IN FEE

James Atcheson to
Robert Smith

     MG

County of Lanark)   Robert Moffat of the town of
                  Perth in the County of Lanark,
    To Wit   )   Gentleman.

     in the within Memorial named, maketh oath and
saith, that he was present, and did see the Indenture to which the said Memorial relates, duly
executed.
Signed, Sealed and delivered by the therein named
James Atchison and Robert Smith.

     and that he is subscribing Witness to the
Execution of the said Indenture, that he, this
Deponent, also saw the said Memorial duly signed
and sealed by the therein named James Atchison --
for Registry thereof. Which said Memorial was at-
tested by him, this Deponent, and another subscribing Witness, and that both said Instruments were
executed at Perth in the County of Lanark.

                Robert Moffat

Sworn before me at Perth in the
County of Lanark this twenty-
second day of August AD 1861.
D. Fraser (?writing not clear)
A Commissioner in B.R. etc.,
in and for the County of Lanark and Renfrew.

A MEMORIAL to be Registered of an Indenture of
Mortgage, bearing date the twentieth - day of
August --- in the year of our Lord, one thousand
eight hundred and sixty-one --- made between James
Atchison of the Village of Smiths Falls in the
County of Lanark and Province of Canada, Physician
-- of the first part and Robert Smith of the City
of Toronto in the County of York and Province aforesaid, gentleman ... of the second part. Whereby
it is witnessed that the said party of the first
part in consideration of the sum of two hundred
and forty-six pounds ... of lawful money of Canada
to him paid by the said party of the second part,
(the receipt is hereby acknowledged) did grant,
bargain, sell, alien, transfer, assure, release,
convey and confirm unto the said party of the
second part his heirs and assigns ALL and singular
those certain parcels or tracts of land and premises, situate lying and being in the Township of
Beckwith in the County of Lanark and Province of
Canada, containing by admeasurement three hundred
acres be the same more or less being composed of
Lot Number Fourteen and the South West half of Lot
Number Fifteen, both in the sixth Concession of
the said Township of Beckwith.....

Together with the appurtenances TO HOLD the same
with the appurtenances unto the said party of the
second part, his heir and assigns. To the sole
and only use of the said party of the second part,
his heirs and assigns forever. Subject to the
reservations, limitations, provisoes and conditions expressed in the original grant thereof
from the Crown. And in the said Indenture is
contained a proviso for making void the same, on
payment, by the said party of the first part, his
heirs, executors, administrators or assigns, unto
the said party of the second part, his executors,
administrators or assigns, of the sum of Two
hundred and forty-six pounds ... with interest
thereon at seven per cent per annum, at the times
and in manner in said Indenture more fully set
forth.

235

Which said Indenture is Witnessed by Robert
Moffat of the Town of Perth in the County of
Lanark, Gentleman.

And this Memorial thereof is hereby required to
be registered by me, James Atchison the said
Grantee therein named.
Herein, my Hand and Seal this twentieth day of
August, in the year of our Lord, one thousand
eight hundred and sixty-one.

(signed) James Atchison.

In the presence of
Robert Moffat
M.B.Stanley

Thursday the twenty-second day of August AD 1861
at three of the clock. B. Beckwith. Folios 490
and 491. Memorial No. 323. A.S. Sinclair Dy.
Regr. South Riding of Lanark.

Folio 536
Memorial No. 353.

James Atcheson and wife to
Robert Smith

Paterson Harrison - Toronto.

Memorial - Sale on the thirty-first day of March
1862, between James Atcheson of Village of Smith
Falls in the County of Lanark - Physician, first
part, and Helen Atcheson of same place, wife of
first party - second part, and Robert Smith of the
City of Toronto County of York, Gentleman, third
part... whereby witnessed that said party for the
sum of three hundred and ninety-six pounds hath
granted unto said party of third part, his heirs
and assigns those parcels or tracts being in Township of Beckwith in County of Lanark - containing
by admeasurement three hundred acres be the same
more or less being composed of Lot Number 14 and
the south west half of lot Number 15, both of the
sixth concession of the said Township of Beckwith.

Witnessed by George Carr Shaw of Village of Smiths
Falls.

```
County of Carleton )   William Horatio Radenhurst of
                   )   the City of Ottawa in the
        To Wit:    )   County of Carleton, Esquire,
                       in the within Memorial named,
                       maketh Oath that he was pre-
                       sent and saw; ROBERT SMITH
                       therein named duly execute
                       the Deed to which the annexed
                       Memorial relates; also saw the
                       said Robert Smith duly execu-
                       te the said Memorial and that
                       he, Deponent, is a subscri-
                       bing witness to said Deed and
                       Memorial, which said Memorial
                       was executed in presence of
                       another subscribing witness,
                       and that both the said Inst-
                       truments were executed at
                       Ottawa aforesaid.
```

SWORN before me at the City of Ottawa in the County
of Carleton this twenty-sixth day of November A.D.
1863.

W. H. Walker

Wm. H. Radenhurst.

Commissioner for taking Affidavits in the Queen's
Bench, in and for the County of Carleton.

Liber B. Beckwith
Folio 680
Memorial No. 444.

Robert Smith to
Charles D. Morson.

Registered on Friday the eleventh day of December
A.D. 1863 at eleven of the clock in the forenoon.
Liber B. Beckwith. Folio 680. Memorial No. 444.

A. L. Sinclair

Dy. of Regt. S.R. Lanark.

paid.

Mortgage Memorial without Dower.

A Memorial to be Registered of an Indenture of
Bargain and Sale by way of Mortgage made the twenty-
fifth day of November in the year of our Lord, one
thousand eight hundred and sixty-three, by and
between Robert Smith of the City of Ottawa in the
County of Carleton, Gentleman, of the first part,
and Charles Day Morson of the same place, Esquire,
of the second part.

Whereby the said party of the first part, in consideration of the sum of four hundred pounds of
lawful money of the Province of Canada to him in
hand paid by the said party of the second part,
the receipt whereof is acknowledged, did grant,
bargain, sell, alien, transfer, release, convey
and confirm unto the said party of the second part,
his heirs and assigns, all and singular those
certain parcels or tracts of land situate in the
Township of Beckwith in the County of Lanark and
Province of Canada containing by admeasurement
three hundred acres by the same more or less being
composed of Lot Number Fourteen and the South West
half of Lot Number Fifteen both in the sixth
concession of the said township of Beckwith.

To have and to hold the said above granted premises, with all the privileges and appurtenances
thereof, to the said party of the second part, his
heirs and assigns to his and their own use forever.
Subject, nevertheless, to a provision therein
contained, that the said Indenture, and everything
therein contained, shall be absolutely void on
payment of the sum of Four hundred pounds of lawful money of Canada, with interest thereon, after
the rate of twelve per cent per annum, on the days
and times and in manner therein mentioned.

Which said Indenture is witnessed by William
Haratio Radenhurst of the City of Ottawa, Esquire.

And this Memorial thereof is hereby required to be
Registered by me, the said grantor therein named.

239

Witness my Hand and Seal the twenty-sixth day
of November in the year of our Lord, one thousand
eight hundred and sixty-three.

(signed) R. Smith.

Signed and sealed in the
presence of
Nicholas Sparks
Wm. H. Radenhurst.

(Copy of Opposite Page)

LIBER B BECKWITH
FOLIO----------829, 830 and 831
MEMORIAL NO. 538

JAMES ATCHESON

TO

THOMAS JAMIESON

PAID

Seles B Beckwith.
of Moon $24.820 & 54
Memoras 20 — 558

James Meice on
v
Thomas Semiew

County of Lanark } I John Holliday of the Town of Perth in the
To Wit: } County of Lanark in the Province of Canada
Gentleman make oath and say that I was
present and saw the Indenture to which the within or
annexed Memorial relates duly executed signed sealed and
Delivered by the therein named and described James Atcheson
to the therein named Thomas Jamieson at the Town of
Perth in the County of Lanark: Also together with another
subscribing witness saw the said James Atcheson duly
execute the annexed or within Memorial at the said
Town of Perth, and further that I am a subscribing
witness to both said Deed and Memorial thereof

Sworn before me at the Town of Perth
in the County of Lanark this Twenty-
Ninth day of November A.D. 1864:

John Holliday

John Deacon Jr
A Commissioner in B.R. for taking Affts in and
for the United Counties of Lanark & Renfrew

A Memorial to be registered pursuant to the Statute in such case made and provided of An Indenture in the words and figures following, that is to Say:

This Indenture made the Twenty Eighth day of November, in the year of our Lord one thousand Eight hundred and sixty four :—

Between James Atcheson of the Township of South Elmsley in the County of Leeds in the Province of Canada Physician of the first part. and

Thomas Jamieson of the Town of Perth, in the x County of Lanark, in the said Province of Canada Saddler of the Second part

Whereas by an Indenture bearing date the thirty first day of March in the year of our Lord one thousand Eight hundred and Sixty two, made between Robert Smith of the City of Toronto in the County of York and Province of Canada Gentleman, of the first part, and the said James Atcheson (then residing in the Village of Smiths Falls in the County of Lanark in the said Province) of the second part, the said Robert Smith in consideration of the Sum of one hundred and Eighty eight pounds five shillings of lawful money of Canada, then paid by the said James Atcheson to him Did grant unto the said James Atcheson his Heirs and assigns forever. All and Singular that certain parcel or tract of Land and premises situate, lying and being in the Township of Beckwith in the County of Lanark and Province of Canada, Containing by admeasurement Three hundred acres, be the same more or less, Being Composed of Lot Number Fourteen and the South West Half of Lot Number Fifteen both in the x Sixth Concession of the said Township of Beckwith. To have and to hold the same with the appurtenances unto the said James Atcheson his heirs and assigns forever. Subject however to a Proviso therein

244

Contained, that if the said Robert Smith, his Heirs Executors or administrators, did and should well and truly pay or cause to be paid to the said James Atchison his Executors, administrators or assigns the full sum of one hundred and Eighty Eight pounds five shillings of lawful money of Canada, and interest thereon in manner and at the certain time therein after mentioned that is to say: the said principal Sum of one hundred and Eighty eight Pounds and five Shillings to be paid on the First day of January in the year of our Lord one thousand eight hundred and sixty-four, with interest on the same at the rate of Twelve per cent per annum, the first instalment of interest to be due and payable on the thirty first day of March in the year of our Lord one thousand eight hundred and sixty three, And the interest to accrue due and become payable at the rate aforesaid up to the said first day of January in the year of our Lord one thousand eight hundred and sixty four to be paid at the same time as the principal money hereinbefore mentioned, without any default or abatement whatsoever, then these presents should cease and be void to all intents and purposes whatsoever. And it was by the same indenture further declared and agreed by and between the parties to these presents, that if the said party of the first part his heirs executors or administrators, should make default in payment of any or either of the said payments according to the true intent and meaning of the Proviso hereinbefore in that behalf contained and one half Calendar month should have elapsed without such payment having been made (of which latter default in payment as also if the continuance of the said principal money and interest or some part thereof on that security the production of these

245

present should be conclusive evidence) it should
and might be lawful to and for the said party thereto of the second part his Heirs executors administrators or assigns, without any further consent or con
currence of the said party thereto of the second part his
Heirs and assigns to enter into possession of the
said Lands hereditaments and premises and to receive and take the rents and profits thereof ~~and whether~~
~~no account of possession of the same to make any~~
~~lease or lease thereof~~ as he or they should think fit
and also to sell and absolutely dispose of the said
Lands hereditaments and premises with the appurtenances in such way and manner as to him or
them should seem meet and to convey and assure
the same so sold unto the purchaser or purchasers
thereof his her and their heirs and assigns or as
he, she or they should direct and appoint —
    And Whereas the said Robert Smith did r..
nor did any other person or persons pay to the said
James Atcheson the said sum of One hundred and
Eighty Eight Pounds Five shillings on the First day
of January one thousand eight hundred and sixty
four or before or since that day according to the
true intent and meaning of the said Proviso to
the said Indenture. And Whereas after the said
time so fixed by the said Indenture for the said
payment had expired the said James Atcheson
caused a Notice to be published for Two weeks
before the Twenty Eighth day of November in the
year of our Lord one thousand eight hundred and
sixty four in the ~~the~~ Newspaper Called the "Carleton
Place Herald" published in the said County of
Lanark to the effect that in consequence of the
default of payment of the said principal money
and interest and in pursuance of the said power
of sale the said Mortgaged premises would be sold

by Public Auction at Doran's Auction Room
on Gore street in the Town of Perth in the said County
of Lanark on Monday the Twenty Eighth day of
November aforesaid at Twelve o'clock noon:—
And Whereas at the time and place last aforesaid
the parcel or tract of Land and premises heretofore
by these presents
particularly described and being put up at x
Public Auction the said Thomas Jamieson became the purchaser thereof being the best and
highest bidder therefor at or for the price or
sum of one thousand and fifty dollars ;—
Now this Indenture witnesseth that the said
James Atcheson in pursuance of the powers above
recited and in consideration of the sum of one thousand
and fifty dollars, of Lawful money of Canada to
him in hand paid by the said Thomas Jamieson
at or before the ensealing and delivery of these
presents the receipt whereof is hereby acknowledged
Hath (by way of Conveyance only and not of warranty) granted, bargained, sold, aliened transferred Conveyed, and Confirmed and by
these presents Doth (by way of Conveyance only and
not of warranty) grant, bargain, sell alien transfer
convey and confirm unto the said Thomas Jamieson
his Heirs and assigns forever : All and Singular the said above described parcel or tract
of Land and premises together with the hereditaments and appurtenances to the said premises belonging and all the Estate, right, title,
interest, claim and demand whatsoever
both at Law and in Equity of him the said James
Atcheson and also of the said Robert Smith his
heirs and assigns as far forth as the said James
Atcheson has power to grant and convey the
same of and in the said parcel or tract of Land
and premises and every part and parcel thereof—

247

To have and to hold the said above granted and bargained premises with the appurtenances unto the said Thomas Jamieson his heirs and assigns to he sole and only proper use benefit and behoof of the said Thomas Jamieson his heirs and assigns forever:—

And the said James Atcheson doth hereby for himself his heirs executors and administrators ~~grant~~ covenant promise and agree to and with the said Thomas Jamieson his heirs and assigns that the said Robert Smith his Heirs Executors or administrators did not on the First day of January in the year of our Lord one thousand eight hundred and Sixty four, or at any time before or since then well and truly pay or cause to be paid to him the said James Atcheson or his assigns the said Sum of one hundred and Eighty Eight Pounds and five Shillings according to the true intent and meaning of the said Proviso to the said in part recited Indenture, but the whole of the said principal Sum remains unpaid:

In witness whereof the said parties to these presents have hereunto set their Hands and Seals the day and year first above written and in the Twenty eighth year of Her Majesty's Reign:—

Signed Sealed and Delivered
In presence of—
sd John Holliday
sd John Mathieson

sd James Atcheson [L S]
sd Thomas Jamieson [L S]

Which said Indenture is witnessed by John Holliday of the Town of Perth in the County of Lanark Gentleman and John Mathieson of the same place Gentlemen

And this memorial thereof is hereby required to be Registered by me James

248

Atcheson the said grantor therein Named:
As witness my hand and seal this twenty fifth
day of November in the year of our Lord one
thousand Eight hundred and sixty four:

Signed and Sealed
In presence of
John Mathieson
John Holliday

James Atcheson

Liber B. Beckwith
Folio 832
Memorial No. 539.

Thomas Jamieson (etrx.)
to
JAMES ATCHESON

paid

County of)	John Mathieson ... of the Town ...
Lanark)	of Perth ... in the County of Lanark
)	Gentleman, make Oath and say that I
To Wit:)	was present and saw THOMAS JAMIESON,

Jane Jamieson and James Atcheson....
duly execute the Deed to which the
within Memorial relates; also, (together with another subscribing
Witness,) saw Thomas Jamieson ....
duly execute the said within Memorial, and that I am a subscribing
Witness to said Deed and Memorial,
and further, that both said Instruments were executed at the Town of
Perth in the County of Lanark.
(signed)
JOHN MATHIESON

Sworn before me at the Town
of Perth ... in the County of
Lanark ... this twenty-eighth
day of November A.D. 1864.
(signed) Alex Morris.

A Commissioner for taking affidavits in the Queen's
Bench in and for the United Counties of Lanark and
Renfrew.

Memorial Deed with Dower

A MEMORIAL, to be registered, of an Indenture,
tripartite, made the twenty-eighth day of November,
in the year of our Lord, One thousand eight hundred
and sixty-four. In pursuance of the Act to faci-
litate the Conveyance of Real Property;
BETWEEN:
THOMAS JAMIESON of the Town of Perth in the County
of Lanark and Province of Canada, Saddler, of the
FIRST PART JANE JAMIESON of same place, wife of the
first part, of the second part and JAMES ATCHESON
of the Township of South Elmsley in the County of
Lanark and Province of Canada, Physician, of the
third part. WHEREBY the said party of the first
part, for and in consideration of the sum of ONE
THOUSAND FIFTY DOLLARS of lawful money of Canada,
then paid by the said party of the third part, to
the said party of the first part (the receipt
whereof thereby acknowledge) did grant unto the
said party of the third part, his heirs and assigns
forever, ALL AND SINGULAR that certain parcel or
tract of Land and Premises, situate lying and being
in the Township of Beckwith in the County of Lanark
in the Province of Canada containing by admeasurement - Three hundred acres be the same more or less
BEING COMPOSED OF LOT NUMBER FOURTEEN and the SOUTH
WEST HALF OF LOT NUMBER FIFTEEN, both in the SIXTH
concession of the said Township of Beckwith.

To have and to hold, the said above granted premises, unto the said party of the third part, his
heirs and assigns, to and for his and their sole
and only use forever.

And by the same Indenture it is witnessed that the
said party of the second part, wife of the party
of the first part, thereby barred her Dower in the
said Lands: which said Indenture is

Witnessed by John Mathieson of the Town of Perth
in the County of Lanark, Gentleman and John
Holliday of the same place, Gentleman.

251

And this MEMORIAL thereof is hereby required to be registered by me, the said granter therein named.

As Witness my hand and seal this twenty-eighth day of November, one thousand eight hundred and sixty-four.

(signed)
THOMAS JAMIESON

Signed, and sealed in
presence of
John Matheson
John Holliday.

Registered on Saturday the tenth day of December AD 1864 at one of the clock in the afternoon. Liber B Beckwith Folio 832 Memorial No. 539.

A.L.Sinclair
Dy Regr.
South Riding Lanark

Deed No. 2B592 contains the following information --

I, Edward Holmes, Township of Kitley, County of
Leeds, Yeoman make oath and say that I was present
and saw James Atcheson, Helen Atcheson, his wife,
and James Drummond -- sign Memorial Deed executed
at Smiths Falls in the South riding of the County
of Lanark.

Sworn before me at the Village of Smiths Falls in
the County of Lanark, 3 July 1865.
                                (signed) Edwards Holmes

Indenture Triparite made the 3rd July 1865 between
James Atcheson of the Township of South Elmsley in
the County of Leeds and Province of Canada, Physician of the first part, Helen Atcheson of same
place, wife of the said party of the first part,
of the second part, and James Drummond of the
Township of Kitley in the County and Province
aforesaid, yeoman.

The property sold for the sum of three hundred and
sixty-five pounds and was written up as 300 acres
same more or less composed of lot number 14 and
south west half of lot number 15, concession sixth,
Township of Beckwith in County of Lanark.
                                (signed) James Drummond
                                X (his mark).

The document was signed by

Witnessed by:
1. William Drummond.
2. Edward Holmes.

October 1864, an advertisement - sent to be
printed by Bell and Woodburn printers, central Ottawa,
and sent to Carleton Place with this curious note:

"I want you to have sucalers well taken up in
your village, country, all of Ramsay. Tell Mr.
Poole the editor of the Carleton Place paper to
insert in his paper till day of sale and this will
be a "cappey" for him".
                              Yours respectfully,
                              H. McLean.

It would seem this was C.D.Morson trying to sell the
property in view of document between Robert Smith and
himself, which was never discharged. The ad in the
October 5th, 1864, "Carleton Place Herald" read:

H. McLean, auctioneer, has received instructions
from the heirs of the late Rev. John Smith of
Beckwith, to offer for sale by public auction, on
the 10th of October next, at the hour of 12 o'clock
at Paul Lavallee's Hotel in the Village of Carleton
Place, lot 14 and the S.W. half lot 15 in the 7th
concession of the Township of Lanark comprising 300
acres more or less together with stone dwelling
house, barns, etc., thereon.
Title indisputable.
Terms of Sale $800. down - balance to be secured
by mortgage at 7% sale without reserve.
                              H. McLean, Auctioneer
                              of Ottawa.
Same ad appeared October 21, 1864, with added caption:

FARM PROPERTY TO BE SOLD AT AUCTION.

Then we find an ad in the BATHURST COURIER:

AUCTION SALE

Three hundred acres of land known as lot 14 and
s.w. half of lot 15 in the 6th concession of
Township of Beckwith, property of the heirs of the
late Rev. John Smith of Beckwith, will be offered
for sale on Tuesday November 1st. being Fair Day

at N. Lavalee's Hotel, Village of Carleton Place
at hour of 2 o'clock P.M., the whole of that
valuable farm with stone dwelling house and other
outhouses, barns and well fenced. Farm is well
watered, 5 miles from Carleton Place and within
1 mile of Ottawa and Brockville Railway.
Terms of sale - quarter down, balance to be paid
in one, two and four years.

H. McLean.

"Carleton Place Herald", October 26, 1864. again
carried an ad:

AUCTION SALE

Three hundred acres of land known as lot No. 14
and the SW half of lot 15 in the 6th concession
of Township of Beckwith, County of Lanark, being,
the property of the heirs of the late REV. JOHN
SMITH of Beckwith, will be offered for sale on
Tuesday, November 1st being the Fair Day at N.
Lavallee's Hotel in the Village of Carleton Place,
at the hour of 2 o'clock P.M., the whole of that
valuable farm, stone dwelling house and other outhouses, barns and well fenced. The farm is well
watered, 5 miles from Carleton Place and within 1
mile of the Ottawa and Brockville Railway.
Terms of Sale - quarter down, balance to be paid in
one, two, and three years.

H. McLean. Auctioneer.

The above ad repeated in same paper November 2, 1864.
However, the uncle James Atcheson who held a mortgage
for 188.50 pounds on the property now takes action with
a Mortgage Sale and the notice reads as follows:

Carleton Place Herald, November 16, 1864.

MORTGAGE SALE

Whereas default has been made in payment secured
to be paid by an Indenture of mortgage, dated the
twenty-first day of March in the year of our Lord

one thousand and eight hundred and sixty-two,
made between ROBERT SMITH, of the City of Toronto
in the County of York and the Province of Canada,
gentleman, of the first part, and JAMES ATCHISON
of the Village of Smith Falls in the County of
Lanark and Province aforesaid, Physician, of the
second part, upon all and singular those certain
parcels or tracts of land and premises, situate
lying and being in the Township of Beckwith, in the
County of Lanark, containing by admeasurement
THREE HUNDRED ACRES by the same more or less being
composed of lot number fourteen and the South West
half of lot number fifteen, both in the sixth concession of the Township of Beckwith.

NOTICE IS HEREBY GIVEN THAT PURSUANT TO THE POWER
OF SALE in said mortgage contained, the above
described parcels or tracts of land and premises
will be sold by Public Auction at DORAN'S AUCTION
ROOM on Gore Street in the town of Perth on MONDAY
the twenty-eighth day of November, A.D. 1864, at
the hour of twelve o'clock noon, unless the moneys
due to be sooner paid.
Terms - made known may be inspected at the office
of Messrs. Deacon & Morris, Solicitors, Perth.

Dated this tenth day of November A.D. 1864.

> Alexander Morris
> Solicitor for said
> Mortgagee
> James Atchison.

Thomas Gair, 4th Laird of Nigg
(1707-1771)

Isobella, wife of Thomas

Isobella Rose, daughter of Thomas Gair

Rose ring with Gair Coat of Arms and motto "Sans Sol Seize"

MATERNAL GENEALOGICAL CHART OF THE REVEREND JOHN SMITH

ALEXANDER GAIR (1595-1659) of NIGG
(ROSS & CROMARTY - SCOTLAND)
Married KATHERINE MCCULLOCH
had issue

ALEXANDER b.1620   THOMAS b. 1625   WILLIAM

THOMAS GAIR of NIGG b. ca. 1649 d. 1729
m.MARGARET BREBNER
(Nigg House still has a lintel stone with initials TG MB and date 1705)
had issue

ANDREW d.   ALEXANDER of NIGG   WILLIAM   THOMAS   A DAUGHTER
unmarried   b. 1688 d. 1734
              m. MARGARET CUTHBERT
              d. 1734
              had issue

THOMAS of NIGG (1707-1771)   ALEXANDER 1710-1751
m. ISABELLA ROSS (1702-1795)   the present Laird (1978)

daughter of LAIRD OF CALROSSIE   LT. COL. GAYRE of GAYRE
related to BALNAGOWAN family and   & NIGG derives from here
ROYAL HOUSE OF DENMARK
had issue

THOMAS died in   ISABELLA   (1736-1790)
childhood   m. HUGH ROSE of AITNOCH (1729-1791)
                        (after marriage designated of NIGG)
                        had issue

JOHN died in   BARBARA m. COL WALTER   ISABELLA (died 1814)   CHRISTINA
infancy   ROSS of NIGG   m. REV.ROBERT SMITH   m.WILLIAM MURRAY
                 no issue   1763-1824 m.1791   of PITCULZEAN
                                           had issue   had issue

HISTORY OF GAIR OR GAYRE CLAN

(Celtic) The name derives from the great
Cornish Domesday Manor of Gayre. It first
appears on the Borders in association with
the Mowes of that Ilk, and the next generation
settled in Easter Ross having married the
heiress of MacCulloch of Nigg.

(above information from the Scottish Field
Supplement "A Guide to the Clans and Major
Families of Scotland - May, 1977)

ISABELLA   ROBERT   CATHERINE   HUGH   JOHN (REV.)   MARGARET CRAWFORD
b.1792   b.1797   25/3/794   b.3/11/1795 b.19/1/1801 M.DR.GEO.MACDONALD
died   d.young m.JOHN DUFF   m.JANE MORSON (1777-1862) Cromarty
infancy   MACDONALD (Naval   30/8/1838 at   28/4/1821
                    Lieut.) b.1792   Bytown,Canada had issue
                    d.9/6/1827   d.18/4/1851
                    had issue   had issue

HELEN b.   ROBERT b.153831807   ISABELLA
14/12/1804   Army Surgeon 23rd   30/I/1811 m. rev. GEORGE ROMANES (1806-1871)
m. John James   Fusiliers, served in   of Smiths Falls, CANADA 12/8/1835
Aitchison M.D. Canada. Ret. 21/9/1860 d. LONDON, ENGLAND 2/1/1883
of Elmsley,   d.Stuttgart, Germany   had issue
Canada   29/9/1880
28/10/1852

HELEN   ISABELLA   ANGELA   WILLIAM   GEORGE   HUGH
m.1)REV.ALX MCLEAN m.REV.ROSS m.DAVIDSON m.ESTHER MACKAY
2)HOASSACK   TAYLOR   MINISTER HALKIRK (2nd wife)
had issue   had issue   had issue   had issue

ALEX. CHRISTINE MARG.
b.1817 b.1819 b.1820
or 1818 m.Dr. m.PROVOST DR.WALTER ESTHER   FITZGERALD MURRAY
m.ANN   SMITH ROSS   TAYLOR   m.ALEX MIDDLETON
CALDER DINGWALL   (Esther Mackay Murray bought
                                                 back Nigg from Flora Ross
                                                 Taylor in 1843)
ALEX   SIR JOSHUA
MACLEAN   MACLEAN ROSS ROSS TAYLOR
               family   a quo
                       WALTER   Middletons of
                                  ROSEFARM CROMARTY

DAUGHTER   SON   JOHN DUFF MACDONALD
d. infancy d. 1835 b. Cromarty 18/11 1819
                    m. Brockville, Canada, 26/12/1850
                    SARAH ANN MALLOCH
                    eldest daughter Judge of Leeds and Grenville
                    Counties, George Malloch, d.Hamilton 3/10/1901
                    had issue

CHILDREN OF MARGARET CRAWFORD SMITH MACDONALD

ROBERT died North America
JOHN Queensland
GEORGE 1874 married LYDIA MACINTOSH
HUGH 1841-1886 ..1874 MARY HELEN
HISLOP (1852-1930)
DUNCAN died India
CHESBOROUGH died Cromarty
JESSY died Cromarty
MARGARET died Cromarty
CAROLINE married KENNEDY
BARBARA ROSE 1828-1896 m.WILLIAM
MCDONALD no issue
CATHERINE ROSS (1839-1912) died Wellington, N.Z.
The genealogy of this family has been compiled by Bruce F.McDonald in the book
THE FAMILY MCDONALD - 100 years 1866-1966

CHILDREN OF REV. GEORGE AND ISABELLA ROMANES

JAMES   ROBERT   GEORGINA   GEORGE JOHN (Prof.) CHARLOTTE
b. Smiths Falls, m. 29/12/1838 b. Smiths Falls, b. Kingston, Canada ELIZABETH
CANADA. 4/8/1836 died young   CANADA, 17/10/1842 d.Eng. 24/5/1894 died Scotland
d. Scotland 1902   d. England 1878   m. Ethel Duncan   unmarried
m. MARGARET WARDROPE   unmarried   had issue   1911

ISABELLA STEWART   MRS RUST   SARA
m.WILLIAM HUGH   lived in Trinidad 1901
WARDROPE of Hamilton
had issue

WILLIAM HUGH MASON
b.6/9/1897

ROBERT
b. 16/8/1839 ISABELLA   MARY MATILDA MARGARET   JANE MORSON   JOHN ROSE
              b. 4/10/1830 OTTLEY FELLOWES CRAWFORD   b. 9/7/1847   b.Aug. 1849
              m. 11/12/1913 b. 12/8/1842 b. 1844   d. 28/12/1915 d. 18/10 1947
              m. A.R.WARDELL b. 23/11/1922 d. 25/4/1920 Ottawa   Toronto
              Dundas, Canada Ottawa, Canada Ottawa   unmarried   unmarried
              had issue   Unmarried   m.WILLIAM WYLD
                                                    (1854-1905)
                                                    8/5/1879
                                                    had issue

ETHEL GEORGINA   GEORGE   JAMES GERALD PAGET   FRANCIS JOHN   NORMAN HUGH   EDMUND GILES
d. 1914   ERNEST   (LT.COL D.S.O.)   m. DORIS HELEN m. CICELY   RADCLIFFE
                 d. 1910   d. 1946   WRIGHT   ANNE MITCHELL d. 1915
                 m. MINA ALEXANDRA SCOTT   INGHAM
                 had issue   had issue

GEORGE CHRISTOPHER   WALTER JOHN   HUGH GILES   JOAN CICELY
b. 1907   b. 1910   INGHAM   MARY
                                                  b. 1921   b. 1922
                                                                 m. PATRICK
                                                                 WESTMACOTT
                                                                 had issue

MAUDE OTTLEY   REGINALD   ALLEN   LINDSAY   ALEXANDER   GERTRUDE MAY NAOMI KATE
CUNNIGHAM   STEWART ROSE AP ROBERTS AITCHESON   b. 13/1/1879 b. 12/8/1881 b.4/3/1885
b. 7/10/1872   b. 9/6/1874 GREIR   b. 13/3/1879 d. 13/1/1962 d. 18/11/1951 d.Aug. 1849
d. 29/11/1872 d. 21/6/1910 b. 12/3/1877 d. 13/1/1962 m. 29/9/1908 unmarried m.2A/8/1910
                                        MABEL THERESA BARRIE   KENNETH D.
                                        had issue   HARRIS, Ottawa
                                                                         had issue

GILES JOHN   CYNTHIA JOY
b 1919   b. 1920
m. MARGARET GEE m. LEWIS
had, issue   CASTLEDON
                had issue

DOROTHY WILMA HENRY (S.J.) THOMAS   JOHN LINDSAY   KENNETH 28/191?
CINNIGHAM   b.19/9/1911 b. 6/12/1912 b. 11/12/1917   stillborn
b. 6/12/19 10 d. 9/12/1975 d. 9/10/1974 m. 5/4/1946   NAOMI JEAN
                                         THERESA CAROLINE   b. 1918
                                         ROCHE   (MRS.BAND)
                                         had issue   had daughter

JAMES RAOUL GRIER   ISOBEL MARION OTTLY
b. 28/8/1883   b. 17/9/1887
d. 20/5/1931   m. 10/9/1909
m. 16/11/1909   PHILIP LESLIE NEAME (b 1886)
HATTIE SCOTT of   had issue
Gagetown, N.B.
d. 13/10/1953   SHIRLEY LESLIE WILLIAMS
had issue   b. 17/10/1910
                    Portland, Oregon, U.S.A.

WILLIAM GREIR
b 29/9/1911
m. 5/7/1934
MARIE BABINEAU
b. 1913 Newcastle, New Brunswick
had issue

JAMES   ROSALIND   JULIAN
b. 1946 h. 1949   b. 1951

Two daughters of Lindsay Wardell's
family died in infancy

KATHLEEN MARY b.26/5/1916 d. 7/9/1916
MARY b.11/1/1919 lived only a few hours

WILLVERNON   ANDREW   CHRISTIAN   HEINA
b. 1943   b. 1945   h. 1947   b. 1952

MICHAEL JOSEPH   ROBERT JOHN   MARY CATHERINE
B 1/12/1948   b. 7/5/1951   b. 11/1/1963

PAUL LINDSAY
b 18/8/1952
m. 18/9/1975
DONNA HELEN MARX
b 8/1/1958
had issue

JANE RENEE
b. 30/4/1976

DIANA ELIZABETH   RODNEY DAWSON   DONALD GREIR
B. 29/4/1935   b. 31/5/1938   b. 29/6/1944
m. DAVID GARINGER m. ELIZABETH LUCY MAHER M. in Germany 3/12/64
Mass. U.S.A.   Nelson, B.C. 5/?/?? had issue
had issue

LISA NOEL CRAIG DAVID
b.21/11/196? b.1 /2/1965
California California,
U.S.A.   U.S.A.

MARCUS
b.5/5/1965

GARY JOHN   SANDRA   GREGORY CECIL TANYA ANN
B.9/9/1958 ELIZABETH b. 17/11/1965 b.9/3/1969
            b 22/7

JUDITH BARBARA
b. 29/6/1946
m. HUGH ANTHONY MOAR
b. 23/10/1941
19/1/1966
had issue

BETTINA ELKA WYLD
b. 23/3/1968
m. 2)ALICE SONJA JANSEN
of Koege, Denmark 1975
had issue

HEATHER MARIE   TROY ANTHONY   SCOTT BERNARD
b. 13/1/1967   b. 26/7/1968   b. 2/11/1972

JAMIE GREIR WYLD
b. 9/9/1977